D0537347

CLASSIC STARS DESSERTS

I had eyed the pastry department from across the kitchen and realized my heart lay there among the sugar and flour. In 1987, Jeremiah gave me the opportunity and I switched to making desserts. I have never looked back. While I appreciate the merits of other courses and feel that my experience with savory cooking has refined my palate and given me the ability to invent distinctive desserts, creating desserts comes from my heart rather than my brain. Besides, at the end of the day, I would rather smell like chocolate and strawberries than garlic and shrimp!

One of the best things about Stars was the eclectic mix of customers that came in every evening. There were birthday and anniversary celebrants, businesspeople making deals, sports fans after a Giants or 49ers game, symphony and opera buffs on their way to a performance, and out-of-town visitors at the bar wanting only a martini, some oysters, and a bite of something sweet. Together, they created the energy of the restaurant. People often asked me if it was difficult to come up with desserts for such a wide spectrum of customers. But that is what made my work both fun and a welcome challenge. If a menu offers an interesting assortment of desserts—a light and creamy caramel custard, a bright fresh plum sorbet, crêpes suzette, a sexy ice-cream concoction, a crisp napoleon or fruit-filled pie, and at least two chocolate desserts—you are sure to please everyone.

Throughout my pastry career, my dessert style has stayed the same: simple but elegant and luscious, colorful, and composed yet spontaneous and natural. In concept and design, my desserts are imaginative and interesting without being too technical or esoteric. They are updated versions of American and European classics that have not lost the essence of their original idea, making them familiar and straightforward in their composition yet inviting because of an added twist. I use the freshest, best-quality ingredients available and never mask their basic flavors by adding too much sugar. Chocolate

One of the best things about Stars was the eclectic mix of customers that came in every evening.

··· ୭ ···

desserts taste like rich bittersweet chocolate; peach desserts taste like ripe, juicy peaches. Components of each dessert stand on their own, but combined, they enhance one another and create something unforgettable. A flaky, buttery crust becomes even better when filled with lime mousse and sliced mango; a chocolate almond torte is taken to a new level when served with an orange custard sauce and espresso ice cream.

For Stars as well as Stars Café, we made seven different desserts daily, which we served to an average of four hundred people; we also made pizza dough, focaccia, and brioche for the main kitchen. Each week we used 200 pounds of butter, 40 gallons of cream, 80 pounds of chocolate, 450 pounds each of sugar and flour, and more than 1,500 eggs. On a

The ovens were hot in the pastry kitchen at Stars long before most people in San Francisco turned off their alarm clocks, and stayed hot long after those same people's heads hit the pillow at night.

··· ⟲ ···

busy summer weekend, we could easily use 10 cases of raspberries, 8 cases of boysenberries, 4 cases of strawberries, 2 cases of peaches, and 1 case of cherries.

Like most restaurants today, the staff at Stars maintained a close relationship with suppliers and depended on them to deliver the freshest and best produce, dairy products, and other baking staples, from vanilla and nuts to dried fruits. Because high-quality ingredients are essential for making great-tasting food, these relationships are vital to the success of any restaurant. There was one produce supplier named Rocky who invariably failed to show up when he said he would. Often two days late, nursing the worst hangover, he would appear

at our back door with cases and cases of the most succulent berries. It was frustrating not to know when he was going to be there, and I felt like a hostage to his erratic schedule. But his berries were so incredible that I would always take them whenever he decided to materialize.

Although you probably don't have access to the same number of suppliers that a professional pastry chef does, you can still get good-quality ingredients. Investigate your local produce stores and ask which fruits are available, when the freshest produce is delivered, and what is grown locally. Seek out organic produce at both stores and farmers' markets. The growth of the Internet has also made a wide range of baking products available to home bakers in even the most remote locations.

··· ⟲ ···

The ovens were hot in the pastry kitchen at Stars long before most people in San Francisco turned off their alarm clocks, and stayed hot long after those same people's heads hit the pillow at night. My day began with the production of morning pastries—cinnamon rolls, oatmeal scones, muffins— for Stars Café. Next, I reviewed the day's menu that had been devised the night before, organized the production of the desserts we needed to make that day, and discussed any last-minute changes with the pastry cooks. Once the daily produce order came in, the menu was often adjusted because what we

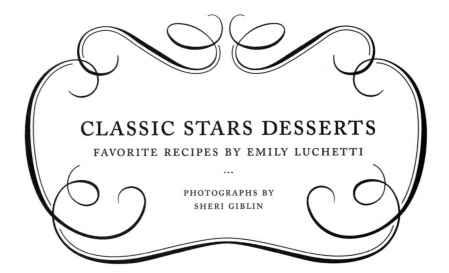

CLASSIC STARS DESSERTS

FAVORITE RECIPES BY EMILY LUCHETTI

...

PHOTOGRAPHS BY
SHERI GIBLIN

CHRONICLE BOOKS
SAN FRANCISCO

Library of Congress Cataloging-in-Publication Data available.

ISBN-10: 0-8118-4703-9
ISBN-13: 978-0-8118-4703-2

Manufactured in Canada.

Designed by Katie Heit
Prop styling by Leigh Noe
Food styling by Dan Becker
Food Stylist Assistants: Christine Wolheim and Nani Steele
Photographer's Assistant: Jennifer Martine

Distributed in Canada by Raincoast Books
9050 Shaughnessy Street
Vancouver, British Columbia V6P 6E5

10 9 8 7 6 5 4 3 2 1

Chronicle Books LLC
680 Second Street
San Francisco, California 94107

www.chroniclebooks.com

TO JEREMIAH, *who created Stars and sent me on my pastry life path*

— CONTENTS —

8
INTRODUCTION

14
INGREDIENTS & EQUIPMENT

18
THINGS THAT MAKE A DIFFERENCE

23
SWEETS & STICKIES

35
CHAPTER 1
PUDDINGS, CUSTARDS, MOUSSES
& TRIFLES

59
CHAPTER 2
CHOCOLATE DESSERTS

91
CHAPTER 3
HOT DESSERTS

117
CHAPTER 4
FRUIT DESSERTS

151
CHAPTER 5
TARTS, PIES & PASTRIES

181
CHAPTER 6
CAKES

213
CHAPTER 7
COOKIES & CANDIES

257
CHAPTER 8
BREAKFAST

273
CHAPTER 9
BUILDING BLOCKS

303
ACKNOWLEDGMENTS

304
INDEX

312
TABLE OF EQUIVALENTS

I found my first cooking job through a classified ad titled "No Typing Required" in the *New York Times*. It was placed by a precious-metals trading company looking for a chef's assistant for its downtown Manhattan

office, near Wall Street. I served breakfast to the president of the company: he ate the top half of a New York–deli bran muffin and I ate the bottom half. The chef and I prepared and served lunch, occasional business breakfasts, and cocktail receptions for the top twenty executives in the company. We worked in a high-rise with a view of the East River, and I got a free cab ride to work (I had to be there really early), making it a great first job in the food world.

A year and a half later, while my friends were selling insurance or agonizing over law- or business-school applications, I attended the New York Restaurant School. After school I worked variously at The Silver Palate, the first gourmet takeout in New York; Manhattan Market, owned by David and Susan Leiderman; and Caliban, a little restaurant on the corner of Twenty-Sixth Street and Third Avenue. These experiences made me crave even more culinary adventures, and I headed off to France for a year and worked as a *stagiaire* (for free) at several restaurants, most notably Gérard Pangaud's, near the Bois de Boulogne in Paris.

I returned to the States in 1984 and headed west to California to be part of the blossoming of American regional cuisine. The state promised a bounty of locally grown produce and fresh seafood, and chefs and customers had just begun to recognize how unique that was. Today it is hard to imagine that cooking local foods in straightforward ways was ever a new idea.

When I accepted a job at the about-to-be-opened Stars, a restaurant patterned after the old brasseries of Europe and New York, no one had any idea how this new spot would capture the hearts and stomachs of people all over the country. Nor could I appreciate how my career and food style would be so formidably shaped by its influence. Owner and executive chef Jeremiah Tower was the creative genius behind Stars. It was his passion and perseverance, in concert with an incredible group of chefs and cooks, that made Stars an institution.

I spent several years cooking in the main part of the Stars kitchen, but something was missing.

received did not meet our standards for flavor and freshness. We all worked in fifth gear throughout the day: melting chocolate, turning puff pastries, assembling trifles, frosting cakes, baking tarts and cookies, making sabayon, and freezing sorbets and ice creams. The production was intense, and each cook had to be able to execute several tasks at once. With the constant assistance of several timers (one being the cook's sense when something is done), a cook learned to juggle all these different duties and stay a step ahead. As we worked, we would toss ideas back and forth about the next day's menu.

When the evening pastry cooks arrived, I outlined the night's work schedule. We reviewed the presentation of all the desserts, including the best plates to use and the appropriate sauces. We plated all the new desserts and presented them to the waiters for tasting. In the restaurant business, this is called "lineup." You have never seen people devour a dessert until you have seen eleven waiters attack a new creation. It is a fork-stabbing frenzy.

The evening service started off quickly, with many guests dining early before the symphony, ballet, or opera. Within an hour, the pastry plater was faced with a long line of tickets. He or she rapidly plated cakes, sautéed bananas for shortcakes, warmed crêpes, and at the same time kept an eye out for the waiter whose desserts were being assembled. Desserts were put together as fast as the tickets came in. Waiters were not let out of the kitchen without

several plates in both hands, so that hot desserts and soufflés would never sit for even a moment before they were whisked to diners. The pace remained steadily furious all evening, and then, before you knew it, it was time for the after-dinner rush. We had a large number of guests who came to Stars just for dessert, stopping by to prolong an evening with a nightcap of a Pear Napoleon with Ginger Pastry Cream or Frozen Kir Royale.

I varied the dessert menu daily, which allowed us to take advantage of the best of the seasonal produce. It was not unusual to switch the evening's desserts in the afternoon. A late arrival of delicious, sweet raspberries, ripened to perfection, would be immediately used in a tart with Grand Marnier cream. But San Francisco's famous fog can cause a quick change in the weather, and at the last minute, we would switch and put the berries in a warm, soothing lemon pudding soufflé, a dessert that would ward off the chill and possibly even make you welcome the cold blast.

··· ❧ ···

Creating desserts is an ongoing process. I am always thinking about new desserts and constantly trying different ideas and testing recipes. As I work throughout the day, I exchange ideas with the pastry cooks. "What if we decreased the sugar in this recipe?" "Do you think the mousse would taste better if we used espresso instead of coffee?" New desserts are created in various ways. Sometimes they are the result of a group effort. For example, one cook will envision an apple tart with a brown-sugar custard, and another one will suggest adding ground pecans to the dough. Variations on desserts also occur when two cooks work simultaneously on separate projects. The sight of the ingredients placed side by side often suggests combinations that were not previously considered. One day, a pastry cook was making fantasy cream, a rich mascarpone custard, while another was making a caramel sauce. I happened to walk by, saw the two at work, and caramel fantasy cream was born.

To make certain a dessert has just the right flavor, I test and taste, retest and taste again, before putting it on the menu. Throughout my career, I have had the good fortune to work alongside Mark Franz, first as the chef at Stars and now as the chef-owner of Farallon. He has a great palate not only for savory food but for desserts as well. Over the years, I have gone to him when I was not quite sure if a dessert was finished, relying on him to give me either a thumbs-up or a suggestion on how to improve it.

In the late 1970s and early 1980s, restaurant-goers started paying as much attention to desserts as they did to the rest of the menu. Before then, of course, there were some wonderful traditional desserts like soufflés and crêpes, but the dessert menu was presented more as an afterthought. Chefs responded to this new interest by putting their own spins on such classic American desserts as crisps,

layer cakes, and sundaes. Architectural desserts, with twisted tuile cookies and dots of colorful sauces decorating the plates, became popular as pastry chefs realized there were no rules. Today, pastry chefs across the country show a wide array of styles that synthesize classic and architectural styles. Their desserts are as unique as the savory dishes created by the chefs in the main part of the kitchen. Many restaurant customers ask for the dessert menu when they are presented with the main menu, and some even select a restaurant on the appeal of the desserts.

Today, pastry chefs across the country show a wide array of styles that synthesize classic and architectural styles.

··· ⟳ ···

Over the last ten years, dessert wines have become part of the dessert course. Sometimes they are served with a simple cookie, like the traditional union of *vin santo* and biscotti. But more often, menus recommend pairing a specific wine with a particular dessert. Also, because dessert wines are typically sold by the glass, customers have the opportunity to experiment with a variety of wines and desserts, gradually becoming knowledgeable about how a wine and a dessert can each contribute to a new taste experience. In "Sweets and Stickies" (pages 23–33), Peter Palmer, the wine director at Farallon restaurant in San Francisco, discusses the different types of dessert grapes, the wines that are made from the grapes, and which types of desserts each wine complements.

The recipes in this book are my favorites from *Stars Desserts* and *Four Star Desserts*. Since the books' publications in 1991 and 1995, respectively, these are the desserts that I have found myself going back to time after time. They are also the recipes that people tell me are their favorites, with most of them not difficult to execute. Other recipes, although more involved, need only to be broken down into separate steps. As a result, this book is ideal for both the novice and the accomplished baker. Although both books were written for the home cook, I have been pleasantly surprised over the years to discover how many professional chefs use my recipes in their restaurant kitchens. A slight change here and there, like switching fruits or adding sauces, turns the desserts into something different. At home, you can do the same. Make the recipe, understand it, and then use your imagination to create something new.

Preparing desserts brings satisfaction on two levels. First, making a beautiful fruit tart or a luscious trifle layered with chocolate zabaglione brings creative fulfillment and a sense of personal accomplishment. Then, when you serve it to friends and family, you take pleasure in seeing the dessert enjoyed by others.

Too many people falsely believe that you have to sacrifice desserts to be healthy and physically fit. But the key is moderation, not abstention. Regardless of which diet is in vogue, it all comes down to two things: calories eaten versus calories expended and portion size. Avoid processed foods and enjoy an occasional dessert. I eat healthful foods—skim milk and nonfat plain yogurt on my cereal in the morning and lots of fruits, vegetables, low-fat proteins, and seafood for lunch and dinner—and I exercise—run, swim, play tennis, bike, attend Pilates classes—regularly. I eat well and exercise to stay healthy but also because I want to be able to eat desserts. What better way to reward yourself for completing a twenty-mile bike ride or a four-mile jog than with a slice of blueberry pie?

Dessert is important for our emotional well-being and tastes better when we don't feel guilty eating it. Like most people, I am more apt to stick to a healthful diet if I know I can have a treat now and then. When a dessert is made with great ingredients and has maximum flavor, you don't need a huge portion to feel satiated. If we cannot eat desserts all the time, we don't want to waste calories on mediocre desserts. They must have the most intense flavor possible and be made with the best ingredients available. And that is where these recipes come in. Not only are they timeless, but they are also worth every calorie.

··· *Ingredients & Equipment* ···

The starting point of any incredible dessert is high-quality ingredients. Some you can gather quickly in your grocery cart as you scurry down each aisle, but others, like those included here, require a bit more attention.

CHOCOLATE

I prefer bittersweet over semisweet chocolate. It has less sugar and more of a chocolate taste. One exception is Scharffen Berger semisweet chocolate, which is 62 percent cacao and is delicious. For bittersweet chocolate, I use Callebaut, E. Guittard, El Rey, Scharffen Berger, Lindt, or Valrhona. I always use bittersweet chocolate chips, too, for their more intense flavor. I like Valrhona cocoa powder, but it can be difficult to find. Droste cocoa powder is another good choice and is more readily available. Both are Dutch-process cocoa powders, which means they have been treated with an alkali. They are darker than nonalkalized powders and dissolve more readily in liquids. Specialty chocolate brands are stocked in some cookware stores and in finer grocery stores. You can also find most brands at the Chocosphere online chocolate store at www.chocosphere.com.

DAIRY PRODUCTS

Use heavy whipping cream (sometimes labeled heavy cream), which has a slightly higher fat content than whipping cream. Try to avoid ultrapasteurized cream, which does not increase in volume as fully as pasteurized cream, does not hold its shape as well when whipped, and has a slightly "cooked" flavor. When possible, use organic cream. Its taste cannot be beat. And always use whole milk, preferably organic.

Mascarpone is a triple-cream cheese that is thickened by warming together cream and a little tartaric acid, allowing the mixture to rest and thicken, and then draining it and discarding the whey. Look for it in cheese shops and well-stocked supermarkets.

Use unsalted butter, rather than salted butter. If you are making the dough for a special tart, European-style unsalted butter is a treat. It has a higher butterfat content than conventional unsalted butter, and thus a richer taste.

DRY INGREDIENTS

I use unbleached all-purpose flour for almost all of my recipes. (I use cake flour for making certain cakes.) Bleached flours are chemically treated to make them whiter, but the difference in color is usually undetectable in baked goods. Nor do most baked goods need to be bright white. Also, I find that bleached flour can give some desserts an unpleasant aftertaste.

Use kosher salt. It dissolves more quickly than regular table salt and heightens the flavor of desserts without imparting an iodine aftertaste. When I call for a pinch of salt, it is what you can easily grasp between you index finger and your thumb.

Dark brown sugar has a more pronounced molasses flavor than light brown (sometimes called golden brown) sugar, but they are generally inter-changeable in recipes. However, I prefer one over the other in some desserts and have indicated my preference. In other recipes, you may use either type.

You may use superfine sugar if you prefer, but regular granulated sugar works fine in all the recipes. Always use pure cane sugar, rather than beet sugar, for the best results.

Cornstarch, all-purpose flour, or tapioca flour may be used to thicken fruit in desserts. Look for tapioca flour in Asian markets.

VANILLA

Use high-quality pure vanilla extract, never imitation. Nielsen-Massey and Flavorganics are good brands. Select vanilla beans that are plump and moist, and store them double bagged in lock-top plastic bags to keep them fresh longer.

EQUIPMENT, BIG AND SMALL

You don't need much equipment to make most of the recipes in this book, and you probably already have most of what you need in your kitchen. If you have to buy a few things, bakeware doesn't cost much. Just make sure that what you purchase is heavy duty, rather than flimsy. You can use nonstick or not, whichever you prefer. Also keep in mind that pans, from baking sheets to tart pans, often vary slightly in size—perhaps only ¼ inch or maybe ½ inch—depending on the manufacturer. Try to use the size pan that most closely matches what is called for in a recipe. Here is a list of what I suggest to friends for stocking a basic pastry kitchen and what you will need to make the recipes in this book.

BIGGER STUFF

* Three 9-inch round cake pans (It is easier to bake each layer in its own pan, rather than split a layer.)
* 9-by-13-inch baking pan
* 9-inch square baking pan
* 8-inch square baking pan
* 9 ½-inch metal pie pan or ovenproof glass (Pyrex) pie dish (whichever you prefer)
* 9 ½-inch tart pan with removable bottom
* Six 4-inch tartlet pans or rings with ½- to ¾-inch sides
* 2 or 3 baking sheets, preferably 11½ by 17½ inches with 1-inch sides (The 1-inch sides allow

you to use the baking sheets for cakes and candies as well as cookies.)

* 10-inch (12-cup) Bundt pan
* 9-inch round springform pan
* 10-inch angel food cake pan, preferably with removable bottom and small feet around rim
* Two 8½-by-4½-by-2¾-inch loaf pans
* 1½- and 2-quart baking dishes
* Muffin pans (enough for 18 muffins) with standard wells (2¾ inches wide at the top)
* Madeleine pan and individual savarin molds
* 6-inch nonstick or well-seasoned crêpe pan or nonstick frying pan with flared sides
* 12-inch sauté pan (This item is worth spending money on. You will find yourself using it often for baking and general cooking.)
* Eight 5-ounce (⅔-cup) porcelain ramekins
* 2 ½-quart glass bowl (for trifles)
* 2 ½-quart soufflé dish
* 2-quart steamed pudding mold
* Stand mixer or handheld mixer (The latter is not as powerful or efficient as a stand mixer. All of the recipes were tested with a stand mixer, so keep in mind that if you use a handheld mixer, the mixing times will be longer. My KitchenAid stand mixer has been part of my kitchen for many years.)
* Food processor
* Digital scale
* Cooling rack

* Ice-cream maker (KitchenAid, Cuisinart, and White Mountain are all good choices.)

SMALLER STUFF

* Measuring spoons (I have two sets, so I don't have to search for them in the sink.)
* Measuring cups, for both dry measures (metal or heavy-duty plastic) and liquid measures (clear glass)
* Ice-cream scoops in various sizes, from ½ inch up to 2 inches in diameter
* Rolling pin
* Wire whisks, small and medium
* Offset spatulas, large (for frosting cakes) and small (for frosting cookies, removing some baked goods from pans, and other tasks)
* Heat-resistant silicone spatulas (for hot mixtures)
* Wooden spatulas
* Large metal (barbecue-type) spatula (for moving cake layers and larger pieces of pastry)
* Ruler (for measuring dough)
* Nonstick baking liners (such as Silpat brand)
* Parchment paper
* Mixing bowls in assorted sizes (I like stainless steel)
* Sieves, medium and fine mesh
* Cookie cutters, plain and fluted, round and other shapes, in various sizes
* Knives, chef's, paring, and serrated

* Microplane or other rasp-type grater (for citrus zest and nutmeg)
* Citrus juicers, handheld reamer or electric
* Pastry blender for making doughs (if you don't have a stand mixer)
* Metal or plastic pastry scraper
* Pastry brush
* Disposable pastry bags and star and plain pastry tips
* Thermometers, instant read and candy
* Slotted spoons
* Short-handled tongs
* Sugar shaker (for dusting tops of desserts with confectioners' sugar)
* Plastic airtight containers (for storing cookies and the like)

PLATING DESSERTS

Once I have created a dessert, it is both fun and a challenge to figure out what plate it will look good on. There is no prescribed plate for any dessert. If you have the following plates, bowls, and glassware at home, you can serve all the desserts in this book. The less ornate the plate, the better. A simpler look lets the dessert stand out.

For individual desserts
* 8- to 9-inch plates
* Individual wide bowls
* Stemmed glasses (wineglasses work well)

For whole desserts
* Large square and rectangular 12- to 14-inch platters

··· *Things That Make a Difference* ···

Some techniques are used over and over again in baking. Because I am
a professional pastry chef, I get to use and develop these skills more
than home bakers. Here are some things that I have discovered over the
years that will make your baking easier and more fun. Don't become
discouraged if you make a mistake. We all do at one time or the other.
I learned many of these techniques the hard way, too.

Reading Recipes. Cookbooks often tell you to read
a recipe in its entirety before you begin to make it.
It is good advice and bears repeating here. Even I
occasionally fall victim to being in a hurry and failing
to do it, and then always wish I had. Familiarizing
yourself with the whole recipe so that you know all
the steps involved increases your chances of making
a great dessert.

Using an Ice Bath. Ice baths are necessary to cool
liquids quickly to stop the cooking process. To make
an ice bath: Fill a bowl one-third full with ice. Add
cold water to cover the ice. Rest the bowl holding the
hot mixture in the ice bath. Whisk or stir occasionally
until the mixture cools to room temperature.

Using a Double Boiler. A standard double boiler—
two pans, one nested inside of the other—is good
for melting chocolate and making curds. Sabayons
are also cooked over water, but they require a "home-

made" double boiler, which consists of a stainless-
steel bowl over a pan of simmering water. Whisking
the ingredients in a bowl guarantees that they will
not get stuck in the corners and curdle the mixture,
especially important for eggs. A bowl also allows
more room for whisking and for the sabayon to
increase in volume.

To make a double boiler: Fill a medium-sized
saucepan one-third full with water. Bring the water
to a simmer. Rest a stainless-steel bowl in the rim of
the pan. It should be a tight fit and the bowl should
extend about one-third of the way into the pan. The
bottom of the bowl must not touch the water. If
it does, the bowl is too deep and must be replaced
with a shallower bowl.

Judging Room-Temperature Butter. When a recipe
calls for room-temperature butter, the butter should
not be so soft that it looks greasy. To test for the
correct softness, press lightly against the butter with

your index finger. It should leave an imprint, but the butter should hold its shape.

Melting Chocolate. There are two basic ways to melt chocolate. You can use a traditional or homemade double boiler as described previously or, for smaller amounts, you can use a microwave. Finely chop the chocolate for both methods. If using a double boiler, turn off the heat before you rest the pan or bowl with the chocolate in the pan. The residual heat will melt the chocolate. Stir the chocolate occasionally as it melts, and then, once it is melted, whisk or stir until smooth. If using a microwave, place the chopped chocolate in a microwave-safe bowl, microwave for 1 minute, and then stir. If the chocolate is not completely melted, repeat in 15- to 30-second intervals until the chocolate is melted, stirring after each interval. (The chocolate will not become completely smooth until it is stirred.) Many pastry chefs use a microwave for large amounts of chocolate, but I find that the chocolate burns easily, so I prefer to use a double boiler when melting a big quantity. Also, white chocolate melts at a lower temperature than dark chocolate.

I don't call for tempering chocolate (carefully heating and then cooling the chocolate to ensure that it is evenly colored, shiny, and malleable) in this book. In cases where the chocolate may bloom—develop a speckled appearance—because it hasn't been tempered, such as on top of toffee,

melt it at the minimum temperature possible so that it doesn't get hot. Remember, too, the speckling is only a visual imperfection. The dessert will still be delicious.

Mixing Ingredients. Three terms—beat, whip, and fold—are used repeatedly in baking, and what is meant by each of them can sometimes be confusing. If you are instructed to beat ingredients, you should try to combine them without incorporating a lot of air. If you have a stand mixer, use the paddle attachment; if you are beating by hand, use a wooden spoon or spatula. (A wooden utensil is stiffer than a rubber spatula and makes mixing easier.) Creaming is another word for beating. If you are told to whip ingredients, you want to incorporate air into them. Use the whip attachment on your stand mixer, or a whisk if whipping by hand.

When you are directed to fold two mixtures together, work as gently as possible. Use a rubber spatula and begin by putting the lighter mixture on top of the denser one. Position the spatula in the middle of the stacked mixtures and draw it straight down through them, carrying some of the lighter mixture to the bottom of the bowl. Then, run the spatula along the bottom of the bowl and up one side in a fluid motion, carrying some of the heavier mixture with it up over the surface. Rotate the bowl one-quarter turn and repeat the folding action. Work quickly but lightly, so that you deflate the lighter mixture as little as possible, and halt the folding the moment the two mixtures are just combined.

Scraping the Bowl. When mixing ingredients, always scrape the bottom and the sides of the bowl well to incorporate all the ingredients. If you don't, butter or flour sticking to them will not get mixed in and can affect the outcome of the dessert.

Using a Stand Mixer. Desserts are easier and quicker to make when you use a stand mixer; plus, this efficient machine comes in various vivid colors that are sure to brighten your kitchen. It is what I use, and the recipe directions in this book are written for the stand mixer. You can make nearly all of the recipes with a handheld mixer, but you will need to increase the mixing time by a minute or two.

Sifting Dry Ingredients. It is important to sift dry ingredients—flour, baking powder, baking soda— to aerate them and to rid them of any lumps or hard pieces. I use kosher salt, which doesn't fit through the holes of a sifter, so you will need to add the salt to the dry ingredients after sifting.

Greasing Pans. You can either grease pans with butter or coat them with nonstick spray. I have called for buttering the pans in most of the recipes, but nonstick spray is quicker and less messy. Use a brand that doesn't have a lot of water in it.

Too much water will cause baked items to stick to the pan.

Toasting Nuts. To prevent sogginess and to ensure maximum flavor, always toast nuts before adding them to a recipe. Spread them in a shallow pan and place in a preheated 300°F oven for about 20 minutes. They will take on color and become fragrant. Nuts with a higher fat content, such as macadamias, walnuts, and pecans, will toast more quickly than those with less fat, such as almonds and peanuts. To check whether almonds are ready, cut a whole nut in half and look at the interior color. It should be golden brown.

Skinning hazelnuts is a thankless job, so purchase skinned hazelnuts if you can find them. If you can only find hazelnuts with their skins intact, toast them as directed, checking not only for a change in color and fragrance but also loosening skins, then put them in a colander and swirl them around, letting the loose skins fall through the holes. Don't worry about getting every bit of skin off, just the loose pieces.

Making Caramel. If you are a novice at making caramel, set aside some quiet time and focus on learning how to do it. Once you master it, it will no longer be intimidating. You need to be attentive through the process, however, so that you don't burn the caramel or yourself. To be safe, keep a bowl of cold water nearby for soothing burns in case you are splattered. Once you have made caramel several times, you will be able to recognize when it has reached the proper color. If it is too light, your sauce will be thin; it if it is too dark, it will be bitter.

To begin, gently stir together the sugar and water in a heavy pan, being careful not to splash the sugar on the sides of the pan where it can stick and later crystallize. Place the pan over medium heat to dissolve the sugar, stirring occasionally. When the mixture begins to boil, increase the heat to high and do not stir the mixture again while it boils. Use a wet pastry brush to wash down any sugar crystals clinging to the sides of the pan. Cook until the sugar becomes a golden amber, which usually takes 3 to 5 minutes. When the mixture starts to change from light to medium amber, remove the pan from the heat. This lets the bubbles subside so that you can more easily see the color and slows down the cooking so that you don't overcook the caramel. If it is not yet golden amber, return it to the heat for a littler longer. Once the caramel is the correct color and off the heat, you can start adding the liquid a couple of tablespoons at a time. The caramel will bubble up as you add the liquid. Using a long-handled wooden spoon or a whisk, stir gently so the bubbles subside. If the caramel sputters rapidly, stop stirring and let the bubbles subside on their own. Once the mixture has cooled a bit, you can add the liquid more quickly.

Shaving Chocolate. The easiest way to shave chocolate is to start with a big block. Put the chocolate on a piece of parchment paper or plastic wrap. Using a melon baller or the end of an apple corer, scrape the chocolate toward you to make curls. Alternately, with a smaller piece of chocolate, slip a plastic bag over your hand and grasp the chocolate. Using a vegetable peeler, shave the narrow edge of the chocolate. Then, using the side of the knife blade, transfer the curls to a plate. Be careful not to crush them. To grate chocolate, use a Microplane or similar fine-rasp grater.

Using Parchment Paper. Parchment paper is a baker's savior. You may use it to line cake and cookie pans to prevent sticking and to simplify cleanup. It is easier to sift dry ingredients onto parchment than it is into a bowl. Then you need only make a chute out of the parchment to add the sifted dry ingredients to other ingredients, forgoing the often messy transfer from one bowl to another. If you have access to a restaurant-supply store, buy parchment paper in sheets. You won't have to worry about it curling up as you do when you tear it from a roll.

Using Vanilla Beans. These tropical beans are expensive, so you want to get every bit of flavor from them. To get the seeds out, cut the bean in half lengthwise. With a knife blade, scrape out the seeds. Use both the seeds and the pod halves. After using the pod halves, rinse and allow to air-dry. Slip them into a canister of sugar to flavor it, or grind them to a powder in a spice grinder.

Toasting Coconut. Coconut tastes and looks better and has a better texture if it is toasted before you use it in recipes. Spread the coconut in a single layer on a baking sheet and place in a preheated 350°F oven. Stir the coconut every few minutes, as it will color around the edges faster than it will in the middle. Cook until evenly brown, which should take about 8 minutes. Be careful, as it burns easily.

Measuring Dry Ingredients. Professional pastry chefs weigh their ingredients, and for larger amounts it yields a better result. For smaller amounts, such as those in home baking, measuring by volume is fine, though it must be done accurately. To measure dry ingredients, dip the measuring cup in the ingredient so that it is overflowing. Using a table knife, sweep away the excess level with the rim, being careful not to pack down the ingredients. To measure in a measuring spoon, also fill it to overflowing and sweep away the excess. For greater accuracy, measure chocolate by weight. The size of the chocolate pieces will affect how much chocolate fits into a measuring cup.

Using a Water Bath. Some cakes, custards, puddings, and other desserts need to be cooked in a water bath, which calls for putting the pan or dish holding the uncooked dessert in a larger pan of water. This allows the dessert to cook more gently and evenly. It can be hard to find a pan that will hold a standard cake pan, but I have discovered that a large (12-inch) sauté pan with 2-inch sides works well. For other desserts, a baking pan or roasting pan can be used. It is easier to fill the pan with water when it is already on the rack, so place the item or items to be baked in the empty pan, place the pan on the middle rack of the oven, and then pour in the water to the depth indicated in individual recipes.

Knowing Your Oven. Most ovens, even professional ones, have one side that is hotter than the other. If you are using two shelves at the same time, such as when baking multiple cake layers or baking sheets of cookies, halfway through baking switch the pans between the shelves. Rotate the baking sheets 180 degrees at the same time.

Cutting Desserts. For nice-looking slices, run a knife under hot water (or dip it in a pitcher of hot water), dry it off with a towel, and then make a cut. Clean the knife between cuts to ensure each slice is neat. The towel and the water container can look messy, so you can serve the dessert already plated, or present it whole and then return to the kitchen to slice it.

⸱⸱⸱ *Sweets & Stickies* ⸱⸱⸱

BY PETER PALMER

FARALLON WINE DIRECTOR

Dessert and dessert wine, enjoyed together or alone, provide some of the most memorable moments of any meal. From a simple fresh fruit preparation paired with a delicate, flowery Muscat Beaumes de Venise or Moscato d'Asti to a golden, honeyed glass of Sauternes alongside a slab of Stilton or a wedge of tarte Tatin, the possibilities and combinations awaiting the expectant diner are countless.

People remember dessert. Indeed, humans have an unarguable penchant for most things sweet. Just witness the outrageous success of the soft-drinks industry. Sugar is even slipped into some savory recipes to tempt and satisfy the palate. Meat has an inherent sweetness; bottled salad dressings and other prepared foods contain surprising, hidden amounts of sugar; and fast food is absolutely loaded with sweeteners. Chefs will sometimes utilize an accent of fruit or a drizzle of a *gastrique*, an ever-so-slightly-sweet reduction, as part of a main course to deliver a subtle contrast to the starch, protein, and vegetables on the plate and to heighten the complexity of the dish. But because it arrives at the end of the meal and it satisfies our natural cravings, we tend to recall easily what the pastry chef whipped up for dessert.

My own love affair with the world of dessert wines—at least those made from white grapes— began with a half bottle of Château Rieussec, the much-lauded property in Bordeaux, shared with a

friend in the early 1990s. At the time it was unlike anything I had previously experienced, with a full-blown, exotic complexity of aroma and taste, a luxurious palate balanced by fresh acidity, and a finish that seemed to go on forever. Simply put, it blew me away.

My objective here is to explore briefly some of the world's best-known stickies (what the Australians affectionately call sweet wines) and offer ideas for enjoying them with dessert. Wines from Europe and a few of their New World counterparts are considered, along with suggestions for pairing them with that little something sweet at the end of a meal. Do not view this as an all-encompassing bible to dessert-and-wine pairing, however. Look on it instead as a reflection on some of my favorite discoveries and as a springboard to your own exploration and experimentation.

Dessert wines can be expensive or relatively modest, simple or beguilingly complex. They can be sipped as dessert itself, or matched with a favorite sweet ending to create an even more remarkable experience.

FOOD FOR THOUGHT

RESIDUAL SUGAR

The dessert wine should *always* (I hate to say "always," as there are exceptions to almost every rule) have the same or a slightly higher sense of sweetness as the dessert. If it doesn't, the sugar in the dessert tends to strip the wine of its mouthfeel and fruit, leaving it with an exaggerated leanness. Many wine bottles sport residual sugar amounts somewhere on the label. This information can be useful, but nothing beats first-hand experience of the wine region and producer, and learning to trust your palate.

ACIDITY

Acidity in wine, as in food, is usually a good thing. It cuts through fat and richness and refreshes the palate, making the mouth anticipate the next bite, sip, taste. Add sugar to water and you create simple syrup, which, of course, no one drinks. Add a dash or more of lemon juice and you get lemonade, the quintessential refresher. Acid is good.

BALANCE

Consider a peach. In the summer, if left to ripen on the tree for a brief yet precise time, a peach will achieve a sublime yin and yang of sweetness and juiciness, of flavor, and of, well, peachiness. Taken too early, the fruit is hollow and acidic, tough and forgettable; plucked too late, it loses its attractive liveliness. Picked even later and it is mushy and rotten. But for a couple of weeks the elements of sugar, texture, flavor, and acidity combine to create a whole that is more than the sum of its parts. This is balance. And like the peach, or like an apple or strawberry or any fruit, the elements of wine must also be in sync. Start with a wine that is not balanced and food will just exacerbate its flaws.

PERSONAL PREFERENCE

I'm an acid freak and I know it. I also like bitterness, which is why I find myself drawn to the darker chocolates. But clearly some people prefer softer, less intense milk chocolate. Just as clearly, some people don't care for peaches, and instead crave melon or bananas or some other fruit. So it is with the world of wine. Not everyone will appreciate the high-wire acid and sugar act of authentic German *Eiswein*, but luckily the earth is not limited to only one expression of dessert wine. The world is your oyster—or at least a molded white chocolate Joseph Schmidt bivalve—so dive in and discover the remarkable sea of options available at your local wine shop or restaurant. Ask for advice and recommendations. You will soon learn which wines you like the best.

NOBLE ROT

Sounds yummy . . . I'll take a double. No discussion of sweet late-harvest wines would be complete, or as interesting, without mold. And not just any mold, mind you, but the benevolent strain fondly known as *Botrytis cinerea*. In the right place at the right time—autumn by the banks of a river, perhaps—botrytis attacks healthy, ultraripe grapes and sucks out all the water, dehydrating them and leaving nothing behind but the moldy grape, of course, and the very essence of concentrated grape sugars and flavors.

Left to Mother Nature, this good mold—this *pourriture noble*, or "noble rot"—doesn't occur every year, which is one reason these shriveled grapes, and the wine they produce, can be so expensive. Several factors must be in alignment for the mold to occur in a positive fashion: warm, but not too hot, weather; morning mists and high humidity; ripe, unbroken grape skins; and its slow, even spread throughout the vineyard. If all the elements are in place, and the estate harvests the grapes and ferments and ages the wine with care, the resulting liquid is transformed from humble juice to what some consider the nectar of the gods.

GRAPES AND WINES

MUSCAT

The family of grapes collectively known as muscat is large and diverse. It is one of the oldest of wine varieties, part of the luggage of both the ancient Greeks and ancient Romans as they explored and conquered new lands. The grape is grown throughout the world now, producing a plethora of wines, some dry, some sweet, some white, some red, but all disarmingly aromatic and flowery. The finest variety goes by several different names but delivers, according to the experts, superior grapes and wine. Muscat Blanc à Petits Grains, Moscato di Canelli, Muscat d'Alsace, Muscat de Frontignan, Muskateller, and many more are all synonyms for this one variety. Two of the best-known examples are the low-alcohol, frothy Moscato d'Asti from Italy's Piedmont region and the fortified, but still lighter-bodied Muscat Beaumes de Venise from the southern Rhône Valley of France. New World examples include the popular Bonny Doon Muscat Vin de Glacière from California, a modern and consistently delicious example of ice wine.

The many different styles of muscat, just like the foods they match, span the dessert spectrum. The lighter expressions like Beaumes de Venise pair especially well with fruit-based preparations and simple cakes, tarts, and cookies. Moscato d'Asti is versatile at the table, pairs well with a host of sweets (even chocolate), and can be a wonderful pick-me-up at the end of a long meal. Richer styles include Passito di Pantelleria, from a small island near Sicily, and Moscato Passito from the Piedmont, both made from partially dried grapes. The decadent muscat- and Muscadelle-based wines of Chambers Rosewood Vineyards in Rutherglen, Australia, are top-notch examples from Down Under, expertly blended from stocks of fortified, old, and rare wines.

Muscat and Dessert Pairings
Lemon-Raspberry Pudding Soufflé (page 98)
Crêpes Suzette (page 99)
Lemon Blueberry Trifle (page 48)
Poppyseed Shortcakes with Strawberries (page 148)
Cornmeal Tartlets with Orange Crème Fraîche
    and Strawberries (page 168)
Passion Fruit–Meringue Tartlets (page 166)

SAUTERNES
Sémillon, Sauvignon Blanc, and Muscadelle— these three grapes, in varying proportions, are responsible for one of the most heralded, most age-worthy, and most sumptuous sweet wines in the world. Produced in only a handful of *communes* south of the city of Bordeaux, true Sauternes is difficult, time-consuming, and expensive to make. Individual berries, and only those rife with botrytis, are harvested one grape at a time, and multiple passes, sometimes seven or eight or more, through the vineyard are made to ensure that only perfect grapes—actually the shriveled raisins that pass as grapes—are picked at their optimum. The climate, of course, does not always favor the healthy development of botrytis. Maybe three years in

every decade deliver the right raw material and the right autumn weather for a truly great vintage. But the mere fact that it does happen keeps wine folk clamoring, hoping for more.

Sauternes are unfortified but lush, heady, and decadent wines, vanilla tinged from oak aging, honeyed, decayed, and sometimes smoky. They can last and develop in a bottle for a long, long time, becoming even more complex and deserving candidates for sipping alone, coveted as dessert in their own right. When served with food, Sauternes usually complement full-bodied preparations: caramel sauce and crème brûlée, tarte Tatin, sweets based on nuts and honey, *financiers*. The much-sought-after Dolce, a late-harvest Sémillon and Sauvignon blend from California's Napa Valley, is considered a fine example of a New World Sauternes-style dessert wine.

Sauternes and Dessert Pairings
Walnut Rum Steamed Pudding (page 52)
Apple Pandowdy (page 104)
Pear Charlotte (page 106)
French Apple Tartlets (page 165)
Banana Napoleons with Warm Caramel
    Walnut Sauce (page 170)

RIESLING
Riesling, in all its expressions, is misunderstood by much of the wine-drinking world, which sees it as

a sweet, sticky, flabby beverage that only grand-mothers and wine newbies find attractive. In reality, it is one of the most, if not *the* most, riveting and versatile grape varieties on earth, able to produce wines of complexity, depth of flavor, and a trans-parency that reflects its origins.

Dessert-style wines made from Riesling can be botrytis-infected or not. *Eiswein* from Germany, somewhat rare and expensive, is the best example of the rot-free type: an intense, sweet, high-acid wine made from grapes left to freeze on the vine and then harvested in the cold morning hours very late in the year (sometimes even in January). The resulting ice crystals are left behind in the press and only the concentrated grape juice and sugar is fermented into wine. Inniskillin Winery in Canada has made New World ice wine its specialty. Bonny Doon in Cali-fornia makes the previously mentioned Muscat Vin de Glacière, and other countries (Austria and Aus-tralia) and a handful of locations within the United States (California, Ohio, New York, Washington) have wineries devoted to producing high-quality ice wines from Rieslings and other grapes.

When the autumn weather in Germany is favorable and noble rot attacks the Riesling grape (only a couple times each decade), the late-harvest, botrytis-infected wines are classified on the label with the mind-numbing, tongue-twisting Trocken-beerenauslese (TBA) designation. Across the border, in the Alsace region of France, Riesling (along with muscat, Gewürztraminer, and Pinot Gris) can also succumb to botrytis, with the resulting wine labeled Selection des Grains Nobles (SGN). German TBA and Alsace SGN are rare and expensive, but the wines are a hedonist's dream-come-true: luscious, exotic, concentrated, and complex expressions of deca-dence in a bottle. A tad easier on the pocketbook is Navarro Cluster Select Late Harvest Riesling from the Anderson Valley in Mendocino County, California. Although hard to find because it is not produced every year, it is worth the search.

Most of these wines will match well with rich desserts (and some are superb with foie gras, but that is another story); they have the flavor, the extract, the acid, and the sugar to stand up to full-flavored foods.

Riesling and Dessert Pairings
Pear Riesling Trifle (*Eiswein*) (page 47)
Maple Banana Compote with Ginger
    Ice Cream (page 94)
Pumpkin Steamed Pudding (page 56)
Poached Pears with Walnut Cream (page 132)
Summer Pudding (*Eiswein*) (page 145)
Maple Pecan Pie (page 175)

CHENIN BLANC
Along with the Riesling grape, Chenin Blanc con-spires to produce, in the right area and with favorable growing conditions, sweet wines of incomparable depth and balance. The best-known growing region

is Vouvray in France's Loire Valley. The area produces many distinct styles: very dry and mineral-like, off-dry but still refreshingly acidic, sparkling, *moelleux* (soft, medium-sweet, and mellow), and, of course, late-harvest, botrytis-infected dessert wines.

The latter are stupendous with a wide range of cheeses, making them much more versatile than port. The natural high acid and residual sugar pairs well with everything from goat cheese to a big, bold blue. Vouvray and other sweet wines made from Chenin Blanc (Quarts de Chaumes, Coteaux du Layon, Bonnezeaux) are terrific accompaniments to many fruit-based desserts (apple and lemon), will hold their own with holiday cakes and pies, and have the richness and acid to pair well with fuller, sweeter preparations.

Chenin Blanc and Dessert Pairings
Summer Trifle (page 46)
Persimmon Pudding (page 57)
Peach Boysenberry Cobbler (page 108)
Goat Cheese Cake with Mixed Berries (page 188)
Orange Spice Cake with Berries (page 196)
Gingerbread with Warm Apples and Cider
    Sabayon (page 206)
Lemon Custards (page 44)

TOKAJI

Never heard of Furmint? You are not alone, but I am sure you know its most famous expression:

Hungarian Tokaji. A unique and historic specialty of Hungary's far northwest region, Tokaji is a combination of fully fermented wine (Furmint, muscat, and others) with the controlled addition of Aszú, the local name for a paste made from botrytis-infected grapes. The standard measure of these berries and the sweet paste made from them (the amount of Aszú added back into the base wine) is based on an old measure called *puttonyos*. This traditional moniker still appears on the label of Tokaji Aszú wine (3, 4, 5, or 6 *puttonyos* and so on) and offers clues to the wine's body and style. A level 6 *puttonyos* Tokaji Aszú will be fuller, sweeter, and more intense than one labeled 3 *puttonyos*. All of the wines (at least the ones that are traditionally made) should be a beautiful orange-amber, have a pronounced, zesty acidity and a taste reminiscent of spiced apricots and honey, and offer a tinge of sherrylike complexity that adds to their individuality and allure.

Tokaji and Dessert Pairings
Walnut Rum Steamed Pudding (page 52)
Pumpkin Pie (page 174)
Apricot Custard Tart (page 154)
Russian Tea Cakes (page 223)
Savarin with Grand Marnier Sabayon and
    Mixed Berries (page 134)

VIN SANTO

Made from a combination of grapes, mostly

Trebbiano and Malvasia, *vin santo*, literally "holy wine," is a specialty of Tuscany. It is an example of a *passito* wine, the traditional practice of drying or partially drying the harvested grapes on straw mats. A warm, dry, well-ventilated area is used for the controlled "raisining" of the fruit before it is crushed and fermented. The resulting wine, depending on the producer and choice of grape, can vary widely in quality and sweetness: some almost dry; some syrupy sweet; some young, vibrant, and inexpensive; some mature, vintage-dated rarities. Most *vin santo* will be amber hued and have a bit of the *rancio* character associated with fino sherry. It can be served simply with a plate of crunchy biscotti (dip the cookies into the wine) and pairs well with other desserts based on nuts and dried fruits.

Vin Santo and Dessert Pairings
Macaroon Nut Tart (page 159)
Honey-Marsala Baked Figs with Ginger
    Sabayon (page 126)
Torta Regina (page 195)
Almond Biscotti (page 232)
Tuscan Cream Cake (page 203)

SHERRY

True sherry, which hails from Andalusia in southwest Spain, comes in many different styles, from salty and bone-dry to dark, creamy, and syrupy sweet. Along with Madeira, sherry remains one of the greatest wine values on earth, and can be enjoyed from the first course through dessert. Cream sherry and East India sherry, the richer, sweeter versions, take center stage for our purposes. Both are made from Palomino, the workhorse grape of sherry, with or without additions of Pedro Ximénez and Muscat of Alexandria, and are a distinctive, delicious, and unique alternative at the table. They traditionally have a slight oxidative edge, derived from the *solera* system of aging and blending, which adds to their character.

Cream sherry is soft, velvety, and viscous, pairing well with rich cookies, dried fruits, oats, raisins, and nut-based cakes. East India distinguishes itself by being baked, or cooked, like Madeira. It complements some of the same foods as cream sherry, but it can also shine with chocolate presentations, especially ones that combine fruit and nuts.

Sherry and Dessert Pairings
Tiramisu (page 51)
Chocolate-Filled Filo Triangles (page 73)
Chocolate Truffle Tart (page 158)
Maple Pecan Pie (page 175)
Chocolate-Hazelnut Pound Cake with
    Espresso-Cinnamon Cream (page 192)

MADEIRA

The islands of Madeira, a group of lonely volcanic mountains off the west coast of Africa, produce an utterly delicious, truly distinctive style of wine. And it is one that I happen to adore. It is probably the combination of a luscious sweetness and a cornucopia of dried fruit, caramel, and nut flavors contrasted with laserlike acidity and a unique something-or-other that comes from treating the wine so poorly. Madeira, you see, suffers abuses that few other wines would tolerate as well. It is baked, cooked, exposed to damaging temperature and humidity, and oxidized. In other words, it is basically thrashed throughout its upbringing but somehow turns out fine.

Perhaps the most charming part of the Madeira story is the historical practice of using barrels of the young wine as ballast for ships—and, naturally, as refreshment for the sailors on them—traveling from Europe, stopping at the islands, and then continuing on to the Americas. This is how Madeira as we know it—and love it—was born. Sloshed around in the hold of an eighteenth-century ship, crossing the equator once, sometimes twice, with no refrigeration, would ruin any wine or foodstuff. But Madeira survived, even blossomed, and the early colonists quickly developed a taste for it.

Malvasia (also known as Malmsey) and Bual, two of the handful of grapes grown on steep terraces on the islands, yield the richest styles of Madeira and the ones that suit the needs of dessert. The young fermented and fortified wine is now barrel aged in an *estufa*, basically a modern hothouse,

that re-creates the seafaring voyages of old, or it is simply left outside to ripen in the unrelenting sun and heat. When made with care, and from good grapes, these wines are utterly unique, and practically indestructible: an open bottle will remain fresh for a good while.

Bual-Malmsey wines stand up to rich cookies, marzipan, holiday-spiced cakes and pies, and many cheeses, easily matching their fullness and refreshing the palate with that telltale acidity. There is plenty of modern Madeira that lacks character and authenticity, so take pains to search out a reputable producer. Blandy's and Broadbent Selections are two prominent quality shippers, but wines from many smaller estates are now reaching American shores as well.

Madeira and Dessert Pairings
Maple Pecan Pie (page 175)
Caramel Almond Tartlets with Warm
   Blueberries (page 162)
Pumpkin Cheesecake (page 189)
Marmalade Window Cookies (page 230)
Walnut Rum Steamed Pudding (page 52)

BRACHETTO
Made from a light red grape variety from northwest Italy, in the area of Asti, Roero, and Alessandra, Brachetto is an odd little wine, rarely seen outside its home base, but definitely worth trying. From

its charming pink color and slightly fizzy mouth-feel to its inviting aroma of wild strawberries, rose petals, and subtle spice, the wine is lovely and distinctive. As you might imagine, it is a good partner with desserts featuring delicate red fruits but is surprisingly adept with chocolate preparations as well.

Brachetto and Dessert Pairings
Three-Chocolate Brownies (page 236)
Strawberry Grand Marnier Trifle (page 50)
Strawberry Compote with Rhubarb
   Ice Cream (page 96)
Bing Cherry Tart (page 155)
Persimmon Pudding (page 57)

BANYULS
A popular alternative to port, Banyuls is a fortified red wine from the southern reaches of France's Roussillon region, perched above the shores of the Mediterranean and just across the border with Spain. The main grape variety is the noble Grenache Noir, the same grape used in Châteauneuf-du-Pape and other southern Rhône Valley wines. When the fermentation is partially finished, alcohol is added to the must, arresting the process and leaving behind residual grape sugars. The resulting wine is left to macerate further, barrel aged, and then bottled. The style of Banyuls depends greatly on the aim of the estate. The wines may be sweet, spicy,

and liqueur-like, reminiscent of the fruit of an earthy framboise, or they may be mature and complex, slightly *rancio* expressions that can age magnificently. They are considered a great foil for rich chocolate desserts, especially in their heady, unbridled youth.

Banyuls and Dessert Pairings
Chocolate Espresso Frozen Cream
   Sandwiches (page 82)
Stareos (page 239)
Gâteau Royale (page 88)
Chocolate Almond Bark (page 251)
Hazelnut Shortcakes with Plum Compote (page 124)
Orange Spice Cake with Berries (page 196)

PORT
There are some eighty different grape varieties that may be used in the production of port. Luckily, no one is going to test you on all the names. If, however, you feel like impressing your dinner guests, you can always memorize a few of the most important grapes, although the details may be a bit fuzzy after a multicourse dinner of food and wine. Touriga Nacional, Tinta Barroca, Touriga Francesa, Tinta Roriz, and Tinta Cão—there they are, ready for your next round of Trivial Pursuit.

What is important to understand are the different styles of Portugal's most famous wine—the granddaddy of fortified reds—and the area in which they are made. Real port comes from the Douro Valley, a hot, dry inland region that wants to produce dark, intense, thick-skinned grapes. The land is divided into hundreds of different *quintas* (farms, or vineyards), some individually owned and some owned by the major port houses. The bottled product usually combines grapes and wines from all of a producer's holdings or contracts.

After harvesting, maceration, and the beginnings of that wonderful chemical transformation we wine lovers call fermentation, grape brandy is added to the vats. This stops the process, raises the alcohol level, and leaves behind unfermented grape sugar, the sweetness in port. At this point, the sturdy young wine is drawn off into barrels, where it rests for a couple years while the estate decides its fate.

In addition to white port, there are two basic categories: ruby and tawny. Basic ruby port is a multivintage blend of many wines, combined to produce a consistent house style year after year, much like a nonvintage Champagne. It is, as the name suggests, a healthy ruby red, with a grapy, sweet, and fruity personality that marries well with chocolate, cherries, and the sturdier cheeses. All the major port houses offer their own version, labeled with proprietary names like Fonseca Bin 27, Graham's Six Grapes, and Warre's Warrior, to name a few.

Basic tawny port, also a blend, is labeled as ten year, twenty year, and even forty year (the older,

the more expensive) and is made from wines left to mature in barrel for years. The year on the bottle is an average of the different ages used. During this extended aging process, the wine loses its young ruby color (fading to amber) and the flavors mellow, becoming more delicate, fig-like, dried, and nutty. It is suited to desserts based on nuts, caramel, brown sugar, and dried fruits.

Other port styles include Colheita, a vintage-dated tawny that spends decades in barrel and is bottled only when the house decides to release it. These ports are usually rare and expensive, though worth the search as some can be magnificent. LBV, or Late Bottled Vintage, is a vintage dated, ruby style port that has seen a few more years of barrel aging and is ready to drink on release. It should, in theory, be a step up in complexity and intensity from basic nonvintage ruby port. Single-*quinta* port comes from one estate (or farm), will be vintage dated, and has the name of the *quinta* on the label. These are sturdy, structured, intense wines that can age well in bottle and throw sediment just like vintage port.

Ah . . . vintage port. Just a mention of the wine calls to mind regal celebrations, gastronomic feats of unrivaled gluttony, bottles a century old, history, pomp, and circumstance. In the Douro Valley, when all the varied elements involved in grape growing and wine production come together just right, a port house will "declare" a vintage. They will bottle what should be their finest wine. The stuff of legends, of birth years, of royalty, vintage port is meant to age for decades and then be carefully decanted and enjoyed in its maturity. It can certainly be served alongside dessert, but, as with old Sauternes, it is probably relished best by itself, with blue cheese and nuts, or with very simple presentations.

Several other countries produce splendid port-style wines made from such grapes as Zinfandel, Grenache, and Shiraz. They are usually full-bodied, spicy, fruity, sweet wines that can stand in beautifully if a bottle of true port is not in the liquor cabinet.

Ruby Port and Dessert Pairings
Warm Bittersweet Chocolate Tartlets with
    Spiced Almonds (page 164)
Chocolate Truffle Tart (page 158)
Bing Cherry Tart (page 155)
Plum Vanilla Creamsicle Bombe with Plum
    Caramel Sauce (page 122)
Black-and-White Brownies (page 238)

Tawny Port and Dessert Pairings
Chocolate Caramel Bread Pudding (page 64)
Caramel Almond Tartlets with Warm
    Blueberries (page 162)
Walnut Rum Steamed Pudding (page 52)
Chocolate-Hazelnut Pound Cake with
    Espresso-Cinnamon Cream (page 192)

PUDDINGS,
CUSTARDS,
MOUSSES &
TRIFLES

— CHAPTER 1 —

The recipes in this chapter, because of their creaminess, are often wrongfully belittled as "comfort desserts." In truth, they are among the best ways to cap off a meal—or to enjoy at any time. Custards, simple in design and small in size, have a silky texture that never leaves you wanting more. Steamed puddings do not have to be the too-familiar cannonballs of winter holiday entertaining. Properly assembled and cooked, they are just firm enough to be cut like a cake but still very moist, and even after several days, they still taste as if freshly made. Trifles are ethereal, with complexities of flavor other desserts cannot match. They are wonderful for larger parties, as they are both dramatic and may be assembled a day ahead. Just be sure to hide the trifle in the back of the refrigerator, so it does not disappear before the party starts.

38
CARAMEL CUSTARDS

48
LEMON BLUEBERRY TRIFLE

40
ORANGE CRÈME CARAMELS WITH RASPBERRIES

50
STRAWBERRY GRAND MARNIER TRIFLE

42
CHOCOLATE "BRÛLÉE" GINGER CUSTARDS

51
TIRAMISU

44
LEMON CUSTARDS

52
WALNUT RUM STEAMED PUDDING

45
FRENCH CREAM WITH BERRIES

54
BLUEBERRY STEAMED PUDDING

46
SUMMER TRIFLE

56
PUMPKIN STEAMED PUDDING

47
PEAR RIESLING TRIFLE

57
PERSIMMON PUDDING

CARAMEL CUSTARDS

— SERVES 6 —

A custard is like a cookie: its ingredients and presentation are simple, yet its taste is anything but. The depth of the caramel flavor gives these custards the sophistication of a much fancier and more difficult-to-prepare dessert. After all these years, this is still one of my favorite endings to a meal.

6 LARGE EGG YOLKS

¼ CUP WATER

1 CUP GRANULATED SUGAR

2 CUPS HEAVY WHIPPING CREAM

1 CUP MILK

In a large bowl, whisk together the egg yolks until blended. Set aside.

In a heavy, nonreactive saucepan large enough to eventually hold the milk and cream, stir together the water and sugar. Place over medium heat and cook, stirring occasionally, until the sugar dissolves and the mixture comes to a boil. Increase the heat to high and cook, without stirring, until the syrup becomes a golden amber. (See page 20 for tips on making caramel.)

While the sugar is cooking, put the cream in a small, heavy saucepan and place over medium heat until small bubbles appear around the edges of the pan, then remove from the heat. Prepare an ice bath. (See page 18 for tips on using an ice bath.)

As soon as the caramel is golden amber, remove from the heat and let the bubbles subside for a few seconds. Stir in about ¼ cup of the hot cream. Be careful as you stir, as the caramel will bubble up when you add the cream. Continue to add the cream about ½ cup at a time, stirring and waiting for the bubbles to subside before adding more. Once all the cream has been added, whisk in the milk.

While whisking constantly, pour the caramel mixture into the egg yolks in a slow, steady stream. Place the bowl in the ice bath and let cool to room temperature, whisking occasionally. Meanwhile, preheat the oven to 300°F.

Strain the custard through a fine-mesh sieve into a bowl. Place six 5-ounce ramekins in a 9-by-13-inch baking pan. (See page 22 for tips on using a water bath.) Fill the ramekins with the caramel cream. Cover the pan with aluminum foil but leave one corner open. Place the baking pan in the middle of the oven. Carefully pour hot water into the pan so that the water comes halfway up the sides of the ramekins. Cover the pan completely with the foil.

Bake the custards for 50 minutes. To check if the custards are ready, carefully remove the foil and gently shake a ramekin. The custard should be set around the edges, yet have an area in the middle—about the size of a quarter—that is not completely firm. Remove the pan from the oven. Remove the ramekins from the pan with tongs or a dish towel to protect your fingers. Cover and refrigerate for at least 2 hours before serving.

PLANNING AHEAD

The custard base may be made 2 days in advance and kept refrigerated. The custards may be baked a day in advance and kept refrigerated.

ORANGE CRÈME CARAMELS WITH RASPBERRIES

— SERVES 6 —

A crème caramel is often passed over in favor of the more popular crème brûlée. Both depend on caramel for their predominate flavor, but in a crème caramel the caramel is soft and the custard is unmolded. Raspberries or other fresh fruits are the perfect accompaniment. To make pouring the caramel into the ramekins easy, transfer from the pan into a heatproof measuring cup.

ORANGE CUSTARD BASE

⅔ CUP MILK

2 CUPS HEAVY WHIPPING CREAM

PEEL OF 1 ORANGE

4 LARGE EGG YOLKS

1 LARGE WHOLE EGG

⅔ CUP GRANULATED SUGAR

PINCH OF KOSHER SALT

CARAMEL

⅔ CUP GRANULATED SUGAR

5 TABLESPOONS WATER

1 PINT RASPBERRIES (ABOUT 2 CUPS)

1 TABLESPOON GRAND MARNIER (OPTIONAL)

To make the custard base: In a heavy, nonreactive saucepan, combine the milk, cream, and orange peel over medium heat and heat until small bubbles appear around the edges of the pan. Remove from the heat, cover, and let steep for 10 minutes.

Meanwhile, prepare an ice bath. (See page 18 for tips on using an ice bath.) In a large stainless-steel bowl, whisk together the egg yolks, whole egg, sugar, and salt until blended.

While whisking constantly, pour the milk mixture into the egg mixture in a slow, steady stream. Place the bowl in the ice bath and let cool to room temperature, whisking occasionally. Strain through a fine-mesh sieve into a bowl and discard the orange peel.

To make the caramel: While the custard base is cooling, arrange six 5-ounce ramekins in a 9-by-13-inch baking pan. (See page 22 for tips on using a water bath.) In a small, heavy saucepan, stir together the sugar and 3 tablespoons of the water. Place over medium heat and cook, stirring occasionally, until the sugar dissolves and comes to a boil. Increase the heat to high and cook, without stirring, until the mixture becomes a golden amber. (See page 20 for tips on making caramel.) Remove from the heat and let the bubbles subside for a few seconds. Stir in the remaining 2 tablespoons water. Be careful as you stir, as the caramel will bubble up when you add the water.

Pour the caramel into the bottoms of six 5-ounce ramekins. If necessary, pick up each ramekin and rotate it so that the caramel completely coats the bottom. Set aside until the caramel hardens, about 10 minutes. Meanwhile, preheat the oven to 300°F.

Fill the caramel-lined ramekins with the custard base. Cover the pan with aluminum foil but leave one corner open. Place the baking pan in the middle of the oven. Carefully pour hot water into the pan so that the water comes halfway up the sides of the ramekins. Cover the pan completely with the foil.

Bake the custards for 50 to 55 minutes. To check if the custards are ready, carefully remove the foil and gently shake a ramekin. The custard should be set around the edges, yet have an area in the middle—about the size of a quarter—that is not completely firm. Remove the pan from the oven. Remove the ramekins from the pan with tongs or a dish towel to protect your fingers. Cover and refrigerate for at least 2 hours before serving.

Carefully run a small knife around the inside edge of each ramekin and unmold the custards onto individual plates. In a bowl, toss the raspberries with the Grand Marnier, if desired. Scatter some raspberries around each custard.

··· ⌒⌒ ···

PLANNING AHEAD

The custard base may be made 2 days in advance and kept refrigerated. The custards may be baked a day in advance and kept refrigerated.

CHOCOLATE "BRÛLÉE" GINGER CUSTARDS

— SERVES 6 —

A crème brûlée is traditionally made with a very thin layer of burnt sugar on top of the custard. Here, I have substituted a layer of chocolate for the caramel, creating a similar effect that will satisfy chocolate lovers.

GINGER CUSTARD BASE

2 CUPS HEAVY WHIPPING CREAM

1 CUP MILK

½ OUNCE (1½-INCH PIECE) UNPEELED FRESH GINGER, CUT INTO QUARTERS

5 LARGE EGG YOLKS

1 LARGE WHOLE EGG

½ CUP PLUS 1 TABLESPOON GRANULATED SUGAR

PINCH OF KOSHER SALT

1½ OUNCES BITTERSWEET CHOCOLATE, FINELY CHOPPED

To make the custard base: In a heavy, nonreactive saucepan, combine the cream, milk, and ginger and place over medium heat until small bubbles appear around the edges of the pan. Remove from the heat, cover, and let steep for 10 minutes.

Meanwhile, prepare an ice bath. (See page 18 for tips on using an ice bath.) In a large stainless-steel bowl, whisk together the egg yolks, whole egg, sugar, and salt until blended.

While whisking constantly, pour the cream mixture into the egg mixture in a slow, steady stream. Place the bowl in the ice bath and let cool to room temperature, whisking occasionally. Meanwhile, preheat the oven to 300°F.

Strain through a fine-mesh sieve into a bowl and discard the ginger. Place six 5-ounce ramekins in a 9-by-13-inch baking pan. (See page 22 for tips on using a water bath.) Fill the ramekins with the custard. Cover the pan with aluminum foil but leave one corner open. Place the baking pan in the middle of the oven. Carefully pour hot water into the pan so that the water comes halfway up the sides of the ramekins. Cover the pan completely with the foil.

Bake the custards for 1 hour. To check if the custards are ready, carefully remove the foil and gently shake a ramekin. The custard should be set around the edges, yet have an area in the middle—about the size of a quarter—that is not completely firm. Remove the pan from the oven. Remove the ramekins from the pan with tongs or a dish towel to protect your fingers. Cover and refrigerate for at least 2 hours before serving.

Melt the chocolate, then whisk until smooth. (See page 19 for tips on melting chocolate.) With the back of a spoon, gently spread 1 teaspoon of the melted chocolate over the top of each custard.

Refrigerate the custards until the chocolate is set, about 30 minutes, before serving.

··· ❧ ···

PLANNING AHEAD

The custard base may be made 2 days in advance, and the custards may be baked 1 day ahead. Keep them refrigerated. Spread the chocolate on the custards the same day you serve them.

LEMON CUSTARDS

— SERVES 6 —

If you are looking for a quick, simple, and delicious dessert, this is the one. For an added lemon boost, pipe a little lemon curd (you can use the lemon cream, minus the cream, in Lemon Blueberry Trifle, page 48) into the middle of each custard 5 minutes after you remove them from the oven. Be sure the pastry-bag tip is about ½ inch below the surface of the custard when you pipe. These custards are incredible with Ginger Cookies (page 218).

3 LARGE EGG YOLKS

1 LARGE WHOLE EGG

½ CUP GRANULATED SUGAR

6 TABLESPOONS FRESHLY SQUEEZED LEMON JUICE

1⅓ CUPS HEAVY WHIPPING CREAM

GRATED ZEST OF 1 LEMON

In a stainless-steel bowl, whisk together the egg yolks, whole egg, and sugar until blended. Whisk in the lemon juice. Prepare an ice bath. (See page 18 for tips on using an ice bath.)

In a heavy, nonreactive saucepan, combine the cream and lemon zest and place over medium heat until small bubbles appear around the edges of the pan. Remove from the heat.

While whisking constantly, pour the cream mixture into the egg mixture in a slow, steady stream. Place the bowl in the ice bath and let cool to room temperature, whisking occasionally. Meanwhile, preheat the oven to 300°.

Strain the custard through a medium-mesh sieve into a bowl and discard the zest. Place six 5-ounce ramekins in a 9-by-13-inch baking pan.

(See page 22 for tips on using a water bath.) Fill the ramekins with the custard. Cover the pan with aluminum foil but leave one corner open. Place the baking pan in the middle of the oven. Carefully pour hot water into the pan so that the water comes halfway up the sides of the ramekins. Cover the pan completely with the foil.

Bake the custards for 35 minutes. To check if the custards are ready, carefully remove the foil and gently shake a ramekin. The custard should be set around the edges, yet have an area in the middle—about the size of a quarter—that is not completely firm. Remove the pan from the oven. Remove the ramekins from the pan with tongs or a dish towel to protect your fingers.

Cover and refrigerate the custards for at least 2 hours before serving.

··· ⌘ ···

PLANNING AHEAD

The custard base may be made 2 days in advance and kept refrigerated. The custards may be baked 1 day ahead and kept refrigerated.

FRENCH CREAM WITH BERRIES

— SERVES 6 —

Julia Orenstein, a pastry cook at Stars, created this dessert. It combines the creamy consistency of a custard with the rich flavor of a cheesecake. Since her baking days, she has become fluent in French and has taught at a major California university. Not surprisingly, her love for desserts has not diminished.

2 TEASPOONS POWDERED GELATIN

2 TABLESPOONS COLD WATER

1 CUP HEAVY WHIPPING CREAM

½ CUP GRANULATED SUGAR

1⅔ CUPS SOUR CREAM

⅓ CUP MASCARPONE CHEESE

1½ TEASPOONS VANILLA EXTRACT

1 TABLESPOON FRESHLY SQUEEZED LEMON JUICE

1 PINT RASPBERRIES (ABOUT 2 CUPS)

1 PINT BLACKBERRIES (ABOUT 2 CUPS)

1½ CUPS BERRY SAUCE (PAGE 289) MADE
   WITH RASPBERRIES

In a small heatproof bowl, sprinkle the gelatin over the cold water and let stand for 10 minutes to soften.

In a stainless-steel bowl, whisk together the cream, sugar, sour cream, and mascarpone until well blended. Place the bowl over a pan of simmering water, making sure the bottom of the bowl does not touch the water. (See page 18 for tips on using and making a double boiler.) Stirring occasionally, heat the cream mixture until it is warm. Remove the bowl from the pan and remove the pan from the heat.

Place the bowl of gelatin in the pan of hot water, being careful that the water does not rise above the sides of the bowl. Heat the gelatin until it is dissolved and no longer cloudy, about 3 minutes. Whisk the gelatin into the cream mixture. Stir in the vanilla and lemon juice. Strain the custard through a fine-mesh sieve into a bowl.

Divide the cream mixture evenly among six 5-ounce ramekins. Cover and refrigerate for about 4 hours until set.

When ready to serve, dip the base of each ramekin in hot water for several seconds, then run a knife around the inside edge of the ramekin and invert the cream onto a dessert plate. (Or, you may serve the creams in the ramekins.) Serve chilled with the raspberries, blackberries, and berry sauce.

PLANNING AHEAD

The creams may be made a day in advance and kept refrigerated.

SUMMER TRIFLE

— SERVES 8 TO 10 —

Sitting outside on a cool evening after a hot day is a highlight of
summer. You want the day to never end. Serve this trifle to your friends
and they will never want to go home.

PEACH CREAM

4 LARGE EGGS, SEPARATED

⅓ CUP GRANULATED SUGAR

PINCH OF KOSHER SALT

1½ CUPS MASCARPONE CHEESE

2½ CUPS PEELED AND COARSELY CHOPPED PEACHES
     (ABOUT 4 PEACHES)

PINCH OF CREAM OF TARTAR

1 RECIPE SPONGE CAKE (PAGE 296)

¾ CUP BERRY SAUCE (PAGE 289) MADE
     WITH BLACKBERRIES

¾ CUP BERRY SAUCE (PAGE 289) MADE
     WITH RASPBERRIES

To make the cream: Combine the egg yolks, sugar,
and salt in the bowl of a stand mixer fitted with
the whip attachment and whip on high speed until
thick, about 2 minutes. Add the mascarpone and
mix on medium speed until smooth and thick. Fold
in the chopped peaches.

Wash and dry the whip attachment. Put the
egg whites in a clean mixer bowl, fit the mixer with
the clean whip, and whip on medium speed until
foamy. Add the cream of tartar, increase the speed
to high, and whip until soft peaks form. Using a

spatula, fold the egg whites into the peach cream
just until combined.

With a serrated knife, cut the sponge cake into
quarters and then split each quarter in half horizontally. Pour 2 tablespoons of the blackberry
sauce into the bottom of a 2½-quart glass bowl.
Top with a layer of peach cream ½ inch thick.
Place some of the cake pieces, cutting to fit as
needed, over the peach cream, arranging them in
a single layer. Cover the cake layer with about
2 tablespoons of the raspberry sauce and top with
another ½-inch-thick layer of the peach cream.
Repeat the layers, beginning with the cake pieces,
alternating the berry sauces, and topping with the
peach cream, until the bowl is full, ending with
the peach cream.

Cover the trifle and refrigerate for at least
4 hours before serving. Spoon into individual
bowls to serve.

PLANNING AHEAD

The trifle may be made up to a day in advance and
kept refrigerated.

PEAR RIESLING TRIFLE

— SERVES 8 TO 10 —

When making many desserts, it is important to taste for sweetness
as you go, just as you taste for salt in savory recipes. If you use a sweeter
Riesling here, don't add quite as much sugar to the pears. Add
most of it and cook the pears for a few minutes with the wine, salt, and
lemon juice. Then taste for sweetness and add the rest of the sugar
as needed. The use of Riesling in this recipe makes this trifle a
bit more sophisticated than some of the other trifles in this chapter,
so I sometimes assemble it in wineglasses or stemmed dessert
dishes for a fancier presentation.

PEARS

6   RIPE PEARS, PEELED, HALVED, CORED, AND
    SLICED ½ INCH THICK

½ CUP GRANULATED SUGAR

¼ CUP RIESLING

PINCH OF SALT

2   TABLESPOONS FRESHLY SQUEEZED LEMON JUICE

1   RECIPE SPONGE CAKE (PAGE 296)

2   RECIPES RIESLING SABAYON (PAGE 281)

To prepare the pears: In a large sauté pan, combine
the pears, sugar, Riesling, salt, and lemon juice
and place over medium-high heat. Cook, stirring
occasionally, until the juices start to evaporate, 10 to
15 minutes. Remove from the heat, transfer to a
food processor, and process until coarsely puréed.
Set aside to cool.

With a serrated knife, cut the sponge cake into
quarters and then split each quarter in half horizontally. Spread a thin layer of pear purée in the
bottom of a 2 ½-quart glass bowl. Place the cake
pieces, cutting to fit as needed, in a single layer over
the pear purée. Cover with ⅔ cup of the pear purée
and then 1 cup of the sabayon. Repeat the layers—
cake, purée, sabayon—until the bowl is full, ending
with the sabayon.

Cover the trifle and refrigerate for at least
4 hours before serving. Spoon into individual
bowls to serve.

PLANNING AHEAD

The trifle may be made up to a day in advance and
kept refrigerated.

LEMON BLUEBERRY TRIFLE

— SERVES 8 TO 10 —

In this trifle, blueberry sauce and lemon curd lightened with cream
alternate with layers of cake. Puréeing half of the blueberries and leaving
half of them whole give the trifle a yummy sauce as well as pieces of
fruit for texture. You can make the blueberry sauce the same way
for serving over pancakes or ice cream. Also, the lemon cream, minus the
addition of the cream, is a good basic lemon curd recipe that can be
used in other desserts.

LEMON CREAM

6 LARGE EGG YOLKS

2 LARGE WHOLE EGGS

¾ CUP GRANULATED SUGAR

¾ CUP FRESHLY SQUEEZED LEMON JUICE

1¾ CUPS HEAVY WHIPPING CREAM

BLUEBERRY SAUCE

3 PINTS BLUEBERRIES (ABOUT 6 CUPS)

½ CUP GRANULATED SUGAR

1 TEASPOON FRESHLY SQUEEZED LEMON JUICE

1 RECIPE SPONGE CAKE (PAGE 296)

To make the lemon cream: In a stainless-steel bowl,
whisk together the egg yolks, whole eggs, and sugar
until blended. Whisk in the lemon juice.

Pour the lemon mixture into a heavy, nonreactive saucepan, place over low heat, and cook,
stirring constantly with a heat-resistant spatula,

until the mixture has thickened, about 8 minutes.
Switch to a whisk and whisk until smooth. Remove
from the heat and strain through a fine-mesh sieve
into a clean bowl. Cover with plastic wrap, pressing
it directly onto the surface to prevent a skin from
forming. Refrigerate until cold, about 1 hour.

Put the cream in the bowl of a stand mixer fitted
with the whip attachment and whip on medium-
high speed until soft peaks form. Using a spatula,
fold the cream into the cold lemon curd just until
combined. Cover and refrigerate until needed.

To make the blueberry sauce: In a heavy saucepan,
combine the blueberries, sugar, and lemon juice and
place over medium heat. Cook, stirring occasionally,
until the berries begin to release their juice and
become soft, about 5 minutes. Remove from the
heat and purée half the blueberries in a food processor. Stir the purée back into the berries remaining
in the saucepan. Let cool to room temperature.

With a serrated knife, cut the sponge cake into quarters and then split each quarter in half horizontally. Spread a thin layer of the blueberry sauce in the bottom of a 2½-quart glass bowl. Top with a layer of lemon cream ½ inch thick. Place some of the cake pieces, cutting to fit as needed, over the lemon cream, arranging them in a single layer. Cover the cake layer with about 2 tablespoons of the blueberry sauce and top with another ½-inch-thick layer of the lemon cream. Repeat the layers—

cake, blueberry sauce, lemon cream—until the bowl is full, ending with the lemon cream.

Cover the trifle and refrigerate for at least 4 hours before serving. Spoon into individual bowls to serve.

PLANNING AHEAD

The trifle may be made up to a day in advance and kept refrigerated.

STRAWBERRY GRAND MARNIER TRIFLE

— SERVES 8 TO 10 —

In the spring, when I first see strawberries in the market, I always
buy too many. It's so nice to see a different fruit that I can't resist.
I created this trifle to use up an overabundance of berries. Everyone
liked it so much that I had to go back to the store to buy more
strawberries and make it again for my friends.

3½ PINTS STRAWBERRIES (ABOUT 7 CUPS), HULLED

2 TABLESPOONS GRANULATED SUGAR

1 RECIPE SPONGE CAKE (PAGE 296)

2 RECIPES GRAND MARNIER SABAYON (PAGE 281)

In a food processor, combine the strawberries and
sugar and pulse until coarsely chopped.

With a serrated knife, cut the sponge cake
into quarters and then split each quarter in half
horizontally. Place a layer of strawberries in the
bottom of a 9-by-13-inch baking pan. Place the
cake pieces, cutting to fit as needed, in a single layer
over the berries. Cover with 1 cup of the sabayon.
Repeat the layers, beginning with the berries and
ending with a layer of sabayon, until the pan is full.
There should be 3 layers of cake.

Cover the trifle and refrigerate for at least
4 hours before serving. To serve, cut the trifle into
pieces with a sharp knife.

··· ❧ ···

PLANNING AHEAD

The trifle may be made up to a day in advance and
kept refrigerated.

TIRAMISU

— SERVES 8 TO 10 —

Tiramisu, which became fashionable in the early 1980s, has undergone countless variations over the years. Because many of these changes weren't very good, the dessert's reputation has suffered. That's a shame, as a well-made tiramisu is one of the best desserts in the world. This was one of the most popular recipes in *Stars Desserts*. If you are concerned about eating raw eggs, use eggs pasteurized in the shell.

MASCARPONE CREAM

6 LARGE EGGS, SEPARATED

½ CUP GRANULATED SUGAR

PINCH OF KOSHER SALT

2 CUPS MASCARPONE CHEESE

PINCH OF CREAM OF TARTAR

1 RECIPE SPONGE CAKE (PAGE 296)

8 OUNCES BITTERSWEET CHOCOLATE, SHAVED OR GRATED (SEE PAGE 21)

1¾ CUPS BREWED ESPRESSO OR DOUBLE-STRENGTH COFFEE (REGULAR OR DECAFFEINATED), AT ROOM TEMPERATURE

To make the mascarpone cream: Combine the egg yolks, sugar, and salt in the bowl of a stand mixer fitted with the whip attachment and whip on high speed until thick, about 3 minutes. Reduce the speed to medium, add the mascarpone, and whip until smooth and thick, about 30 seconds.

Wash and dry the whip attachment. Put the egg whites in a clean mixer bowl, fit the mixer with the clean whip, and whip on medium speed until foamy. Add the cream of tartar, increase the speed to high, and whip until soft peaks form. Using a spatula, gently fold the egg whites into the mascarpone cream in 2 additions.

With a serrated knife, slice the sponge cake into quarters and then split each piece in half horizontally. Spread a layer of mascarpone cream about ½ inch thick in the bottom of a 2½-quart glass bowl. Sprinkle some of the chocolate on top. Place the cake pieces, cutting to fit as needed, in a single layer over the mascarpone cream. Brush the cake with some of the espresso and top with more mascarpone cream and chocolate shavings. Repeat the layers—cake, espresso, mascarpone cream, chocolate—until the bowl is full, ending with the chocolate.

Cover and refrigerate for at least 4 hours before serving. Spoon into individual bowls to serve.

PLANNING AHEAD

The tiramisu may be made up to 2 days in advance.

WALNUT RUM STEAMED PUDDING

— SERVES 8 TO 10 —

This steamed pudding is wonderful year-round. In summer, serve it with sliced fresh peaches. When the temperature drops and stone fruits are out of season, serve it as suggested here, with coffee ice cream and chocolate sauce. You need a steamed-pudding mold to make this recipe, but I have included a trio of other steamed puddings in this chapter, making the mold a sound investment.

BUTTER FOR THE MOLD

1½ CUPS (5 OUNCES) WALNUTS, TOASTED (SEE PAGE 20) AND FINELY CHOPPED

1½ CUPS ALL-PURPOSE FLOUR

¾ TEASPOON BAKING SODA

1½ TEASPOONS BAKING POWDER

PINCH OF KOSHER SALT

6 OUNCES (12 TABLESPOONS) UNSALTED BUTTER, AT ROOM TEMPERATURE

1½ CUPS GRANULATED SUGAR

4 LARGE EGGS

3 TABLESPOONS DARK RUM

1 RECIPE CHOCOLATE SAUCE (PAGE 284)

1 PINT COFFEE ICE CREAM

Butter the underside of the top and the inside of a 2-quart steamed-pudding mold. Sprinkle 2 tablespoons of the walnuts in the bottom of the prepared mold.

Sift together the flour, baking soda, and baking powder onto a piece of parchment paper or into a bowl. Add the salt and set aside.

Put the butter and sugar in the bowl of a stand mixer fitted with the paddle attachment and beat on medium speed until light and creamy, about 30 seconds. Add the eggs two at a time, mixing well after each addition. Scrape the sides of the bowl and mix again until smooth. Add the rum and the remaining walnuts and beat until incorporated. Reduce the speed to low, add the dry ingredients, and mix just until combined. Spread the batter into the prepared mold and cover the mold with the lid.

Place the pudding mold in a pot large enough to accommodate the mold with at least 1½ inches of clearance on the top and sides. Fill the pot with hot water to reach one-third of the way up the sides of the mold. Cover the pot and bring the water to a low boil over medium-high heat. Reduce the heat to maintain a simmer. Steam the pudding for 1½ to 2 hours, checking the water periodically to make sure that it is just simmering. (Rapidly boiling water will cause the pudding to rise prematurely and then sink). The pudding is ready when a skewer inserted into the center comes out clean.

Let the pudding cool to room temperature. To unmold, invert a platter on top of the mold and then invert the plate and mold together. Lift off the mold. Slice the pudding and serve with the chocolate sauce and coffee ice cream.

PLANNING AHEAD

The pudding may be made 2 days ahead. Wrap in plastic wrap and store at room temperature.

BLUEBERRY STEAMED PUDDING

— SERVES 8 TO 10 —

This recipe was in my great-grandmother Florence's recipe box. Neither my grandmother nor my father remember her baking much, so we were thrilled to discover that even after fifty years, the simplicity and clear flavors of the pudding make it a winner.

BUTTER FOR THE MOLD

1½ CUPS BLUEBERRIES

½ CUP GRANULATED SUGAR

1 TEASPOON FRESHLY SQUEEZED LEMON JUICE

PINCH PLUS ¼ TEASPOON KOSHER SALT

1½ CUPS ALL-PURPOSE FLOUR

½ TEASPOON BAKING SODA

1 TEASPOON BAKING POWDER

¾ TEASPOON GROUND GINGER

½ CUP DARK MOLASSES

½ CUP MILK

1 LARGE EGG

1 TABLESPOON UNSALTED BUTTER, MELTED

1 TEASPOON GRATED LEMON ZEST

1 RECIPE CHANTILLY CREAM (PAGE 276)

Butter the underside of the top and the inside of a 2-quart steamed-pudding mold.

Put the blueberries in a bowl. Add the sugar, lemon juice, and the pinch of salt and toss to mix. Place the berries in the bottom of the prepared pudding mold.

Sift together the flour, baking soda, baking powder, and ginger onto a piece of parchment paper or into a bowl. Add the ¼ teaspoon salt and set aside.

In a large bowl, whisk together the molasses, milk, egg, melted butter, and lemon zest. Add the dry ingredients to the molasses mixture and whisk until smooth. Pour the batter into the mold over the blueberries and cover the mold with the lid.

Place the pudding mold in a pot large enough to accommodate the mold with at least 1½ inches of clearance on the top and sides. Fill the pot with hot water to reach one-third of the way up the sides of the mold. Cover the pot and bring the water to a low boil over medium-high heat. Reduce the heat to maintain a simmer. Steam the pudding for about 1 hour, checking the water periodically to make sure that it is just simmering. (Rapidly boiling water will cause the pudding to rise prematurely and then sink). The pudding is ready when a skewer inserted into the center comes out clean.

Let the pudding cool for 10 minutes. To unmold, invert a platter on top of the mold and then invert the plate and mold together. Lift off the mold. Let cool to room temperature, then slice the pudding and serve with the chantilly cream.

PLANNING AHEAD

The pudding may be made a day ahead. Wrap in plastic wrap and store at room temperature.

PUMPKIN STEAMED PUDDING

— SERVES 8 TO 10 —

Firm enough to cut like a cake, this moist steamed pudding may be made in advance, which means that it is ideal for serving on Thanksgiving.

BUTTER FOR THE MOLD

2 ¼ CUPS ALL-PURPOSE FLOUR

½ TEASPOON GROUND GINGER

2 ¼ TEASPOONS BAKING POWDER

1 ¼ TEASPOONS GROUND CINNAMON

¼ TEASPOON GROUND ALLSPICE

¼ TEASPOON KOSHER SALT

6 OUNCES (12 TABLESPOONS) UNSALTED BUTTER, AT ROOM TEMPERATURE

2 ¼ CUPS GRANULATED SUGAR

3 LARGE EGGS

3 TABLESPOONS FRESHLY SQUEEZED LEMON JUICE

1 ½ CUPS PUMPKIN PURÉE, HOMEMADE (PAGE 301) OR PURCHASED

1 RECIPE CHANTILLY CREAM (PAGE 276)

1 CUP CARAMEL SAUCE (PAGE 285), WARMED

Butter the underside of the top and the inside of a 2-quart steamed-pudding mold.

Sift together the flour, ginger, baking powder, cinnamon, and allspice onto a piece of parchment paper or into a bowl. Add the salt and set aside.

Put the butter and sugar in the bowl of a stand mixer fitted with the paddle attachment and beat on medium speed until light and creamy, about 30 seconds. Add the eggs one at a time, mixing well after each addition. Scrape the sides of the bowl and mix again until smooth. Reduce the speed to medium-low, add the lemon juice and pumpkin purée, and beat until incorporated. Reduce the speed to low, add the dry ingredients, and mix just until combined. Spread the batter in the prepared mold and cover the mold with the lid.

Place the pudding mold in a pot large enough to accommodate the mold with at least 1 ½ inches of clearance on the top and sides. Fill the pot with hot water to reach one-third of the way up the sides of the mold. Cover the pot and bring the water to a low boil over medium-high heat. Reduce the heat to maintain a simmer. Steam the pudding for 1 ½ to 2 hours, checking the water periodically to make sure that it is just simmering. (Rapidly boiling water will cause the pudding to rise prematurely and then sink). The pudding is ready when a skewer inserted into the center comes out clean.

Let the pudding cool to room temperature. To unmold, invert a platter on top of the mold and then invert the plate and mold together. Lift off the mold. Slice the pudding and serve with the chantilly cream and caramel sauce.

PLANNING AHEAD

The pudding may be made 2 days ahead. Wrap in plastic wrap and store at room temperature.

PERSIMMON PUDDING

— SERVES 8 —

Serve this dessert in fall when persimmons are in season and you want a warm pudding for a chilly night. It is delicious accompanied with Caramel Cream (page 277), or Vanilla Ice Cream (page 299) and Caramel Sauce (page 285). To quicken the ripening time of persimmons, put them in the freezer overnight and then thaw them the next day on the countertop. Once thawed, they will be soft and ready to use.

BUTTER FOR THE PAN

ABOUT 5 RIPE HACHIYA PERSIMMONS

3 LARGE EGGS

1 CUP GRANULATED SUGAR

4 OUNCES (8 TABLESPOONS) UNSALTED BUTTER,
   MELTED AND COOLED TO WARM

1½ CUPS ALL-PURPOSE FLOUR

1 TEASPOON BAKING SODA

1 TEASPOON BAKING POWDER

½ TEASPOON GROUND GINGER

½ TEASPOON GROUND CINNAMON

½ TEASPOON GROUND ALLSPICE

PINCH OF GROUND CLOVES

½ TEASPOON KOSHER SALT

1 CUP MILK

1 CUP HEAVY WHIPPING CREAM

Preheat the oven to 350°F. Butter a 9-inch square baking pan.

Remove the stems from the persimmons and cut the flesh into pieces. Purée the persimmon flesh in a food processor until smooth. Strain the purée through a medium-mesh sieve to eliminate any bits of skin and seed. You should have 2 cups purée.

In a large bowl, whisk together the eggs and sugar until blended. Whisk in the melted butter.

Sift together the flour, baking soda, baking powder, ginger, cinnamon, allspice, and cloves onto a piece of parchment paper or into a bowl. Add the salt. Stir the dry ingredients into the egg mixture. Slowly pour in the milk and cream, stirring until combined. Stir in the persimmon purée.

Pour the batter into the prepared pan. Bake until a skewer inserted into the center comes out clean, 40 to 45 minutes. Let cool for about 10 minutes before serving. The pudding will sink as it cools.

Serve the pudding warm, scooped into bowls. If it cools completely before serving, reheat it in a 325°F oven for about 15 minutes.

··· ⌒⌒⌒ ···

PLANNING AHEAD

The pudding may be made a day in advance, covered, and refrigerated. Reheat before serving.

CHOCOLATE DESSERTS

— CHAPTER 2 —

— CHAPTER 2 —

Chocolate belongs to the botanical genus *Theobroma*, literally "food of the gods." Whether or not you believe that chocolate sustained superior beings, the reverse is certainly true. After eating chocolate you feel godlike, as though you can lead nations, conquer enemies, entice lovers, or at least finish that overdue project on your desk. In this chapter, you will discover more than a dozen wonderful chocolate desserts, ranging from a simple, creamy pudding to an ornate construction that tucks hazelnut cream into chocolate crêpes.

For anyone who likes extra-rich chocolate desserts, I have included Chocolate–Peanut Butter Terrine with Sugared Peanuts, a favorite at Stars, and Warm Bittersweet Chocolate Pudding Cakes. Chocolate Caramel Bread Pudding and White Chocolate–Espresso Parfait are on the lighter side but still chocolatey enough to satisfy any craving. And this is not the only chapter where you will find scrumptious chocolate creations. Chocolate Truffle Tart (page 158), French Silk (page 200), Black-and-White Brownies (page 238), and more lie ahead.

62
WARM BITTERSWEET CHOCOLATE
PUDDING CAKES

64
CHOCOLATE CARAMEL BREAD PUDDING

73
CHOCOLATE-FILLED FILO TRIANGLES

74
CHOCOLATE PUDDING

75
CHOCOLATE ZABAGLIONE TRIFLE

76
CHOCOLATE–PEANUT BUTTER TERRINE
WITH SUGARED PEANUTS

78
TRIPLE-STRIPED CHOCOLATE SEMIFREDDO

80
COCOA WAFERS WITH FROZEN
HAZELNUT SABAYON

82
CHOCOLATE ESPRESSO FROZEN
CREAM SANDWICHES

84
WHITE CHOCOLATE–ESPRESSO PARFAIT

86
ESPRESSO GRANITA WITH CHOCOLATE CREAM

87
CHOCOLATE HAZELNUT CRÊPES

88
GÂTEAU ROYALE

WARM BITTERSWEET CHOCOLATE
PUDDING CAKES

— SERVES 6 —

You only need to serve small portions of this dessert because it is so
rich. But even a small serving will fill you up. The pudding cakes
are actually made up of two parts: a thick pudding over a cocoa sauce.
For the optimal amount of sauce in the bottom, serve the cakes
hot from the oven. If you bake them ahead, they may be reheated, but
there won't be quite as much sauce.

1⅓ CUPS ALL-PURPOSE FLOUR

¾ TEASPOON BAKING SODA

⅓ CUP PLUS 1½ TEASPOONS UNSWEETENED
  COCOA POWDER

¼ TEASPOON KOSHER SALT

6 OUNCES (12 TABLESPOONS) UNSALTED BUTTER,
  AT ROOM TEMPERATURE

1½ CUPS FIRMLY PACKED BROWN SUGAR

3 LARGE EGGS

1 TEASPOON VANILLA EXTRACT

2 TABLESPOONS COLD WATER

6 TABLESPOONS HOT WATER

1 RECIPE CHANTILLY CREAM (PAGE 276)

Preheat the oven to 350°F. Place six 5-ounce
ramekins in a 9-by-13-inch baking pan. (See page
22 for tips on using a water bath.)

Sift together the flour, baking soda, and
⅓ cup of the cocoa powder onto a piece of
parchment paper or into a bowl. Add the salt and
set aside.

Put the butter and 1 cup of the brown sugar
in the bowl of a stand mixer fitted with the paddle attachment and beat on medium speed until
smooth, about 30 seconds. Add the eggs one at a
time, mixing well after each addition, and then mix
in the vanilla. Scrape the sides of the bowl and mix
again until smooth. Reduce the speed to low, add
the dry ingredients, and mix until incorporated.
Mix in the cold water. Divide the batter evenly
among the ramekins.

In a small bowl, stir together the remaining
½ cup brown sugar, the remaining 1½ teaspoons
cocoa powder, and the hot water until the sugar

and cocoa are dissolved. Spoon the cocoa liquid evenly over the top of the batter in the ramekins.

Place the baking pan in the middle of the oven. Carefully pour hot water into the pan so that the water comes halfway up the sides of the ramekins. Bake the pudding cakes for about 25 minutes. They are ready when the tops crack and the sides pull slightly away from the sides of the ramekins. Remove the pan from the oven. Remove the ramekins from the pan with tongs or a dish towel to protect your fingers.

Place the ramekins on individual plates. Serve the chantilly cream in a bowl on the side, so that guests can top their pudding cakes as desired.

PLANNING AHEAD

The pudding cakes are best when eaten directly from the oven. If necessary, they may be baked up to 3 hours in advance and stored at room temperature. Reheat in a 350°F oven for about 5 minutes.

CHOCOLATE CARAMEL BREAD PUDDING

— SERVES 6 —

Bread puddings have always been comfort food and are popular both at home and at fancy restaurants. This irresistible version, with chocolate cake and caramel custard, gives the term comfort a whole new meaning. You can use the pound cake recipe on page 192, omitting the hazelnuts, or any chocolate cake with a pound-cake texture.

6 LARGE EGG YOLKS

4 LARGE WHOLE EGGS

¼ TEASPOON KOSHER SALT

½ CUP WATER

1 CUP GRANULATED SUGAR

1½ CUPS HEAVY WHIPPING CREAM

3 CUPS MILK

5 CUPS ½-INCH-CUBED CHOCOLATE CAKE

Preheat the oven to 325°F.

In a bowl, lightly whisk together the egg yolks, whole eggs, and salt. Set aside.

In a heavy, nonreactive saucepan large enough eventually to hold the cream, stir together the water and sugar. Place over medium heat and cook, stirring occasionally, until the sugar dissolves and comes to a boil. Increase the heat to high and cook, without stirring, until the mixture becomes a golden amber. (See page 20 for tips on making caramel.)

While the sugar is cooking, put the cream in a small, heavy nonreactive saucepan and place over medium heat until small bubbles appear around the edges of the pan, then remove from the heat.

As soon as the caramel is golden amber, remove from the heat and let the bubbles subside for a few seconds. Stir in about ¼ cup of the hot cream. Be careful when you stir, as the caramel will bubble up when you add the cream. Continue to add the cream about ½ cup at a time, stirring and waiting for the bubbles to subside before adding more. Once all the cream has been added, whisk the caramel cream into the reserved egg mixture. Then whisk in the milk.

Place the chocolate cake pieces in a 9-by-13-inch baking pan. Pour the caramel custard evenly over the cake.

Bake until a knife inserted into the center comes out almost completely clean, 30 minutes. Serve warm.

PLANNING AHEAD

The bread pudding may be made up to a day ahead. It will keep for several hours at room temperature, or cover and refrigerate if keeping overnight. Reheat in a 325°F oven for about 15 minutes.

>> CHOCOLATE CARAMEL BREAD PUDDING

NECTARINE BLUEBERRY BLINTZES ··· PAGE 102

<< STRAWBERRY COMPOTE WITH RHUBARB ICE CREAM ··· PAGE 96

BLUEBERRY STEAMED PUDDING ··· PAGE 54

>> CARAMEL CUSTARDS ··· PAGE 38

CHOCOLATE–PEANUT BUTTER TERRINE WITH SUGARED PEANUTS ··· PAGE 76

<< WHITE CHOCOLATE–ESPRESSO PARFAIT ··· PAGE 84

CHOCOLATE-FILLED FILO TRIANGLES

— SERVES 8 —

These triangles are like a crunchy *pain au chocolate*, with filo replacing the traditional yeasted dough. If you wish, put a little raspberry jam on top of the chocolate before you fold each triangle.

6 OUNCES BITTERSWEET CHOCOLATE

½ CUP GRANULATED SUGAR

8 SHEETS FILO, THAWED IF FROZEN

4 OUNCES (8 TABLESPOONS) UNSALTED
   BUTTER, MELTED

Preheat the oven to 350°F. Line a baking sheet with parchment paper.

Break up 4 ounces of the chocolate into ½-ounce pieces. In a food processor, finely grind the remaining 2 ounces chocolate with the sugar.

Lay a stack of 8 sheets of filo on a work surface. Remove 1 sheet and place it lengthwise in front of you. Keep the remaining sheets covered with a damp towel.

Brush the sheet with some of the melted butter. Sprinkle it evenly with 1½ tablespoons of the chocolate-sugar mixture. Place a second sheet of filo on top, brush it with butter, and sprinkle it with 1½ tablespoons of the chocolate-sugar mixture. Add 2 more sheets in the same manner, brushing each with butter and topping each with the chocolate-sugar mixture.

Cut the filled stack of filo sheets lengthwise into 4 even strips. Starting at the left end of 1 strip, place a ½-ounce piece of chocolate 2 inches from the edge. Fold the end of the filo diagonally over the chocolate, enclosing the chocolate completely and creating a 3-inch triangle; the bottom edge of the strip should now be even with the left side of the strip. Next, fold the bottom of the triangle up, so that it meets the straight edge evenly. Now fold again on the diagonal, so that the left edge is even with the right side. Repeat this folding pattern, alternating the direction with each fold, until you reach the end of the strip. Repeat with the remaining 3 strips, to make 3 more triangles. Place the triangles on the prepared baking sheet.

Make 4 more chocolate-filled triangles in the same manner, using the remaining filo sheets, melted butter, chocolate-sugar mixture, and chocolate pieces. Add the triangles to the baking sheet. If there is any butter left over, brush it on top of the triangles.

Bake the triangles until golden brown, about 15 minutes. Serve warm.

PLANNING AHEAD

The triangles are best served the day they are made. If they have cooled completely before you are ready to serve them, reheat them in a 350°F oven for 8 minutes.

CHOCOLATE PUDDING

— SERVES 6 —

Here is a chocolate pudding that is just as good as what mom used to make. It tastes even better if you make a hole in the middle and pour in some organic heavy whipping cream. Although chocolate puddings are a type of custard, they should not be cooked quite as long as other custards, because the chocolate makes them set up more as they cool.

5 LARGE EGG YOLKS

1 TABLESPOON GRANULATED SUGAR

PINCH OF KOSHER SALT

1 TEASPOON VANILLA EXTRACT

2 CUPS HEAVY WHIPPING CREAM

3 OUNCES BITTERSWEET CHOCOLATE,
   FINELY CHOPPED

Preheat the oven to 300°F. Place six 5-ounce ramekins in a 9-by-13-inch baking pan. (See page 22 for tips on using a water bath.)

In a large bowl, whisk together the egg yolks, sugar, salt, and vanilla until blended. Set aside.

In a heavy, nonreactive saucepan, heat the cream over medium heat until small bubbles appear around the edges of the pan. Remove from the heat and add the chocolate. Cover and let stand for 5 minutes. Stir until smooth.

While whisking constantly, pour the chocolate mixture into the egg mixture in a slow, steady stream. Continue whisking until smooth.

Fill the ramekins with the chocolate cream. Cover the pan with aluminum foil but leave one corner open. Place the baking pan in the middle of the oven. Carefully pour hot water into the pan so that the water comes halfway up the sides of the ramekins. Cover the pan completely with the foil.

Bake the puddings for about 30 minutes. To check if the puddings are ready, carefully remove the foil and gently shake a ramekin. The pudding should be set around the edges, yet have an area in the middle—about the size of a half dollar—that is not completely firm. Be careful not to over-cook them. As they cool, they will thicken. Remove the pan from the oven. Remove the ramekins from the pan with tongs or a dish towel to protect your fingers.

Cover and refrigerate for at least 3 hours before serving. Let the puddings sit at room temperature for 10 minutes before serving.

PLANNING AHEAD

The puddings may be made 2 days in advance and kept refrigerated.

CHOCOLATE ZABAGLIONE TRIFLE

— SERVES 8 TO 10 —

I am always trying to think up new trifle recipes, not only because their flavors are so wonderful but also because they must be prepared in advance. That last advantage frees me up, on the day of the party, to do other things—like get a massage! I use a bulb baster to soak the cake with the espresso.

1 RECIPE CHOCOLATE SPONGE CAKE (PAGE 296)

2 RECIPES ZABAGLIONE (PAGE 281)

1½ CUPS COLD BREWED ESPRESSO OR
    DOUBLE-STRENGTH COFFEE (REGULAR
    OR DECAFFEINATED)

6 OUNCES BITTERSWEET CHOCOLATE, SHAVED
   OR GRATED (PAGE 21)

With a serrated knife, cut the sponge cake into quarters and then split each quarter in half horizontally. Spread about 1 cup of the zabaglione in the bottom of a 2½-quart glass bowl. Place some of the cake pieces, cutting to fit as needed, over the zabaglione, arranging them in a single layer. Brush the cake layer with about ½ cup of the espresso. Repeat the layers until the bowl is full, ending with the zabaglione.

Cover the trifle and refrigerate for at least 2 hours before serving. Garnish with the shaved chocolate. Spoon into individual bowls to serve.

PLANNING AHEAD
The trifle may be made up to 2 days in advance and kept refrigerated.

CHOCOLATE–PEANUT BUTTER TERRINE
WITH SUGARED PEANUTS

— SERVES 8 —

This chocolate and peanut butter dessert is for adults who like big flavors. When you are making the terrine, gradually add both the melted chocolate to the eggs and the cream to the chocolate mixture. If you add them too quickly, the mixture will seize, or harden. For the best results, use chocolate with 58 to 62 percent cacao, rather than a chocolate with a higher percentage.

TERRINE

11 OUNCES BITTERSWEET CHOCOLATE,
    FINELY CHOPPED

1 OUNCE (2 TABLESPOONS) UNSALTED BUTTER

6 TABLESPOONS CREAMY PEANUT BUTTER

4 LARGE EGG YOLKS

¼ CUP GRANULATED SUGAR

1¾ CUPS HEAVY WHIPPING CREAM

GLAZE

4 OUNCES BITTERSWEET CHOCOLATE,
    FINELY CHOPPED

2½ OUNCES (5 TABLESPOONS) UNSALTED BUTTER

2 TEASPOONS LIGHT CORN SYRUP

SUGARED PEANUTS

1 LARGE EGG WHITE

6 TABLESPOONS GRANULATED SUGAR

1½ CUPS (7½ OUNCES) UNSALTED PEANUTS

To make the terrine: Spray an 8½-by-4½-by-2¾-inch loaf pan with nonstick spray. Line the sprayed pan with plastic wrap, allowing a 1½-inch overhang on all sides.

In a stainless-steel bowl, combine the chocolate, butter, and peanut butter. Place the bowl over a pan of simmering water, making sure the bottom of the bowl does not touch the water. (See page 18 for tips on using and making a double boiler.) Heat, stirring occasionally, until the chocolate and butter melt. Remove from the heat and whisk until smooth.

Combine the egg yolks and sugar in the bowl of a stand mixer fitted with the whip attachment and whip on high speed until thick, about 1 minute. Remove the bowl from the mixer stand. Using a wooden spoon, stir in the chocolate mixture in 3 equal additions. The mixture will be quite thick.

In a separate bowl, whisk the cream until it starts to thicken. Using a spatula, fold the cream into the chocolate mixture in 4 equal additions. Spread the batter in the prepared pan. Cover with the plastic wrap overhanging the sides and refrigerate until firm, at least 4 hours.

To unmold the terrine, fold back the plastic wrap and invert the pan onto a wire rack. Pull on a corner of the plastic wrap to release the terrine from the pan. Lift off the pan and carefully remove the plastic wrap. Line a baking sheet with parchment paper and place the rack in it. Return the terrine to the refrigerator while you make the glaze.

To make the glaze: In a stainless-steel bowl, combine the chocolate, butter, and corn syrup. Place the bowl over a pan of simmering water, making sure the bottom of the bowl does not touch the water, and heat, stirring occasionally, until the chocolate and butter melt. Remove from over the heat and whisk until smooth. The glaze should be pourable but not so thin that it will run off the terrine. If the glaze is too thin, let it sit at room temperature for about 30 minutes.

Slowly pour the glaze evenly over the top of the terrine, allowing it to stream evenly down the sides. With an offset spatula, spread the glaze to cover the terrine smoothly and completely. Refrigerate until the glaze is set, about 30 minutes.

To make the sugared peanuts: Preheat the oven to 350°F. In a bowl, whisk the egg white until frothy. Whisk in the sugar. Add the peanuts and mix until they are evenly coated with the egg-white mixture.

Spread the peanuts in a single layer on a rimmed baking sheet and place in the oven. Toast the nuts, stirring them every 5 minutes, until dry and golden brown, 15 to 20 minutes.

To serve, transfer the terrine to a serving platter and arrange the sugared peanuts on top. Cut the terrine with a hot, dry knife (see page 22).

PLANNING AHEAD

The terrine may be made 2 days in advance and kept refrigerated. The sugared peanuts will keep for a week in an airtight container at room temperature.

TRIPLE-STRIPED CHOCOLATE SEMIFREDDO

— SERVES 6 TO 8 —

In this recipe, one mousse is divided into thirds, and then each portion is flavored with a different kind of chocolate. The three mousses are then frozen on top of one another, to make three different layers of chocolate.

MOUSSE BASE

5 LARGE EGG YOLKS

6 TABLESPOONS GRANULATED SUGAR

PINCH OF KOSHER SALT

1½ CUPS MILK

1 TEASPOON VANILLA EXTRACT

1½ CUPS HEAVY WHIPPING CREAM

MILK CHOCOLATE LAYER

3 OUNCES MILK CHOCOLATE, FINELY CHOPPED

½ CUP MOUSSE BASE (ABOVE)

WHITE CHOCOLATE LAYER

½ OUNCE WHITE CHOCOLATE, FINELY CHOPPED

½ CUP MOUSSE BASE (ABOVE)

DARK CHOCOLATE LAYER

2 ½ OUNCES BITTERSWEET CHOCOLATE,
   FINELY CHOPPED

½ CUP MOUSSE BASE (ABOVE)

1 RECIPE CHOCOLATE CARAMEL SAUCE
   (PAGE 288), WARMED

To make the mousse base: In a bowl, whisk together the egg yolks, 3 tablespoons of the sugar, and the salt. Set aside.

In a medium, heavy nonreactive saucepan, heat the milk over medium heat until small bubbles appear around the edges of the pan. While whisking constantly, pour the milk into the egg mixture in a slow, steady stream. Pour the mixture back into the pan, place over medium heat, and cook, stirring constantly with a heat-resistant spatula, until it has thickened slightly, about 8 minutes. Stir in the vanilla. Strain the mousse base through a medium-mesh sieve into a clean bowl. Cover and refrigerate until cold, about 2 hours.

Spray an 8-inch square baking pan with nonstick spray. Line the sprayed pan with plastic wrap, making sure to press it into the corners and allowing a 1½-inch overhang on all sides.

Put the cream in the bowl of a stand mixer fitted with the whip attachment and whip on low speed until it begins to thicken. Add the remaining 3 tablespoons sugar and whip on medium-high until soft peaks form. Divide the cream into 3 equal portions, cover, and refrigerate until needed.

To make the milk chocolate layer: Melt the milk chocolate. (For tips on melting chocolate, see page 19.) Whisk until smooth. Slowly whisk ½ cup of the cold mousse base into the chocolate. Using a spatula, fold 1 portion of the whipped cream into the chocolate mixture.

Pour the milk chocolate mousse into the prepared pan. Freeze until firm to the touch, about 30 minutes.

To make the white and dark chocolate layers: Prepare the white and dark chocolate mousses separately in the same manner as the milk chocolate mousse, substituting the white and dark chocolates for the milk chocolate and using the remaining 2 portions of whipped cream. Cover and refrigerate the mousses until needed.

When the milk chocolate mousse is firm to the touch, spread the white chocolate mousse evenly on top. Freeze until firm to the touch, about 45 minutes. (The white chocolate mousse takes longer to freeze than the milk chocolate mousse.) Finally, spread the dark chocolate mousse over the white chocolate mousse. Cover with the plastic wrap overhanging the sides and freeze the triple-layered mousse until it is firm enough to slice, at least 3 hours, depending on your freezer.

To unmold the semifreddo, fold back the plastic wrap, place a cutting board (or invert a large plate) on top of the pan, and invert the pan and board together. Lift off the pan and then peel off the plastic wrap.

Cut the semifreddo into pieces and serve with the warm chocolate caramel sauce. If it is very hard, let it sit at room temperature for 5 minutes before serving.

PLANNING AHEAD

The semifreddo may be made 2 days in advance and stored in the freezer until serving.

COCOA WAFERS WITH FROZEN
HAZELNUT SABAYON

— SERVES 6 —

Freezing sabayon produces a frozen creamy dessert that recalls ice cream without having to use an ice-cream maker. The recipe yields extra wafers in case you break some or have human-size mice in your house.

COCOA WAFERS

5 TABLESPOONS ALL-PURPOSE FLOUR

¼ CUP UNSWEETENED COCOA POWDER

2 LARGE EGG WHITES

½ CUP GRANULATED SUGAR

3 OUNCES (6 TABLESPOONS) UNSALTED BUTTER,
  MELTED

½ TEASPOON VANILLA EXTRACT

HAZELNUT SABAYON

6 LARGE EGG YOLKS

½ CUP GRANULATED SUGAR

PINCH OF SALT

½ CUP FRESHLY SQUEEZED ORANGE JUICE

¼ CUP HAZELNUT LIQUEUR SUCH AS FRANGELICO

1 CUP HEAVY WHIPPING CREAM

1½ CUPS CHOCOLATE CARAMEL SAUCE (PAGE 288)

¾ CUP (3 OUNCES) HAZELNUTS, TOASTED AND SKINNED
  (SEE PAGE 20) AND THEN COARSELY CHOPPED

1 TABLESPOON CONFECTIONERS' SUGAR

Preheat the oven to 350°F. Line 2 baking sheets with parchment paper.

To make the wafers: Sift together the flour and cocoa powder onto a piece of parchment paper or into a bowl. Set aside.

In a bowl, lightly whisk the egg whites until frothy. Whisk in the granulated sugar and then the melted butter and vanilla until blended. Add the flour mixture and stir until smooth.

For each wafer, spoon 1½ teaspoons of the batter onto a prepared baking sheet and, using the back of a spoon, spread the batter into a 3-inch circle. Space the circles about 1 inch apart; you should be able to fit about 8 wafers on each sheet. Bake the wafers, 1 sheet at a time, until they are no longer shiny, 6 to 8 minutes. Remove from the oven and let the wafers cool on the baking sheet for 3 minutes, then use a thin metal spatula to transfer them to a wire rack to cool completely. Continue baking the wafers until all the batter is used. You will need 18 wafers. (The wafers are fragile and break easily. There is extra batter in case some break when you remove them from the pan.)

To make the sabayon: Prepare an ice bath. (See page 18 for tips on using an ice bath.) In a stainless-steel bowl, whisk together the egg yolks, sugar, and salt until blended. Whisk in the orange juice and hazelnut liqueur. Place the bowl over a pan of simmering water, making sure the bottom of the bowl does not touch the water. (See page 18 for tips on using and making a double boiler.) Cook, whisking constantly, until the mixture is thick and there are no air bubbles, about 3 minutes. The mixture should mound slightly when dropped from the whisk. Remove the bowl from the pan and place it in the ice bath. Let cool to room temperature, whisking occasionally.

Put the cream in the bowl of a stand mixer fitted with the whip attachment and whip on medium-high speed until soft peaks form. Using a spatula, fold the cream into the cooled yolk mixture just until combined. Cover and freeze the sabayon for at least 2 hours before serving.

Let the sabayon soften at room temperature for about 5 minutes so the wafers won't crack. Place a cocoa wafer on a dessert plate. Scoop some sabayon onto the middle of the wafer, drizzle with some chocolate caramel sauce, and sprinkle with some nuts. Add a second wafer and again top with sabayon, sauce, and nuts. Top with a third wafer and dust the top with the confectioners' sugar. Drizzle a little chocolate caramel sauce around the stacked wafers. Serve immediately.

PLANNING AHEAD

The cocoa wafers may be made a day ahead and stored in an airtight container at room temperature. If they get soggy, reheat them in a 350°F oven for a couple of minutes to recrisp them. The sabayon may be made 2 days in advance and stored in the freezer until serving. Assemble the stacks just before serving.

CHOCOLATE ESPRESSO
FROZEN CREAM SANDWICHES

— SERVES 8 —

Meringues are by nature dry and brittle, but freezing them makes them soft and chewy. Here, the addition of cocoa powder makes the meringues less sweet than they typically are. Whenever I take these sandwiches to a barbecue, they are quickly devoured. If you don't mind piping lots of small circles, make mini-sandwiches that may be eaten in a single bite. In this case, you can skip the custard sauce.

MERINGUES

¾ CUP CONFECTIONERS' SUGAR

¾ CUP PLUS 2 TABLESPOONS GRANULATED SUGAR

¼ CUP UNSWEETENED COCOA POWDER

5 LARGE EGG WHITES

ESPRESSO CREAM

¾ CUP HEAVY WHIPPING CREAM

1 CUP MASCARPONE

PINCH OF KOSHER SALT

1 TABLESPOON ESPRESSO-GRIND (EXTRAFINE) COFFEE

2 TABLESPOONS GRANULATED SUGAR

CHOCOLATE CREAM

¾ CUP HEAVY WHIPPING CREAM

1 CUP MASCARPONE CHEESE

PINCH OF SALT

3 TABLESPOONS CHOCOLATE SAUCE
  (PAGE 284), CHILLED

1 RECIPE VANILLA CUSTARD SAUCE (PAGE 282)

CONFECTIONERS' SUGAR FOR DUSTING

To make the meringues: Preheat the oven to 225°F. Line 2 baking sheets with parchment paper. With a pencil, draw sixteen 3-inch circles on the parchment paper. Turn the paper over so the pencil side is facedown. (You will be able to see the markings through the paper.) Fit a pastry bag with a ½-inch plain round tip.

Sift together the confectioners' sugar, ¼ cup of the granulated sugar, and the cocoa powder onto a piece of parchment paper or into a bowl. Set aside.

Put the egg whites in the bowl of a stand mixer fitted with the whip attachment and whip on medium speed until frothy. Add 2 tablespoons of the granulated sugar, increase the speed to high, and whip until soft peaks form, about 1 minute. Add the remaining ½ cup granulated sugar in a slow, steady stream and whip until the whites are stiff but still glossy. Fold in the cocoa powder mixture.

Spoon the egg white mixture into the prepared pastry bag. Starting from the center of a penciled circle, pipe the batter in a circular motion, making a solid coil. Form the remaining meringues the same way.

Bake the meringues until they are dry and easily come off the paper when you pick them up. This will take at least 4 hours. (It is even fine to leave the meringues in the oven overnight.) Remove from the oven, let cool completely on the baking sheets, and then store in an airtight container at room temperature until you are ready to assemble the sandwiches.

To make the espresso cream: Place the cream, mascarpone, salt, ground coffee, and sugar in a bowl and whisk until soft peaks form. Cover and refrigerate until you are ready to assemble the sandwiches.

To make the chocolate cream: Place the cream, mascarpone, salt, and chocolate sauce in a bowl and whisk until soft peaks form. Cover and refrigerate until you are ready to assemble the sandwiches.

Fit a pastry bag with a ¼-inch plain round tip and fill with the chocolate cream. Fit a second pastry bag with a ¼-inch plain round tip and fill with the espresso cream. To make each sandwich, pipe about ¼ cup of the chocolate cream onto a meringue disk. Then pipe about ¼ cup of the espresso cream on top of the chocolate cream. (You can also spread the creams with a knife, although the appearance will not be as neat.) Place a second meringue disk on top of the espresso cream. Press lightly to adhere the sandwich together. Wrap well in plastic wrap and freeze for at least 2 hours before serving.

Pour some custard sauce on each plate and top with a sandwich. Dust the tops with the confectioners' sugar. If your freezer is very cold, let the sandwiches sit out at room temperature for 15 minutes before serving. They should not be rock hard.

PLANNING AHEAD

The meringues may be made 1 day in advance of assembling the sandwiches and stored in an airtight container at room temperature. The sandwiches may be assembled 2 days in advance, well wrapped, and kept in the freezer.

WHITE CHOCOLATE–ESPRESSO PARFAIT

— SERVES 6 —

Affogato is an Italian dessert of ice cream "drowned" in espresso.
Here I use some amaretto in the sauce to round out the espresso flavor.
Serve the parfait topped with crushed amaretti or biscotti for crunch.

WHITE CHOCOLATE ICE CREAM

8 OUNCES WHITE CHOCOLATE, FINELY CHOPPED

6 LARGE EGG YOLKS

¾ CUP GRANULATED SUGAR

PINCH OF KOSHER SALT

1½ CUPS MILK

2 CUPS HEAVY WHIPPING CREAM

ESPRESSO-AMARETTO SAUCE

1½ CUPS BREWED ESPRESSO OR DOUBLE-STRENGTH
     COFFEE (REGULAR OR DECAFFEINATED), CHILLED

3 TABLESPOONS HIGH-QUALITY AMARETTO, SUCH
     AS AMARETTO DI SARONNO

1 RECIPE CHANTILLY CREAM (PAGE 276)

½ CUP BITTERSWEET CHOCOLATE SHAVINGS
     (PAGE 21)

½ CUP CRUSHED AMARETTI OR BISCOTTI

To make the ice cream: Prepare an ice bath. (See page 18 for tips on using an ice bath.) Put the white chocolate in a bowl and set aside. In a large bowl, whisk together the egg yolks, ½ cup of the sugar, and the salt until blended.

In a heavy, nonreactive saucepan, combine the milk, cream, and remaining sugar over medium heat and heat until small bubbles appear around the edges of the pan. While whisking constantly, pour the milk mixture into the yolk mixture in a slow, steady stream. Pour the mixture back into the pan, place over medium-low heat, and cook, stirring constantly with a heat-resistant spatula, until it coats the spatula and reaches 175°F on an instant-read thermometer, 3 to 5 minutes.

Pour the hot custard over the white chocolate and whisk until smooth. Strain through a medium-mesh sieve into a clean bowl. Place the bowl in the ice bath. Let cool to room temperature, whisking occasionally. Cover and refrigerate until well chilled, at least 4 hours.

Freeze the custard in an ice-cream maker according to the manufacturer's instructions.

Transfer to a covered container and place in the freezer until scoopable, about 2 hours, depending on your freezer.

To make the sauce: In a pitcher, stir together the espresso and amaretto. Cover and refrigerate until serving.

Scoop the ice cream into glasses and pour an equal amount of the sauce over each serving. Top with the chantilly cream and then with the chocolate shavings and amaretti.

··· ◠◠ ···

PLANNING AHEAD

The custard base for the ice cream may be made a day in advance. The ice cream may be made up to 2 days in advance. The espresso-amaretto sauce may be made up to 8 hours in advance and stored in a covered container in the refrigerator.

ESPRESSO GRANITA WITH CHOCOLATE CREAM

— SERVES 8 —

Unlike ice cream, granita is made by freezing the base in your freezer and using a fork to break up the ice crystals. When served in a tall stemmed glass, the finished dessert sparkles beautifully. Despite their American origin, warm Chocolate Chip Cookies (page 216) are an excellent accompaniment to this typical Italian ice.

ESPRESSO GRANITA

4 CUPS WARM BREWED ESPRESSO

1 CUP GRANULATED SUGAR

CHOCOLATE CREAM

½ CUP CHOCOLATE SAUCE (PAGE 284)

1 CUP HEAVY WHIPPING CREAM

½ TEASPOON GRANULATED SUGAR

To make the granita: In a bowl, whisk together the espresso and sugar until the sugar dissolves. Pour into a 9-by-13-inch baking pan and place in the freezer. Every 30 minutes, remove the pan from the freezer and roughly stir up the mixture with the tines of a fork to prevent the ice crystals from forming a solid mass. Make sure that you scrape up the crystals from the bottom and sides of the pan and break them up each time. This will give the ice a uniformly light, feathery texture. Freeze the mixture until firm, about 4 hours, depending on your freezer.

To make the cream: Warm the chocolate sauce in a microwave or in a double boiler just until it is pourable. (See page 18 for tips on using and making a double boiler.) It should not be hot. In a bowl, combine 2 tablespoons of the chocolate sauce, the cream, and the sugar and whisk until soft peaks form.

Spoon the granita into tall glasses or coffee mugs. Top with a large dollop of the chocolate cream. Drizzle the remaining chocolate sauce over the cream. Serve immediately.

PLANNING AHEAD

The granita may be made 2 days in advance. Break it up with a fork to regain the feathery texture. The chocolate cream may be made up to 4 hours in advance, covered, and stored in the refrigerator. It may need to be lightly rewhipped before serving.

CHOCOLATE HAZELNUT CRÊPES

— SERVES 6 —

This was the last recipe I created for *Stars Desserts*. But because it combines chocolate and hazelnuts, it has always been one of my favorites. Substitute hazelnut ice cream for the hazelnut cream for a frozen variation.

HAZELNUT CREAM

⅓ CUP (2 OUNCES) HAZELNUTS, TOASTED AND SKINNED (SEE PAGE 20) AND THEN COARSELY CHOPPED

¾ CUP MASCARPONE CHEESE

1 TEASPOON HAZELNUT LIQUEUR SUCH AS FRANGELICO

1 TABLESPOON GRANULATED SUGAR

1 TABLESPOON HEAVY WHIPPING CREAM

18 CHOCOLATE CRÊPES (PAGE 298)

½ CUP GRANULATED SUGAR

½ CUP WATER

½ CUP FRESHLY SQUEEZED ORANGE JUICE

2 TEASPOONS FRESHLY SQUEEZED LEMON JUICE

¼ CUP HAZELNUT LIQUEUR SUCH AS FRANGELICO

PINCH OF KOSHER SALT

2 OUNCES (4 TABLESPOONS) UNSALTED BUTTER

½ CUP CHOCOLATE SAUCE (PAGE 284), WARMED

To make the cream: In a small bowl, combine the hazelnuts, mascarpone, liqueur, sugar, and cream and stir until combined. Cover and refrigerate until needed.

Fold each crêpe into quarters. In a large sauté pan, combine the sugar, water, orange juice, lemon juice, liqueur, and salt over medium heat. Cook, stirring, until the sugar dissolves, about 2 minutes. Place 9 of the folded crêpes in the pan and cook them until they are warmed through on the underside, about 10 seconds. Turn them over and cook for 5 seconds to warm through on the second side. Using a spatula, transfer the crêpes to individual plates, placing 3 crêpes on each plate. Heat the remaining crêpes in the same manner and divide evenly among 3 more plates.

Increase the heat to medium-high and add the butter to the pan. Cook, stirring occasionally, until the mixture begins to thicken to a light sauce consistency, about 2 minutes. Spoon the sauce evenly over the crêpes and then top evenly with the hazelnut cream. Drizzle the warm chocolate sauce over the crêpes. Serve immediately.

··· ❧ ···

PLANNING AHEAD

See the crêpe recipe for directions on making the crêpes in advance. The hazelnut cream may be made up to 8 hours in advance, covered, and stored in the refrigerator. The sauce should be made just before serving.

GÂTEAU ROYALE

— SERVES 8 TO 10 —

Lois Murphy, my first cooking instructor and mentor, gave me
this recipe. She and I affectionately nicknamed the cake Gâteau Fatso
because it is hard to resist a second piece. The Grand Marnier
is pronounced, so reduce the amount to 1 tablespoon if you prefer a
lighter taste. Serve the cake with your favorite ice cream. All
flavors seem to complement it.

8 OUNCES BITTERSWEET CHOCOLATE,
  FINELY CHOPPED

8 OUNCES (16 TABLESPOONS) UNSALTED BUTTER,
  AT ROOM TEMPERATURE

1¼ CUPS GRANULATED SUGAR

4 LARGE EGGS

5 TABLESPOONS CORNSTARCH

2 TABLESPOONS GRAND MARNIER

1 PINT ICE CREAM OF CHOICE

Preheat the oven to 350°F. Line the bottom of a
9-inch round springform pan with parchment
paper. Wrap the outside of the cake pan in a double
thickness of aluminum foil.

Melt the chocolate in a double boiler. (See
page 19 for tips on melting chocolate.) Whisk until
smooth, then let cool to room temperature. Add the
butter to the chocolate and whisk until smooth.

Put the sugar and eggs in the bowl of a stand
mixer fitted with the whip attachment and whip on
high speed until thick, about 2 minutes. Reduce the
speed to medium-low and mix in the chocolate-butter
mixture. Stir in the cornstarch and then the Grand
Marnier. Spread the batter into the prepared pan.

Place the springform pan in a baking pan or
large sauté pan with at least a 1-inch clearance
around the sides. (See page 22 for tips on using a
water bath.) Place the baking pan in the middle
of the oven. Carefully pour hot water into the pan
so that the water comes about one-third of the way
up the sides of the springform pan.

Bake the cake until it is crusty on top and a
skewer inserted into the center has a wet crumb,
45 to 50 minutes. Remove the pan from the water
bath and remove the foil from the pan. Let cool to
room temperature on a wire rack.

To unmold the cake, run a knife around the inside edge of the pan to loosen the cake, then remove the pan sides. Invert a platter on top of the cake and then invert the cake and plate together. Lift off the bottom of the cake pan and carefully peel off the parchment paper.

Cut the cake into wedges. Accompany each serving with a scoop of ice cream.

··· ∽ ···

The cake may be made a day in advance. Wrap in plastic wrap and store at room temperature.

HOT
DESSERTS

— CHAPTER 3 —

Too many cooks believe that hot desserts must be limited to rainy nights and elegant dinner parties. But the hot desserts we served at Stars were typically striking in appearance and effect and relatively easy to make, making them suitable for serving on nearly any occasion. For example, although fruit cobblers are commonplace, when they are hot from the oven they rank among the most perfect of all desserts. Compotes can usually be prepared ahead and quickly assembled at the last minute. And contrary to public belief, you don't have to tiptoe around the kitchen and speak in hushed tones when a soufflé is in the oven. Soufflés, like big dogs, just need to be treated with a little respect. Egg whites are delicate, so make sure that you don't overwhip them and that you fold them gently into the soufflé base, and the trickiest parts of making a soufflé are solved.

94
MAPLE BANANA COMPOTE WITH
GINGER ICE CREAM

96
STRAWBERRY COMPOTE WITH
RHUBARB ICE CREAM

98
LEMON-RASPBERRY PUDDING SOUFFLÉ

99
CRÊPES SUZETTE

100
CHESTNUT CRÊPES WITH
ORANGE HONEY ICE CREAM

102
NECTARINE BLUEBERRY BLINTZES

103
STRAWBERRY GRATIN

104
APPLE PANDOWDY

106
PEAR CHARLOTTE

108
PEACH BOYSENBERRY COBBLER

110
BLUEBERRY-PEACH BROWN BETTY

111
PUMPKIN SOUFFLÉ WITH APPLE CARAMEL SAUCE

112
BITTERSWEET CHOCOLATE SOUFFLÉ WITH
ESPRESSO CARAMEL SAUCE

114
ORANGE GRAND MARNIER SOUFFLÉ WITH
CHOCOLATE CUSTARD SAUCE

MAPLE BANANA COMPOTE WITH
GINGER ICE CREAM

— SERVES 6 —

Early New England settlers relied on maple syrup as their sole sweetener. Now more neutral-tasting brown and granulated sugars have taken its place. When you taste the maple syrup in this dessert, you will agree that it should not be limited to pouring over pancakes in the morning.

GINGER ICE CREAM

6 LARGE EGG YOLKS

1 CUP GRANULATED SUGAR

¼ TEASPOON KOSHER SALT

2¼ CUPS MILK

2¼ CUPS HEAVY WHIPPING CREAM

1½ OUNCES (2-INCH PIECE) UNPEELED GINGER,
    CUT INTO 4 PIECES

COMPOTE

5 BANANAS

3 TABLESPOONS FIRMLY PACKED BROWN SUGAR

1⅓ CUPS FRESHLY SQUEEZED ORANGE JUICE

⅓ CUP PURE MAPLE SYRUP

1 TEASPOON FRESHLY SQUEEZED LEMON JUICE

¼ CUP DARK RUM

PINCH OF KOSHER SALT

2 OUNCES (4 TABLESPOONS) UNSALTED BUTTER

¼ CUP (1 OUNCE) PECANS, TOASTED (SEE PAGE 20)
    AND COARSELY CHOPPED

To make the ice cream: Prepare an ice bath. (See page 18 for tips on using an ice bath.) In a stainless-steel bowl, whisk together the egg yolks, ½ cup of the granulated sugar, and the salt. Set aside. In a heavy, nonreactive saucepan, combine the milk, cream, ginger, and the remaining ½ cup granulated sugar and place over medium heat, stirring occasionally until the sugar dissolves and small bubbles appear around the edges of the pan. Remove from the heat, cover, and let steep for 10 minutes.

While whisking constantly, pour the ginger cream into the yolk mixture in a slow, steady stream. Pour the mixture back into the pan, place over medium-low heat, and cook, stirring constantly with a heat-resistant spatula, until it coats the spatula and reaches 175°F on an instant-read thermometer, 3 to 5 minutes.

Pour the custard through a fine-mesh sieve back into the bowl and place in the ice bath. Let cool to room temperature, whisking occasionally. Cover and refrigerate until well chilled, at least 4 hours.

Freeze the custard in an ice-cream maker according to the manufacturer's instructions. Transfer to a covered container and place in the freezer until scoopable, about 2 hours, depending on your freezer.

To make the compote: Peel the bananas and slice them on a slight diagonal ¼ inch thick. In a large sauté pan, combine the brown sugar, orange juice, maple syrup, lemon juice, rum, and salt and bring to a boil over medium-high heat, stirring occasionally. Cook until reduced by half, about 2 minutes. Add the butter and the banana slices and cook until the butter has melted, the bananas are warmed through, and the sauce has thickened slightly, about 2 minutes.

Put a scoop of ice cream in individual bowls and spoon the banana compote on top. Sprinkle with the pecans and serve immediately.

··· ✎ ···

PLANNING AHEAD

The custard base for the ice cream may be made a day in advance. The ice cream may be made up to a week in advance. The compote should be made just before serving.

STRAWBERRY COMPOTE WITH RHUBARB ICE CREAM

— SERVES 6 —

Whenever strawberry-and-rhubarb desserts are mentioned, my first thoughts are of crisp and pie. This is a new and delicious twist to a favorite old-fashioned combination.

RHUBARB ICE CREAM

4 CUPS CUT-UP RHUBARB (1½-INCH PIECES, FROM
   ABOUT 1 POUND)

¾ CUP GRANULATED SUGAR

¼ CUP WATER

LARGE PINCH OF KOSHER SALT

4 LARGE EGG YOLKS

1 CUP MILK

1¼ CUPS HEAVY WHIPPING CREAM

STRAWBERRY COMPOTE

1 TABLESPOON FRESHLY SQUEEZED LEMON JUICE

¼ CUP GRANULATED SUGAR

2 TABLESPOONS GRAND MARNIER (OPTIONAL)

2 PINTS STRAWBERRIES (ABOUT 4 CUPS), HULLED
   AND QUARTERED LENGTHWISE

1 OUNCE (2 TABLESPOONS) UNSALTED BUTTER

To make the ice cream: In a nonreactive saucepan, combine the rhubarb, ¼ cup of the sugar, the water, and the salt and place over medium heat. Cook, stirring occasionally, until the rhubarb is soft, about 10 minutes. Remove from the heat, let cool slightly, transfer to a food processor, and purée until smooth. Strain the purée through a medium-mesh sieve. Let cool to room temperature.

Prepare an ice bath. (For tips on using an ice bath, see page 18). In a bowl, whisk together the egg yolks and the remaining ½ cup sugar. In a heavy, nonreactive saucepan, combine the milk and cream and heat over medium heat until small bubbles appear around the edges of the pan. While whisking constantly, pour the cream mixture into the yolk mixture in a slow, steady stream. Pour the mixture back into the pan, place over medium-low heat, and cook, stirring constantly with a heat-resistant spatula, until it coats the spatula and reaches 175°F on an instant-read thermometer, 3 to 5 minutes.

Pour the custard through a fine-mesh sieve back into the bowl and place in the ice bath. Let cool to room temperature, whisking occasionally. Whisk in the rhubarb purée. Refrigerate until well chilled, at least 4 hours.

Freeze the custard in an ice-cream maker according to the manufacturer's instructions. Transfer to a covered container and place in the freezer until scoopable, about 2 hours, depending on your freezer.

To make the compote: In a large sauté pan, combine the lemon juice, sugar, and Grand Marnier (if using) over medium-high heat. Cook, stirring occasionally, until the sugar dissolves, about 30 seconds. Add the strawberries and the butter and cook, stirring occasionally and gently, until the butter has melted and the strawberries are warmed through, about 1 minute.

Place a scoop of ice cream in individual bowls and spoon the strawberry compote on top. Serve immediately.

··· ⌒⌒ ···

PLANNING AHEAD

The custard base for the ice cream may be made a day in advance. The ice cream may be made up to 1 week in advance. The compote should be made just before serving.

LEMON-RASPBERRY PUDDING SOUFFLÉ

— SERVES 8 —

This is a wonderful dessert: the top half is a soufflé and the bottom half is a thin, puckery sauce that recalls lemon curd. Bake it while you eat your dinner. It can sit for 5 to 10 minutes after baking if you are not quite ready for it. For a delicious variation, use passion fruit juice in place of the lemon juice.

1½ PINTS RASPBERRIES (ABOUT 3 CUPS)

3 OUNCES (6 TABLESPOONS) UNSALTED BUTTER, AT ROOM TEMPERATURE

1 CUP GRANULATED SUGAR

4 LARGE EGGS, SEPARATED

½ CUP ALL-PURPOSE FLOUR

¼ TEASPOON KOSHER SALT

2½ CUPS MILK

½ CUP FRESHLY SQUEEZED LEMON JUICE

CONFECTIONERS' SUGAR FOR DUSTING

Preheat the oven to 325°F. Place 1 cup of the raspberries in the bottom of a 2-quart soufflé dish.

Put the butter and granulated sugar in the bowl of a stand mixer fitted with the paddle attachment and beat on medium-high speed until light and creamy, about 2 minutes. Beat in the egg yolks one at a time, mixing well after each addition. Scrape the sides of the bowl. Reduce the speed to medium-low, add the flour and salt, and mix until incorporated. Mix in the milk and lemon juice. The batter will be thin.

Put the egg whites in another mixer bowl, and whip on medium speed until frothy. Increase the speed to high and continue whipping until soft peaks form. Using a spatula, gently fold the egg whites into the lemon mixture in 2 additions. Gently spread the batter over the raspberries in the soufflé dish.

Place the soufflé dish in a baking pan or large sauté pan with at least a 1-inch clearance around the sides. (See page 22 for tips on using a water bath.) Place the baking pan in the middle of the oven. Carefully pour hot water into the pan so that the water comes about one-third of the way up the sides of the dish.

Bake until the top is golden brown and the sides are pulling away from the dish, about 1¼ hours. Remove from the oven and serve within 15 minutes.

Dust the top with confectioner's sugar and spoon the soufflé into individual bowls. Scatter the remaining 2 cups raspberries on top and serve immediately.

··· ⌾ ···

PLANNING AHEAD

The batter minus the egg whites may be made a day in advance, covered, and refrigerated. Let it sit at room temperature for 1 hour before folding in the egg whites and baking.

CRÊPES SUZETTE

— SERVES 6 —

The great French chef Auguste Escoffier created crêpes suzette, which he prepared with tangerine juice and Curaçao. At Stars, we believed it was the best and purest version, so we always did the same. For a modern twist, add a scoop of vanilla ice cream.

18 CRÊPES (PAGE 297)

1¼ CUPS FRESHLY SQUEEZED TANGERINE JUICE

1½ TEASPOONS FRESHLY SQUEEZED LEMON JUICE

3 TABLESPOONS CURAÇAO

2 TABLESPOONS GRANULATED SUGAR

2 TABLESPOONS WATER

3 OUNCES (6 TABLESPOONS) UNSALTED BUTTER

GRATED ZEST OF 1 ORANGE

Fold the crêpes into quarters. Heat the tangerine and lemon juices, Curaçao, sugar, and water in a large sauté pan over medium heat. Put half the crêpes in the pan and cook for about 15 seconds. Turn them over and cook for another 15 seconds. Remove them from the pan and keep warm on a covered plate while you heat the remaining crêpes in the same manner. Place the second batch of crêpes with the first.

Increase the heat to medium-high and add the butter and orange zest to the pan. Heat until the butter melts and the mixture begins to thicken to a light sauce consistency, about 3 minutes.

Spoon the sauce over the crêpes and serve immediately.

PLANNING AHEAD

See the crêpe recipe for directions on making the crêpes in advance. The sauce should be made just before serving.

CHESTNUT CRÊPES WITH ORANGE HONEY ICE CREAM

— SERVES 6 —

Whole chestnuts and chestnut flour primarily turn up in recipes made during the winter holidays, the same time of the year that you can buy hot roasted chestnuts on the street corners of New York and other cities. Chestnut is often paired with chocolate. Here, I combine it with orange for a lighter dessert. If you are craving chocolate, add a drizzle of warm Chocolate Sauce (page 284).

ORANGE HONEY ICE CREAM

6 LARGE EGG YOLKS

¾ CUP HONEY

PINCH OF KOSHER SALT

2 CUPS MILK

2 CUPS HEAVY WHIPPING CREAM

PEEL FROM 1 LARGE ORANGE

CHESTNUT CRÊPES

½ CUP MILK

½ CUP WATER

2 LARGE EGGS

¼ TEASPOON VANILLA EXTRACT

½ TEASPOON GRATED ORANGE ZEST

½ CUP CHESTNUT FLOUR

½ CUP ALL-PURPOSE FLOUR

¼ CUP GRANULATED SUGAR

⅛ TEASPOON KOSHER SALT

½ OUNCE (1 TABLESPOON) UNSALTED BUTTER, MELTED

SAUCE

1¼ CUPS FRESHLY SQUEEZED ORANGE JUICE

1 TABLESPOON FRESHLY SQUEEZED LEMON JUICE

3 TABLESPOONS GRANULATED SUGAR

PINCH OF KOSHER SALT

2 OUNCES (4 TABLESPOONS) UNSALTED BUTTER, AT ROOM TEMPERATURE

To make the ice cream: Prepare an ice bath. (See page 18 for tips on using an ice bath.) In a stainless-steel bowl, whisk together the egg yolks, honey, and salt. Set aside.

In a heavy saucepan, combine the milk, cream, and orange peel and place over medium heat until small bubbles appear around the edges of the pan. Remove from the heat, cover, and let steep for 20 minutes. Uncover, return the pan to medium heat, and again heat until small bubbles appear around the edges of the pan.

While whisking constantly, pour the cream mixture into the yolk mixture in a slow, steady stream. Pour the mixture back into the pan, place over medium-low heat, and cook, stirring constantly with a heat-resistant spatula, until it coats the spatula and reaches 175°F on an instant-read thermometer, about 5 minutes. Pour the mixture through a medium-mesh strainer back into the bowl and place in the ice bath. Let cool to room temperature, stirring occasionally. Cover and refrigerate until well chilled, at least 2 hours.

Freeze the custard in an ice-cream maker according to the manufacturer's instructions. Transfer to a covered container and place in the freezer until scoopable, about 2 hours, depending on your freezer.

To make the crêpes: In a food processor or blender, combine the milk, water, eggs, and vanilla and process until smooth. Add the orange zest, chestnut flour, all-purpose flour, sugar, salt, and melted butter and process again until smooth. Cover and refrigerate for at least 1 hour.

Heat a nonstick 6-inch crêpe pan or seasoned crêpe pan over medium heat. Pour in 1½ tablespoons of the crêpe batter and quickly rotate the pan, spreading it in a thin layer over the entire bottom. Cook the crêpe until lightly browned, about 30 seconds. Loosen the side of the crêpe with the edge of a knife or your fingers and turn it over. Cook until the second side is lightly browned, about 15 seconds. Transfer the crêpe to a plate. Continue to make crêpes in this manner until you have used all of the batter, stacking the crêpes so that they overlap slightly. You will need 12 crêpes (there will be enough batter for a few extra). Fold the crêpes into quarters and place on a large plate.

To make the sauce: In a large sauté pan, combine the orange juice, lemon juice, sugar, and salt over medium heat and cook, stirring, until the sugar dissolves. Reduce the heat to low, place 6 of the folded crêpes in the pan, and cook them until warmed through on the underside, about 10 seconds. Turn them over and cook for 5 seconds to warm through on the second side. Using a spatula, transfer the crêpes to individual plates, placing 2 crêpes on each plate. Heat the remaining crêpes in the same manner and divide evenly among 3 more plates.

Increase the heat to medium-high and add the butter. Heat until the butter melts and begins to thicken to a light sauce consistency, about 1 minute.

While the sauce is heating, place a scoop of ice cream on top of each serving of crêpes. Spoon the sauce over the ice cream and the crêpes. Serve immediately.

··· ◡ ···

PLANNING AHEAD

The custard base for the ice cream may be made a day in advance. The ice cream may be made up to a week in advance. The crêpe batter may be made a day in advance and kept refrigerated. The crêpes may be made ahead and refrigerated for up to 2 days. They may also be stacked, with pieces of waxed paper between them, well wrapped in plastic wrap, and frozen for up to 1 week. The sauce should be made just before serving.

NECTARINE BLUEBERRY BLINTZES

— SERVES 6 —

Blintzes are filled crêpes that are sautéed so the tops and bottoms are golden brown and crispy. They may be savory or sweet. In this recipe, I stuff them with mascarpone instead of the traditional sour cream and top them with warm fruit.

BLINTZES

1 CUP MASCARPONE CHEESE

1 TABLESPOON GRANULATED SUGAR

¼ TEASPOON VANILLA EXTRACT

PINCH OF KOSHER SALT

12 CRÊPES (PAGE 297)

1½ OUNCES (3 TABLESPOONS) UNSALTED BUTTER

NECTARINE BLUEBERRY COMPOTE

¼ CUP GRANULATED SUGAR

¼ CUP WATER

3 CUPS PITTED AND SLICED NECTARINES (ABOUT 6)

1½ CUPS BLUEBERRIES

2 TABLESPOONS FRESHLY SQUEEZED LEMON JUICE

PINCH OF KOSHER SALT

1 OUNCE (2 TABLESPOONS) UNSALTED BUTTER,
   AT ROOM TEMPERATURE

To make the blintzes: In a small bowl, mix together the mascarpone, sugar, vanilla, and salt. Put about 1 tablespoon of the mascarpone mixture in the center of a crêpe. Fold the sides of the crêpe over the mascarpone, forming a rectangle. Repeat with the remaining crêpes and filling.

In a large sauté pan, melt the butter over medium-high heat. Add half the blintzes, seam-side down, and cook until browned on the underside, 1 to 2 minutes. Carefully turn the blintzes over and brown the second side, about 1 minute. Be careful not to heat for too long or the filling will leak out. Using a spatula, transfer the blintzes to individual plates, placing 2 blintzes on each plate. Heat the remaining blintzes in the same manner and divide evenly among 3 more plates.

To make the compote: Add the sugar and water to the sauté pan over medium heat and cook, stirring occasionally, until the sugar dissolves, about 15 seconds. Add the nectarines, blueberries, lemon juice, salt, and butter and cook until the butter has melted and the fruits are warmed through, about 2 minutes.

Spoon the compote over the blintzes. Serve immediately.

PLANNING AHEAD

The blintzes may be assembled a day in advance, covered, and refrigerated. Cook just before serving. The compote should be prepared just before serving.

STRAWBERRY GRATIN

— SERVES 6 —

I use this recipe when I need a very easy-to-prepare yet amazing dessert. You can substitute almost any summer berries or fruits for the strawberries. Just make sure they are ripe and juicy.

4 PINTS STRAWBERRIES (ABOUT 8 CUPS), HULLED
   AND QUARTERED

1½ CUPS SOUR CREAM

½ TEASPOON VANILLA EXTRACT

PINCH OF KOSHER SALT

3 TABLESPOONS HALF-AND-HALF

½ CUP FIRMLY PACKED DARK BROWN SUGAR

Preheat the broiler. Arrange the strawberries in the bottoms of 6 shallow flameproof ramekins or other individual baking dishes.

In a bowl, whisk together the sour cream, vanilla, salt, and half-and-half. Spoon a thin layer of the mixture evenly over the strawberries. Sprinkle the brown sugar evenly on top.

Arrange the dishes on a baking sheet, slip under the broiler about 4 inches from the heat source, and broil until the sugar has melted, about 1 minute. Serve immediately.

··· ⟳ ···

PLANNING AHEAD

This gratin is so simple to make that there is no need for advance preparation.

APPLE PANDOWDY

— SERVES 8 —

For this and all apple desserts, use firm, juicy apples. Every region of the country has its own varieties, so search out the best in your area.

APPLE FILLING

7 FIRM, JUICY APPLES (ABOUT 3 POUNDS), PEELED,
   HALVED, CORED, AND SLICED ⅛ INCH THICK

4 OUNCES (8 TABLESPOONS) UNSALTED BUTTER

½ CUP GRANULATED SUGAR

2 TABLESPOONS FRESHLY SQUEEZED LEMON JUICE

1 TEASPOON GROUND CINNAMON

½ TEASPOON GROUND ALLSPICE

¼ TEASPOON GROUND GINGER

PINCH OF GROUND CLOVES

PINCH OF KOSHER SALT

1 CUP HEAVY WHIPPING CREAM

1 CUP GOLDEN RAISINS

PECAN TOPPING

1½ CUPS ALL-PURPOSE FLOUR

1 CUP (4 OUNCES) PECANS, TOASTED (SEE PAGE 20)
   AND FINELY CHOPPED

3 TABLESPOONS GRANULATED SUGAR

2 TEASPOONS BAKING POWDER

PINCH OF KOSHER SALT

3 OUNCES (6 TABLESPOONS) COLD UNSALTED
   BUTTER, CUT INTO 1-INCH PIECES

¾ CUP HEAVY WHIPPING CREAM

FLOUR FOR DUSTING

1 RECIPE CARAMEL ICE CREAM (PAGE 300)

1 RECIPE CARAMEL SAUCE (PAGE 285)

To make the filling: In a large, heavy saucepan, combine the apples, butter, sugar, lemon juice, cinnamon, allspice, ginger, cloves, and salt over medium heat. Cook, stirring occasionally, until the apples are soft but still retain their shape, about 10 minutes.

Add the cream to the pan and continue to cook until the liquid thickens slightly, 5 to 10 minutes. Stir in the raisins and transfer the apple mixture to a 1½-quart baking dish.

To make the pecan topping: Preheat the oven to 350°F. Stir together the flour, pecans, sugar, baking powder, and salt in the bowl of a stand mixer fitted with the paddle attachment. Scatter the butter pieces over the top and mix on low speed until the butter is the size of small peas. Slowly pour in the cream and continue to mix on low speed until the dough comes together. (Alternatively, cut the butter into the dry ingredients with a pastry blender until the butter is the size of small peas and then slowly add the cream, stirring and tossing with a fork until the dough comes together.)

On a lightly floured work surface, roll out the dough ¼ inch thick. Using a 3-inch round cutter, cut the dough into circles. Gather together the scraps and reroll as necessary to get 8 circles total. Place the circles in a single layer on top of the apple mixture.

Bake until the topping is golden brown and the apples are beginning to bubble around the edges, about 40 minutes. Let cool for 10 minutes before serving.

Spoon the warm pandowdy into individual bowls. Accompany with a scoop of the ice cream alongside and drizzle the sauce over the pandowdy and ice cream. Serve immediately.

··· ◠◡◠ ···

The pandowdy may be made several hours in advance, kept at room temperature, and reheated in a 350°F for 10 minutes just before serving. It tastes best the day it is made, but leftovers may be covered with plastic wrap, stored at room temperature, and eaten the next day.

PEAR CHARLOTTE

— SERVES 8 —

I use brioche when making charlottes because it produces a buttery and delicate yet crisp crust. You can also use challah or a coarse-textured white bread, such as Pepperidge Farm Toasting White Bread. According to Martha Barnette, author of the wonderful *Ladyfingers and Nun's Tummies: A Lighthearted Look at How Foods Got Their Names*, the dessert got its name from Charlotte, a heroine in a 1774 book by Johann Wolfgang von Goethe.

7 RIPE PEARS (ABOUT 3 POUNDS), PEELED, HALVED, CORED, AND SLICED ⅜ INCH THICK

⅓ CUP PLUS 1 TABLESPOON GRANULATED SUGAR

PINCH OF KOSHER SALT

1½ TABLESPOONS FRESHLY SQUEEZED LEMON JUICE

4 OUNCES (8 TABLESPOONS) UNSALTED BUTTER, AT ROOM TEMPERATURE

½ TEASPOON GROUND CINNAMON

1 LOAF (1 POUND) BRIOCHE (PAGE 293, OR STORE-BOUGHT)

1 RECIPE VANILLA CUSTARD SAUCE (PAGE 282)

1 RECIPE CHANTILLY CREAM (PAGE 276)

Preheat the oven to 350°F. Have ready eight 5-ounce ramekins.

In a large sauté pan, combine the pears, ⅓ cup of the sugar, the salt, and the lemon juice over medium-high heat. Cook, stirring occasionally, until the pears are soft and juicy, about 10 minutes. Increase the heat to high and continue to cook until the liquid evaporates, about 5 minutes. Remove from the heat and let cool to room temperature.

In a bowl, combine the butter, the remaining 1 tablespoon sugar, and the cinnamon and mix until smooth.

Trim off the crusts from the brioche. Lay the side of a ramekin on top of the bread and cut the bread into pieces that are a half inch thicker than the height of the ramekin. (Most ramekins will have 1½-inch sides.) Turn each piece on its side and slice ⅜ inch thick.

Butter one side of each piece of brioche with the cinnamon-sugar butter. With a long side of the bread closest to you, cut each slice vertically into 4 equal pieces. Line the sides of the ramekins with the brioche pieces, buttered side against the ramekin. The bread pieces should fit snugly around the ramekins without any gaps. Fill each ramekin with the pears, dividing them evenly and pressing down on them to ensure a compact fit. With a serrated knife, trim off any brioche that extends above the rim of the ramekins. Place the ramekins on a baking sheet.

Bake until the tops are golden brown, about 20 minutes. Remove from the oven and let cool for 5 minutes, and then invert onto individual plates to unmold.

Drizzle around each charlotte with the custard sauce and top with the chantilly cream. Serve warm.

··· ~~~ ···

PLANNING AHEAD

The charlottes may be made a day ahead. Let cool in the ramekins, cover, and refrigerate overnight. The next day, reheat in a 350°F oven for 10 minutes, then unmold and serve as directed.

PEACH BOYSENBERRY COBBLER

— SERVES 8 —

The essence of all cobblers is seasonal fruit bursting with flavor. Getting fancy or too creative ruins them. This cobbler is also good with vanilla ice cream, homemade (page 299) or your favorite brand, in place of the whipped cream.

FILLING

6 PEACHES (ABOUT 2 POUNDS)

2 TABLESPOONS TAPIOCA FLOUR OR CORNSTARCH

5 TABLESPOONS GRANULATED SUGAR

1 TEASPOON FRESHLY SQUEEZED LEMON JUICE

PINCH OF KOSHER SALT

1½ CUPS BOYSENBERRIES

TOPPING

2 CUPS ALL-PURPOSE FLOUR

2 TEASPOONS BAKING POWDER

½ TEASPOON KOSHER SALT

¼ CUP FIRMLY PACKED LIGHT BROWN SUGAR

3 OUNCES (6 TABLESPOONS) COLD UNSALTED
  BUTTER, AND CUT INTO 1-INCH PIECES

¾ CUP PLUS 2 TABLESPOONS HEAVY
  WHIPPING CREAM

FLOUR FOR DUSTING

1 RECIPE CHANTILLY CREAM (PAGE 276)

To prepare the fruit: Peel and pit the peaches. Cut into ¼-inch-thick slices. There should be about 5 cups.

In a large bowl, combine the peaches, tapioca flour, granulated sugar, lemon juice, and salt and toss to mix evenly. Gently mix in the boysenberries. Transfer the fruit to a 9-inch square baking pan or ovenproof dish of equivalent size and depth. Set aside.

To make the topping: Preheat the oven to 350°F. Stir together the flour, baking powder, salt, and 3 tablespoons of the brown sugar in the bowl of a stand mixer fitted with the paddle attachment. Scatter the butter pieces over the top and mix on low speed until the butter is the size of large peas. Slowly pour in the ¾ cup cream and continue to mix on low speed until the dough comes together. (Alternatively, cut the butter into the dry ingredients with a pastry blender until the butter is the size of large peas, and then slowly add the cream, stirring and tossing with a fork until the dough comes together.)

On a lightly floured work surface, roll out the dough ⅜ inch thick. Using a 2-inch round cutter, cut the dough into circles, cutting as close together as possible to minimize scraps. Place the circles in a single layer on top of the peach mixture. Brush the dough circles with the remaining 2 tablespoons cream. Sprinkle the remaining 1 tablespoon brown sugar evenly over the top.

Bake until the topping is golden brown and the fruit juices are beginning to bubble around the edges, 25 to 30 minutes. Let cool for 10 minutes before serving. Serve warm with the chantilly cream.

··· ᶜ⌒ᵒ ···

PLANNING AHEAD

The cobbler is best served the day it is made. It may be made several hours in advance, kept at room temperature, and then reheated in a 350°F oven for 10 minutes just before serving.

BLUEBERRY–PEACH BROWN BETTY

— SERVES 8 —

A brown betty is typically made by layering fruit with bread crumbs, but I like to use cubes of bread, which give the dessert a buttery crunch that perfectly complements the fresh fruit. I prefer brioche, challah, or Portuguese sweet bread because of their rich flavor.

1 LOAF (1 POUND) BRIOCHE (PAGE 293) OR
   OTHER RICH EGG BREAD

6 OUNCES (12 TABLESPOONS) UNSALTED BUTTER,
   MELTED

1¾ CUPS GRANULATED SUGAR

1 TABLESPOON GROUND CINNAMON

½ TEASPOON FRESHLY GRATED NUTMEG

2 TABLESPOONS ALL-PURPOSE FLOUR

1¾ POUNDS PEACHES, PEELED, PITTED, AND SLICED
   ¼ INCH THICK

1½ PINTS BLUEBERRIES (ABOUT 3 CUPS)

3 TABLESPOONS CORNSTARCH

¼ CUP FIRMLY PACKED DARK BROWN SUGAR

1 RECIPE CHANTILLY CREAM (PAGE 276) OR
   1 QUART VANILLA ICE CREAM (PAGE 299)

Preheat the oven to 350°F. Trim off the crust from the brioche and then cut the loaf into ¾-inch cubes. Place the cubes in a single layer on a baking sheet and toast until light brown, about 10 minutes.

In a bowl, mix together the bread cubes and melted butter, coating the bread cubes evenly. Add 1 cup of the granulated sugar, the cinnamon, nutmeg, and flour and again mix until the bread cubes are evenly coated. Place half of the bread cubes in the bottom of a 9-by-13-inch baking pan.

In a bowl, combine the peaches, blueberries, cornstarch, brown sugar, and the remaining ¾ cup granulated sugar and mix gently until combined. Spoon the fruit mixture evenly over the bread cubes in the baking dish. Top with the remaining bread cubes.

Bake until the topping is browned and the fruit juices are bubbling, 35 to 40 minutes. Let cool for 10 minutes before serving. Serve warm with the chantilly cream.

··· ···

PLANNING AHEAD

The brown betty is best served the day it is made. It may be made several hours in advance, kept at room temperature, and reheated in a 350°F oven for 10 minutes just before serving.

PUMPKIN SOUFFLÉ WITH APPLE CARAMEL SAUCE

— SERVES 8 —

If Sugar pumpkins are available, make your own pumpkin purée for this soufflé. If not, substitute canned pumpkin, but be sure that it doesn't include any seasonings. This soufflé is quicker to prepare than soufflés made with a base of egg yolks and milk.

BUTTER AND GRANULATED SUGAR FOR THE
  SOUFFLÉ DISH
1 CUP PUMPKIN PURÉE, HOMEMADE (PAGE 301)
  OR PURCHASED
½ CUP FIRMLY PACKED DARK BROWN SUGAR
⅛ TEASPOON GROUND CLOVES
½ TEASPOON GROUND CINNAMON
⅛ TEASPOON FRESHLY GRATED NUTMEG
⅛ TEASPOON GROUND GINGER
PINCH OF KOSHER SALT
12 LARGE (ABOUT 1½ CUPS) EGG WHITES
½ CUP GRANULATED SUGAR
¾ CUP APPLE CARAMEL SAUCE (PAGE 287)

Preheat the oven to 375°F. Butter a 2-quart soufflé dish and dust with granulated sugar, tapping out the excess.

In a bowl, combine the pumpkin purée, brown sugar, cloves, cinnamon, nutmeg, ginger, and salt and mix well. Set aside.

Put the egg whites in the bowl of a stand mixer fitted with the whip attachment and whip on medium speed until frothy. Increase the speed to high and slowly add the granulated sugar in a slow, steady stream. Whip until soft peaks form. Using a spatula, gently fold the egg whites into the pumpkin mixture in 2 additions. Gently spread the pumpkin mixture in the prepared dish. Lightly tap the soufflé dish on the counter to remove any air bubbles.

Bake until firm when gently touched on the top and sides, about 30 minutes. Serve immediately with the apple caramel sauce on the side.

··· ᘒ ···

PLANNING AHEAD
The soufflé base may be made a day in advance, covered, and refrigerated. The egg whites must be whipped and folded into the base and the soufflé must be baked just before serving.

BITTERSWEET CHOCOLATE SOUFFLÉ WITH ESPRESSO CARAMEL SAUCE

— SERVES 8 —

Whenever we put a chocolate soufflé on the Stars menu, it produced a love-hate relationship in the kitchen. Customers loved our chocolate soufflé so much that no other dessert was ever ordered. It didn't matter how great the other choices were—nothing could match warm chocolate. When serving a soufflé at home, you don't have someone standing in the kitchen making it for you. Since it must be put together at the last minute, I use the preparation time as a break when guests can stretch their legs and get ready for the grand finale. It is also a good time to get someone else started on the dishes!

3　LARGE EGG YOLKS

⅓ CUP GRANULATED SUGAR

½ CUP ALL-PURPOSE FLOUR

⅛ TEASPOON KOSHER SALT

1½ CUPS MILK

4　OUNCES BITTERSWEET CHOCOLATE,
　　FINELY CHOPPED

BUTTER AND GRANULATED SUGAR FOR THE
　　SOUFFLÉ DISH

10 LARGE (ABOUT 1¼ CUPS) EGG WHITES

½ TEASPOON CREAM OF TARTAR

1　RECIPE ESPRESSO CARAMEL SAUCE (PAGE 288)

In a stainless-steel bowl, whisk together the egg yolks and sugar until blended. Whisk in the flour and salt. In a small, heavy nonreactive saucepan, bring the milk to a full boil over medium-high heat. Pour the milk into the egg mixture all at once and whisk until the mixture is smooth and thick. Add the chocolate and whisk again until smooth. Transfer the chocolate soufflé base to a clean bowl and cover with plastic wrap, pressing it directly onto the surface. Refrigerate until cold, about 2 hours.

Preheat the oven to 350°F. Butter a 2½-quart soufflé dish and dust with granulated sugar, tapping out the excess.

Put the egg whites in the bowl of a stand mixer fitted with the whip attachment and whip on medium speed until frothy. Add the cream of tartar, increase the speed to high, and whip until stiff but still glossy. Using a spatula, gently fold the egg whites into the chocolate mixture in 2 additions. Gently spread the mixture in the prepared dish. Lightly tap the soufflé dish on the counter to remove any air bubbles.

Bake until firm when gently touched on the top and sides, about 55 minutes. Serve immediately by spooning the soufflé onto individual plates and pouring the espresso caramel sauce over the top.

··· ⤳ ···

PLANNING AHEAD

The soufflé base may be made a day in advance, covered, and refrigerated. The egg whites must be whipped and folded into the base and the soufflé must be baked just before serving.

ORANGE GRAND MARNIER SOUFFLÉ WITH CHOCOLATE CUSTARD SAUCE

— SERVES 8 —

At Stars, we put a soufflé on the menu every night. The flavor of the soufflé was whatever inspired us, and sometimes it was difficult to come up with something new. When we weren't feeling particularly creative, we would put our Grand Marnier soufflé on the list. It is elegant, impressive, and full of orange flavor—the perfect ending to any meal, rich or light. It is also good served with raspberry sauce (see Berry Sauce, page 289) instead of the custard sauce.

1½ CUPS MILK

PEEL OF 1 ORANGE

3 LARGE EGG YOLKS

⅓ CUP GRANULATED SUGAR

½ CUP ALL-PURPOSE FLOUR

⅛ TEASPOON KOSHER SALT

⅓ CUP GRAND MARNIER

BUTTER AND GRANULATED SUGAR FOR THE
    SOUFFLÉ DISH

8 LARGE (ABOUT 1 CUP) EGG WHITES

½ TEASPOON CREAM OF TARTAR

1 TABLESPOON CONFECTIONERS' SUGAR

1 RECIPE CHOCOLATE CUSTARD SAUCE (PAGE 283)

In a heavy, nonreactive saucepan, combine the milk and orange peel and place over medium heat until small bubbles appear around the edges of the pan. Remove from the heat, cover, and let steep for 10 minutes.

In a bowl, whisk together the egg yolks and sugar until blended. Whisk in the flour and salt. While whisking constantly, pour the milk through a medium-mesh sieve into the egg mixture in a slow, steady stream. Stir in the Grand Marnier and pour the mixture back into the pan. Place over medium heat and cook, whisking constantly, until thick, 2 to 3 minutes. Transfer the soufflé base to a clean bowl and cover with plastic wrap, pressing it directly onto the surface. Refrigerate until cold, about 2 hours.

Preheat the oven to 350°F. Butter a 2-quart soufflé dish and dust with granulated sugar, tapping out the excess.

Put the egg whites in the bowl of a stand mixer fitted with the whip attachment and whip on medium speed until frothy. Add the cream of tartar, increase the speed to high, and whip until stiff but still glossy. Using a spatula, gently fold the egg whites into the soufflé base in 2 additions. Gently spread the mixture in the prepared dish. Lightly tap the soufflé dish on the counter to remove any air bubbles.

Bake until golden brown and firm when gently touched on the top and sides, about 55 minutes. Dust the top with the confectioners' sugar and serve immediately with the chocolate custard sauce on the side.

PLANNING AHEAD

The soufflé base may be made a day in advance, covered, and refrigerated. The egg whites must be whipped and folded into the base and the soufflé must be baked just before serving.

FRUIT
DESSERTS

— CHAPTER 4 —

Desserts made with fruit should taste as vibrant as the fruit itself. Nature has given us delicious-tasting produce, so it is our job to enhance the flavors of these gifts, not hide them. Not adding too much sweetener to a dessert is crucial in all pastry making, but it is especially true for fruit desserts. The natural sugars in fruits offer some sweetness before you begin. Too much sweetener will only dilute the flavor of a great dessert.

When I see seasonal fruits at their best at the store, I fill up my grocery basket. Summer, with its juicy, fragrant stone fruits and berries, may be the prime period for fruit, but every season has its contributions. Spring has rhubarb and strawberries and an initial flush of figs. Fall brings earthier fruits, such as apples, pears, persimmons, and a bigger crop of figs. While many citrus fruits and tropical fruits are available year-round, winter is when you will find Key limes, Meyer lemons, passion fruits, blood oranges, mangoes, and papayas.

In many of the recipes that follow, the fruits are inter-changeable. Raspberries may be substituted for blackberries or strawberries, nectarine desserts may be made with peaches, and limes and lemons can trade places. Apples and pears may be swapped, too, but keep in mind that pears are juicier than apples, giving off more liquid when baked.

120
OAT CRISPS WITH BLUEBERRIES
AND CRÈME FRAÎCHE

121
RASPBERRY SPRITZER

122
PLUM VANILLA CREAMSICLE BOMBE WITH
PLUM CARAMEL SAUCE

123
BAKED APRICOTS WITH VANILLA ICE CREAM
AND ALMOND PRALINE

124
HAZELNUT SHORTCAKES WITH PLUM COMPOTE

126
HONEY-MARSALA BAKED FIGS WITH
GINGER SABAYON

128
TANGERINE ICE WITH PISTACHIO TUILES

130
LEMON CARAMEL SORBET

131
RIESLING-POACHED PEACHES

132
POACHED PEARS WITH WALNUT CREAM

134
SAVARIN WITH GRAND MARNIER
SABAYON AND MIXED BERRIES

136
FROZEN KIR ROYALE

145
SUMMER PUDDING

146
VANILLA WAFERS WITH ZINFANDEL-
MARINATED RASPBERRIES

148

OAT CRISPS WITH BLUEBERRIES AND CRÈME FRAÎCHE

— SERVES 6 —

I created this recipe as a dessert, but since then some of my friends have told me they like to make it for breakfast. I took their idea one step further and served it with organic nonfat plain yogurt instead of crème fraîche. It gets rave reviews for breakfast or dessert.

1¼ OUNCES (2½ TABLESPOONS) UNSALTED BUTTER, MELTED

¼ CUP FIRMLY PACKED DARK BROWN SUGAR

2 TABLESPOONS GRANULATED SUGAR

2 TABLESPOONS DARK CORN SYRUP

1 CUP OLD-FASHIONED ROLLED OATS

2 PINTS BLUEBERRIES (ABOUT 4 CUPS)

1 CUP CRÈME FRAÎCHE, HOMEMADE (PAGE 279) OR PURCHASED

Preheat the oven to 350°F. Line 2 baking sheets with parchment paper.

In a bowl, combine the butter, brown sugar, granulated sugar, and corn syrup and stir until blended. Stir in the oats, mixing well.

To form the crisps, drop the oats mixture, one tablespoon per cookie, onto the prepared baking sheets, spacing them about 2½ inches apart. Bake, rotating the baking sheets 180 degrees at the midway point, until golden brown and bubbly, about 15 minutes. Let cool for 5 minutes on the baking sheets. Then, using a metal spatula, transfer the crisps to a large flat plate to cool.

To serve, divide the blueberries and crème fraîche among individual bowls and place 2 oat crisps alongside or on top of each serving.

PLANNING AHEAD

The oat crisps may be made a day in advance. Store in an airtight container at room temperature.

RASPBERRY SPRITZER

— SERVES 6 —

The perfect refresher for a hot summer afternoon. All that is missing is the poolside lounge chair and some sunscreen.

1 POUND UNSWEETENED FROZEN RASPBERRIES, THAWED, OR 1½ PINTS (3 CUPS) FRESH RASPBERRIES

1 CUP GRANULATED SUGAR

¼ CUP FRESHLY SQUEEZED LEMON JUICE

PINCH OF KOSHER SALT

6 CUPS SELTZER, CHILLED

6 SCOOPS VANILLA ICE CREAM (PAGE 299)

In a food processor, purée the raspberries until smooth. Strain the purée through a fine-mesh sieve, discarding the seeds. You should have about 1⅓ cups.

In a pitcher, combine the raspberry purée, sugar, lemon juice, and salt. Stir until the sugar is dissolved. Stir in the seltzer and divide evenly among 6 tall glasses. Place a scoop of ice cream in each glass. Serve immediately.

··· ⌒⌒ ···

PLANNING AHEAD

All of the ingredients except for the seltzer and the ice cream may be mixed a day in advance, covered, and refrigerated. Add the seltzer and ice cream just before serving.

PLUM VANILLA CREAMSICLE BOMBE WITH PLUM CARAMEL SAUCE

— SERVES 8 TO 10 —

Plum sorbet and vanilla ice cream make up this unique Creamsicle variation. Once you taste it, you will have second thoughts about going back to the orange-vanilla pairing of the original. Use red plums. They produce a beautiful red-pink sorbet.

PLUM SORBET

2 POUNDS RIPE PLUMS, HALVED AND PITTED

½ CUP GRANULATED SUGAR

¼ CUP WATER

LARGE PINCH OF SALT

1 TEASPOON FRESHLY SQUEEZED LEMON JUICE

1 QUART VANILLA ICE CREAM (PAGE 299)

2 RECIPES PLUM CARAMEL SAUCE (PAGE 286)

To make the plum sorbet: In a food processor, purée the plums until smooth. Strain the purée through a medium-mesh sieve to eliminate any bits of skin. You should have about 2½ cups.

In a bowl, whisk together the plum purée, sugar, water, salt, and lemon juice until the sugar dissolves. Cover and refrigerate until cold, about 1 hour.

Freeze the plum mixture in an ice-cream maker according to the manufacturer's instructions.

Line an 8¼-by-4-by-2¾-inch terrine with plastic wrap, making sure to press it into the corners and allowing a 1½-inch overhang on all sides.

Put half the plum sorbet into the prepared pan, pressing down firmly. Freeze until firm, about 30 minutes. Put half the vanilla ice cream on top of the sorbet, pressing down firmly. Again freeze for 30 minutes until firm. Top with the remaining plum sorbet, again pressing firmly and freezing for 30 minutes. Finally, top with the remaining vanilla ice cream, pressing firmly. Cover with the plastic wrap overhanging the sides and freeze until frozen, at least 3 hours.

To serve, fold back the plastic wrap and invert the loaf pan onto a cutting board. Lift off the pan and carefully peel off the plastic wrap. Slice and place on individual plates. Drizzle with the plum caramel sauce.

PLANNING AHEAD

The bombe may be made 3 to 4 days in advance. You can also slice it 1 day in advance, wrap each slice in parchment paper, place the slices in an airtight container or wrap together in plastic wrap, and return to the freezer until serving.

BAKED APRICOTS WITH VANILLA ICE CREAM AND ALMOND PRALINE

— SERVES 6 —

Baking fruits, especially apricots, helps bring out their delicate perfumes. Any stone fruit may be used in this recipe. Be careful to choose fruits that are ripe but still a little firm, or they will become mushy when baked.

¾ CUP FIRMLY PACKED DARK BROWN SUGAR

2 OUNCES (4 TABLESPOONS) UNSALTED BUTTER, AT ROOM TEMPERATURE

PINCH OF KOSHER SALT

PINCH OF FRESHLY GRATED NUTMEG

PINCH OF GROUND CINNAMON

½ CUP WATER

½ CUP GRANULATED SUGAR

9 RIPE YET FIRM APRICOTS, HALVED AND PITTED

18 SMALL SCOOPS VANILLA ICE CREAM (PAGE 299)

½ CUP CHOPPED ALMOND PRALINE (PAGE 302)

Preheat the oven to 350°F.

In a small bowl, stir together the brown sugar, butter, salt, nutmeg, and cinnamon until well mixed. Set aside.

In a small, heavy saucepan, stir together the water and granulated sugar. Place over high heat,

bring to a boil, and cook until the sugar dissolves, about 1 minute. Remove from the heat and pour into a medium-sized baking dish just large enough to hold the apricots in a single layer.

Place the apricots, cut-side up, in the baking dish. Dab the brown sugar butter evenly on top of the apricots. Bake until the apricots are soft and the brown sugar butter is bubbly, about 15 minutes.

Place 3 warm apricot halves on each plate. Put a small scoop of vanilla ice cream on top of each half. Sprinkle the praline over the ice cream.

PLANNING AHEAD

This dessert must be assembled and baked just before serving, as the apricots should be eaten warm. See the ice cream and praline recipes for information on preparing them in advance.

HAZELNUT SHORTCAKES WITH PLUM COMPOTE

— SERVES 6 —

When you have succulent fruit and you don't quite know what to make, shortcakes are a great standby. Their buttery, crumbly consistency is a good showcase for almost any fruit. For the lightest texture, eat them the day you bake them. Cooking the fruit helps release some of its hidden characteristics and creates a sauce.

HAZELNUT SHORTCAKES

½ CUP (ABOUT 2 OUNCES) HAZELNUTS, TOASTED
   AND SKINNED (SEE PAGE 20)

3 TABLESPOONS PLUS 1 TEASPOON
   GRANULATED SUGAR

1¾ CUPS ALL-PURPOSE FLOUR

½ TEASPOON KOSHER SALT

2¼ TEASPOONS BAKING POWDER

3 OUNCES (6 TABLESPOONS) COLD UNSALTED
   BUTTER, CUT INTO 1-INCH PIECES

¾ CUP PLUS 1 TABLESPOON HEAVY WHIPPING CREAM

FLOUR FOR DUSTING

PLUM COMPOTE

1½ POUNDS (ABOUT 5) RIPE PLUMS, HALVED,
   PITTED, AND SLICED ½ INCH THICK

⅓ CUP GRANULATED SUGAR, OR AS NEEDED

2 TEASPOONS FRESHLY SQUEEZED LEMON JUICE

1 OUNCE (2 TABLESPOONS) UNSALTED BUTTER,
   AT ROOM TEMPERATURE

1 RECIPE CHANTILLY CREAM (PAGE 276)

To make the shortcakes: Preheat the oven to 350°F. Line a baking sheet with parchment paper.

In a food processor, combine the hazelnuts and the 3 tablespoons sugar and pulse to grind coarsely.

Stir together the hazelnuts, flour, salt, and baking powder in the bowl of a stand mixer fitted with the paddle attachment. Scatter the butter pieces over the top and mix on low speed until the butter is the size of small peas. Slowly pour in the ¾ cup cream and continue to mix on low speed just until the dough comes together. (Alternatively, cut the butter into the dry ingredients with a pastry blender until the butter is the size of small peas, and then slowly add the cream, stirring and tossing with a fork until the dough comes together.)

On a lightly floured work surface, pat or roll out the dough 1 inch thick. Using a 2½-inch round cutter, cut the dough into 6 circles, cutting as close together as possible to minimize scraps. Place the shortcakes on the prepared baking sheet. Brush the tops with the remaining 1 tablespoon cream, and sprinkle with the remaining 1 teaspoon sugar.

Bake until golden brown, about 25 minutes. Let cool on the baking sheet to room temperature.

To make the compote: In a large sauté pan, combine the plums, ⅓ cup sugar, and the lemon juice over medium heat. Cook, stirring occasionally, until the sugar dissolves and the juices just begin to bubble. Stir in the butter and cook until the sauce thickens slightly, about 1 minute. If the plums are not quite sweet enough, stir in another tablespoon or two of sugar. Remove from the heat.

Cut the cooled shortcakes in half horizontally and place the bottom of each shortcake, cut-side up, on an individual plate. Spoon an equal amount of the warm plums and the chantilly cream over each shortcake base. Put the tops in place and serve immediately.

PLANNING AHEAD

Bake the shortcakes the day you plan to serve them and keep them at room temperature. The compote must be made just before serving.

HONEY-MARSALA BAKED FIGS WITH GINGER SABAYON

— SERVES 6 —

In California, figs have a short season beginning in late June or early July and then disappear for about a month, reappearing in the late summer and continuing into mid-autumn. My favorite variety is the Black Mission, for both size and color, although Brown Turkey and the green Calimyrna work well in this recipe, too.

FIGS

½ CUP SWEET MARSALA

⅔ CUP HONEY

1 TEASPOON VANILLA EXTRACT

18 RIPE BLACK MISSION FIGS, STEMS TRIMMED

GINGER SABAYON

4 LARGE EGG YOLKS

¼ CUP FRESHLY SQUEEZED ORANGE JUICE

2 TABLESPOONS GRANULATED SUGAR

1½ TEASPOONS PEELED AND GRATED FRESH GINGER

¾ CUP HEAVY WHIPPING CREAM

To prepare the figs: Preheat the oven to 350°F. In a bowl, whisk together the Marsala, honey, and vanilla until blended. Measure out 2 tablespoons and set aside for the sabayon. Mix the figs into the remaining Marsala mixture and let stand for 15 minutes.

Arrange the figs in a baking dish just large enough to hold them in a single layer. Pour the Marsala mixture over them. Cover the dish with aluminum foil and bake for 10 minutes. Turn the figs over and continue to bake until plump and soft, about 10 minutes longer. Remove from the oven and set aside.

To make the sabayon: Prepare an ice bath. (See page 18 for tips on using an ice bath.) In a stainless-steel bowl, whisk together the egg yolks, orange juice, reserved Marsala mixture, sugar, and ginger until blended. Place the bowl over a pan of simmering water, making sure the bottom of the bowl does not touch the water. (See page 18 for tips on using and making a double boiler.) Cook, whisking constantly, until the mixture is thick and there are no air bubbles, about 3 minutes. The mixture should mound slightly when dropped from the whisk. Remove the bowl from the pan and place it in the ice bath. Let cool to room temperature, whisking occasionally.

Put the cream in the bowl of a stand mixer fitted with the whip attachment and whip on medium-high speed until soft peaks form. Using a spatula, fold the cream into the cooled ginger mixture.

To serve, place 3 figs in each individual bowl. Top each serving with a dollop of the sabayon.

··· ⌒ ···

The honey-Marsala mixture and the sabayon may be made a day ahead, covered, and refrigerated. The figs may be baked several hours ahead and served at room temperature or reheated in a 350°F oven for 10 minutes.

TANGERINE ICE WITH PISTACHIO TUILES

— SERVES 8 —

This is my favorite of all citrus sorbets and ices. Tangerines have a particularly distinctive flavor, much more so than most oranges. Look for Honey or Pixie tangerines. The pistachio-flecked tuiles complement the flavor of the ice and deliver a colorful contrast.

TANGERINE ICE

6 CUPS FRESHLY SQUEEZED TANGERINE JUICE

2 TEASPOONS FRESHLY SQUEEZED LEMON JUICE

1¼ CUPS GRANULATED SUGAR

⅛ TEASPOON KOSHER SALT

PISTACHIO TUILES

¾ CUP (3 OUNCES) PISTACHIOS, TOASTED
   (SEE PAGE 20)

¾ CUP GRANULATED SUGAR

3 LARGE EGG WHITES

4 OUNCES (8 TABLESPOONS) UNSALTED BUTTER,
   MELTED AND COOLED

½ TEASPOON VANILLA EXTRACT

¾ CUP ALL-PURPOSE FLOUR

GRATED ZEST OF 1 LEMON

To make the ice: In a bowl, stir together the tangerine juice, lemon juice, sugar, and salt until the sugar dissolves. Pour into a 9-by-13-inch baking pan and place in the freezer. Every 30 minutes, remove the pan from the freezer and roughly stir up the mixture with the tines of a fork to prevent the ice crystals from forming a solid mass. Make sure that you scrape up the crystals from the bottom and sides of the pan and break them up each time. This will give the ice a uniformly light, feathery texture. Freeze the mixture until firm, about 4 hours, depending on your freezer.

To make the tuiles: Preheat the oven to 350°F. Line 2 baking sheets with parchment paper. In a food processor, combine the pistachios and sugar and process until the nuts are finely ground.

In a bowl, whisk the egg whites just until frothy. Stir in the pistachio mixture, followed by the melted butter and vanilla. Then stir in the flour until mixed, and finally the lemon zest.

To form each tuile, spoon 2 teaspoons of the batter onto a prepared baking sheet and, using the back of a spoon, spread the batter into a thin, even circle about 3 inches in diameter, spacing them 1 inch apart. (You will have enough batter to make more tuiles than you need for the recipe.) Bake the cookies, 1 sheet at a time, until light golden brown, about 10 minutes.

As soon as the first sheet is out of the oven, quickly use a thin metal spatula to lift a tuile from the sheet. Immediately place it upside down on a work surface and then roll it around the handle of a wooden spoon, forming a cylinder. Remove the cookie from the handle, set aside, and repeat with the remaining cookies. The tuiles must be rolled while they are hot, or they will crack and break. If they cool too much before you have a chance to roll them, put them back in the oven for 15 to 30 seconds to soften. The tuiles may also be left to cool flat on the baking sheets and enjoyed unrolled.

To serve, scoop the tangerine ice into individual bowls or glasses and place 2 tuiles in each bowl.

··· ❧ ···

PLANNING AHEAD

The ice may be made 2 days in advance. After that it begins to lose its bright, clean taste. Tuile batter will keep for up to 2 weeks in the refrigerator. The tuiles will keep in an airtight container at room temperature for 2 days. (If they have gotten soggy on the second day, put them in a 350°F oven for a couple of minutes to recrisp them.)

LEMON CARAMEL SORBET

— MAKES 1½ QUARTS —

There is just enough caramel in this recipe to eliminate the pucker of the lemon, but the sorbet is not so sweet that it overpowers the lemon flavor. You can use Meyer lemons or the more common Eureka or Lisbon variety. As always, when making caramel, be sure to wear oven mitts to protect against burns.

2¾ CUPS GRANULATED SUGAR

3½ CUPS WATER

2 CUPS FRESHLY SQUEEZED LEMON JUICE

GINGER COOKIES (PAGE 218)

In a heavy, nonreactive saucepan, stir together 2 cups of the sugar and ½ cup of the water. Place over medium heat and cook, stirring occasionally, until the sugar dissolves and comes to a boil. Increase the heat to high and cook, without stirring, until the mixture becomes a golden amber. (See page 20 for tips on making caramel.)

Remove from the heat and let the bubbles subside for a few seconds. Stir in about ¼ cup of the water. Be careful as you stir, as the caramel will bubble up when you add the water. Stir in the remaining 2¾ cups water about ¼ cup at a time. When all the water has been incorporated, add the lemon juice and the remaining ¾ cup sugar, stirring until the sugar dissolves. Cover and refrigerate until cold, about 1 hour.

Freeze the caramel mixture in an ice-cream maker according to the manufacturer's instructions. Transfer to a covered container and place in the freezer until scoopable, about 2 hours, depending on your freezer.

To serve, scoop the sorbet ice into individual bowls and serve with the cookies on the side.

··· ❧ ···

PLANNING AHEAD

The sorbet may be made a day in advance.

RIESLING-POACHED PEACHES

— SERVES 6 —

The female socialites who frequented Stars loved this dessert. It was as healthful as a fruit plate but much more elegant. Whenever we could, we would use white peaches. Their perfume and flavor can't be beaten.

6 RIPE BUT SLIGHTLY FIRM PEACHES

2 CUPS GEWÜRZTRAMINER

1 CUP LATE-HARVEST RIESLING

2¾ CUPS WATER

¾ CUP FRESHLY SQUEEZED ORANGE JUICE

1 TABLESPOON FRESHLY SQUEEZED LEMON JUICE

1 CUP GRANULATED SUGAR

PINCH OF KOSHER SALT

2 STRIPS LEMON PEEL, EACH ABOUT 2 INCHES LONG AND ¼ INCH WIDE

4 STRIPS ORANGE PEEL, EACH ABOUT 2 INCHES LONG AND ¼ INCH WIDE

1 RECIPE CHANTILLY CREAM (PAGE 276)

1 RECIPE BERRY SAUCE (PAGE 289) MADE WITH RASPBERRIES

Halve and pit the peaches. Reserve the pits.

Prepare an ice bath. (See page 18 for tips on using an ice bath.) In a large, nonreactive saucepan, combine the Gewürztraminer, Riesling, water, orange juice, lemon juice, sugar, salt, and lemon and orange peels. Bring to a boil over high heat, stirring to dissolve the sugar. Reduce the heat to a simmer and add the peaches. Cover them with a clean dish towel or a plate to submerge them completely in the liquid. Cook just until the peaches

can be easily pierced with a small knife, about 15 minutes.

Using a slotted spoon, transfer the peaches to a stainless-steel bowl, reserving the poaching liquid, and place the bowl in the ice bath. Let the peaches cool until you can handle them and then peel them, saving the skins.

Add the reserved pits and skins to the poaching liquid and return to a boil over medium-high heat. Cook the liquid until it is slightly syrupy and has reduced to about 1¼ cups, about 5 minutes. Remove from the heat, let cool to room temperature, and then strain through a fine-mesh sieve into a clean bowl, discarding the solids.

To serve, spoon some of the syrup onto each plate. Place 2 peach halves, hollow-side up, onto each pool of syrup and top the peaches with the chantilly cream and raspberry sauce.

PLANNING AHEAD

The peaches may be poached and the poaching liquid may be reduced a day in advance, covered, and refrigerated. Bring to room temperature before serving.

POACHED PEARS WITH WALNUT CREAM

— SERVES 6 —

The secret to poaching pears is slow, careful cooking and a good-quality Sauternes like Château Liot. After poaching the pears, reduce the wine to a syrup for a sweet elixir.

POACHED PEARS

2½ CUPS SAUTERNES

1½ CUPS WATER

2 TABLESPOONS FRESHLY SQUEEZED LEMON JUICE

1 CUP GRANULATED SUGAR

1 STRIP ORANGE PEEL, ABOUT ½ INCH LONG AND ¼ INCH WIDE

1 STRIP LEMON PEEL, ABOUT ½ INCH LONG AND ¼ INCH WIDE

1 PIECE CINNAMON STICK, 2 INCHES LONG

PINCH OF KOSHER SALT

6 RIPE PEARS, PEELED, HALVED, AND CORED

WALNUT CREAM

¼ CUP (1 OUNCE) WALNUTS, TOASTED (SEE PAGE 20)

2 TABLESPOONS MASCARPONE CHEESE

GRATED ZEST FROM 1 ORANGE

1 TABLESPOON GRANULATED SUGAR

PINCH OF SALT

¾ CUP HEAVY WHIPPING CREAM

To prepare the pears: In a heavy, nonreactive saucepan, combine the Sauternes, water, lemon juice, sugar, orange and lemon peels, cinnamon stick, and salt. Bring to a boil over high heat, stirring to dissolve the sugar. Reduce the heat to a simmer and add the pear halves. Cover them with a clean dish towel or a plate to submerge them completely in the liquid. Cook just until the pears can be easily pierced with a small knife, about 20 minutes.

Using a slotted spoon, transfer the pears to a plate, arranging them in a single layer, and let cool to room temperature. Return the poaching liquid to medium-high heat and bring to a boil. Cook until the liquid has reduced and is slightly syrupy, about 8 minutes. Remove from the heat and strain through a fine-mesh sieve into a clean bowl, discarding the solids. Let cool to room temperature. (The syrup will thicken as it cools.)

To make the walnut cream: In a food processor, pulse the walnuts until finely ground. Reserve 2 tablespoons ground nuts for garnish. Put the remaining walnuts, the mascarpone, orange zest, sugar, salt, and cream in the bowl of a mixer fitted with the whip attachment and whip on medium-high speed until soft peaks form.

To serve, arrange 2 pear halves, flat-side up, on individual plates. Fill each half with walnut cream. Drizzle the syrup over and around the pears and sprinkle with the reserved ground nuts.

··· ⚮ ···

The pears may be poached and the poaching liquid may be reduced a day in advance, covered, and refrigerated. Bring to room temperature before serving. Make the walnut cream within 2 hours of serving, cover, and refrigerate. It may need to be lightly rewhipped before serving.

SAVARIN WITH GRAND MARNIER SABAYON AND MIXED BERRIES

— SERVES 8 —

Named for Jean Anthelme Brillat-Savarin, the famed eighteenth-century gastronome and writer, this classic French dessert is seldom seen on menus today, but I keep baking it so people won't forget it. The light, yeast-leavened, breadlike cake may be made in a single large ring mold or individual ring molds. It may be combined with fruit year-round or simply served with ice cream and sauce. The individual molds (typically each about 3¼ inches in diameter) can also be used for baking other kinds of small cakes.

SAVARIN DOUGH

1½ TEASPOONS ACTIVE DRY YEAST

2 TABLESPOONS WARM WATER

1½ TEASPOONS GRANULATED SUGAR

2 TABLESPOONS MILK, WARMED

2 LARGE EGGS

1 CUP ALL-PURPOSE FLOUR

2 OUNCES (4 TABLESPOONS) UNSALTED BUTTER, AT ROOM TEMPERATURE, PLUS EXTRA AS NEEDED

¼ TEASPOON KOSHER SALT

SOAKING SYRUP

1 CUP GRANULATED SUGAR

1 CUP WATER

2 TABLESPOONS FRESHLY SQUEEZED LEMON JUICE

2 TABLESPOONS GRAND MARNIER

⅓ CUP FRESHLY SQUEEZED ORANGE JUICE

½ PINT RASPBERRIES (ABOUT 1 CUP)

½ PINT BLACKBERRIES (ABOUT 1 CUP)

½ PINT BLUEBERRIES (ABOUT 1 CUP)

1 RECIPE GRAND MARNIER SABAYON (PAGE 281)

1 RECIPE BERRY SAUCE (PAGE 289) MADE WITH RASPBERRIES OR BLACKBERRIES

To make the dough: In a bowl, dissolve the yeast in the warm water. Stir in the sugar and let stand for about 5 minutes until foamy. Stir in the warm milk and then the eggs, mixing with a wooden spoon until the ingredients are evenly incorporated. Add the flour and beat until the dough is smooth and elastic, about 30 seconds.

Transfer the dough to a lightly buttered bowl, cover with a kitchen towel, and let the dough rise until doubled in bulk, about 1 hour.

Butter 8 individual savarin molds and place them on a baking sheet. Add the butter and salt to the dough and mix with the wooden spoon until completely incorporated and smooth. Divide the dough evenly among the molds, patting it gently in place. The dough is sticky and will be easier to work with if you coat your fingertips with a little butter. (You can also spoon the dough into a pastry bag fitted with a ½-inch plain round tip and pipe the dough into the molds.) Invert a 9-by-13-inch baking pan over the filled molds (there should be adequate clearance to accommodate the rising dough) and let the dough rise again until doubled in bulk, about 1 hour. The savarins will fill the molds and be rounded on top.

Preheat the oven to 350°F. Uncover the savarins and place in the oven on the baking sheet. Bake until light brown, 15 to 20 minutes. Let cool to room temperature on the baking sheet, then remove the savarins from their molds. If they stick, loosen them first with a knife and then unmold.

To make the soaking syrup: In a saucepan, combine the sugar, water, lemon juice, Grand Marnier, and orange juice over medium heat. Cook, stirring to dissolve the sugar, until the mixture is hot.

To serve, place the savarins in a single layer in the 9-by-13-inch baking pan. Pour the syrup evenly over the savarins and let them soak for 8 minutes. Turn the savarins over and let soak for another 5 minutes. Place a savarin on each plate along with some of the berries and a dollop of the sabayon. Drizzle the berry sauce over the fruit and on top of the sabayon.

PLANNING AHEAD

The savarins may be baked a day in advance, wrapped in plastic wrap, and stored at room temperature. Soak the cakes just before serving.

FROZEN KIR ROYALE

— SERVES 6 —

My husband and I have always enjoyed a classic Kir royale.
Made with Champagne and a splash of cassis (black currant liqueur), it
is the ideal aperitif before almost any meal. This is a frozen variation
made by combining raspberry-cassis sorbet with sabayon flavored with
Champagne. To extend the French theme, serve with Brown
Butter Madeleines (page 228).

RASPBERRY-CASSIS SORBET

1½ POUNDS UNSWEETENED FROZEN RASPBERRIES,
    THAWED

¼ CUP CASSIS

ABOUT ⅔ CUP GRANULATED SUGAR, OR AS NEEDED

1 TEASPOON FRESHLY SQUEEZED LEMON JUICE

PINCH OF KOSHER SALT

½ CUP WATER

1 RECIPE CHAMPAGNE SABAYON (PAGE 281)

To make the sorbet: In a food processor, purée the
raspberries until smooth. Strain through a fine-
mesh sieve into a bowl, discarding the seeds.
You should have just under 2 cups purée. Whisk
in the cassis, sugar, lemon juice, salt, and water,
adjusting the sugar according to the sweetness
of the berries. Cover and refrigerate until well
chilled, at least 2 hours.

Freeze the berry mixture in an ice-cream
maker according to the manufacturer's instructions.
Transfer to a covered container and place in the
freezer until scoopable, about 1 hour.

To serve, place scoops of the sorbet in
beautiful tall glasses. Top with the sabayon and
serve immediately.

PLANNING AHEAD

The sorbet may be made 2 days in advance.

>> FROZEN KIR ROYALE

PEAR CHARLOTTE ··· PAGE 106

<< OAT CRISPS WITH BLUEBERRIES AND CRÈME FRAÎCHE ··· PAGE 120

COCONUT CREAM PIE WITH MANGO AND BLACKBERRY SAUCES ··· PAGE 179

>> FRENCH APPLE TARTLETS ··· PAGE 165

WARM BITTERSWEET CHOCOLATE TARTLETS WITH SPICED ALMONDS ··· PAGE 164

<< BLACKBERRY STREUSEL TART ··· PAGE 157

SUMMER PUDDING

— SERVES 8 —

If I could have just one dessert in summer, this would be my choice.
It is sophisticated and simple at the same time. Since you should make it
only when the berries are at the height of their season, I rationalize having
it for breakfast, too, convincing myself it is glorified bread and jam.

3 PINTS STRAWBERRIES (ABOUT 6 CUPS), HULLED
   AND QUARTERED

1 CUP GRANULATED SUGAR

1 TABLESPOON FRESHLY SQUEEZED LEMON JUICE

PINCH OF KOSHER SALT

2 PINTS BLACKBERRIES (ABOUT 4 CUPS)

2½ PINTS RASPBERRIES (ABOUT 5 CUPS)

1 LOAF (1 POUND) BRIOCHE (PAGE 293)

1 RECIPE CHANTILLY CREAM (PAGE 276)

Spray an 8½-by-4½-by-2¾-inch loaf pan with
nonstick spray. Line the sprayed pan with plastic
wrap, making sure to press it into the corners and
allowing a 1½-inch overhang on all sides.

In a heavy, nonreactive saucepan, combine
the strawberries, sugar, lemon juice, and salt over
medium-low heat and cook, stirring occasionally,
until the strawberries begin to give up some of
their juice, about 10 minutes. Add the blackberries
and raspberries and continue cooking until all the
berries are soft and have broken apart, forming a
sauce, about 10 minutes. Remove from the heat and
let cool to warm.

Trim off the crusts from the brioche and cut
the loaf into 32 slices. Each slice should be about
¼ inch thick.

Spread ½ cup of the berry sauce into the
bottom of the prepared pan. One piece at a time,
dip the brioche into the sauce in the saucepan,
saturating it. Place the berry-soaked brioche
pieces in the pan, forming a single layer and a
snug fit. Spread ½ cup of the berry sauce on top of
the brioche. Repeat the layering, starting with the
berry-soaked brioche, until the pan is full, ending
with the berry sauce.

Cover with the plastic wrap overhanging the
sides and place the loaf pan on a baking sheet.
Cover with a pan just large enough to fit in the loaf
pan and put a large food can or other weight heavy
enough to compress the pudding into the second
pan. Refrigerate for at least 6 hours.

To unmold the pudding, remove the weight
and second pan, fold back the plastic wrap, and
invert the loaf pan onto a cutting board. Lift off the
pan and carefully peel off the plastic. Cut the loaf
into 8 slices and place on individual plates. Top with
the chantilly cream.

PLANNING AHEAD

The pudding may be made 2 days in advance and
kept refrigerated. Unmold just before serving.

<< SUMMER PUDDING

VANILLA WAFERS WITH ZINFANDEL-MARINATED RASPBERRIES

— SERVES 8 —

Red wine and red fruit have been traditionally paired—Cabernet sauce and strawberries with black pepper, for example—and here the peppery quality of Zinfandel goes well with raspberries. Make sure to select a good-quality Zinfandel, since you will still have half a bottle to enjoy after you have made the recipe.

VANILLA WAFERS

2 LARGE EGG WHITES

½ CUP PLUS 1 TABLESPOON GRANULATED SUGAR

3 OUNCES (6 TABLESPOONS) UNSALTED BUTTER, MELTED AND COOLED

½ TEASPOON VANILLA EXTRACT

½ CUP PLUS 1 TABLESPOON ALL-PURPOSE FLOUR

ZINFANDEL-MARINATED RASPBERRIES

1½ CUPS FRUITY ZINFANDEL

7 TABLESPOONS GRANULATED SUGAR

3 STRIPS ORANGE PEEL, EACH ½ INCH LONG AND ¼ INCH WIDE

2 STRIPS LEMON PEEL, EACH ½ INCH LONG AND ¼ INCH WIDE

SMALL PINCH OF GROUND CINNAMON

¾ CUP WATER

4 BLACK PEPPERCORNS

3 PINTS RASPBERRIES (ABOUT 6 CUPS)

1 RECIPE CHANTILLY CREAM (PAGE 276)

To make the vanilla wafers: Preheat the oven to 350°F. Line 3 baking sheets with parchment paper.

In a bowl, whisk together the egg whites and sugar just until incorporated. Whisk in the melted butter and the vanilla. Stir in the flour until well mixed.

To form each wafer, spoon about 1½ teaspoons of the batter onto a prepared baking sheet and, using the back of a tablespoon, spread the batter into a thin, even circle about 2½ inches in diameter. You should be able to fit at least 6 circles on a baking sheet. There will be extra wafer batter in case some break or you want to nibble.

Bake the wafers, 1 sheet at a time, until golden brown, about 5 minutes. Check them often, as they burn quickly. Let cool for 3 minutes on the pan, then use a thin metal spatula to transfer the wafers to a wire rack and let cool completely. Place them in an airtight container until ready to serve.

To prepare the raspberries: In a small, nonreactive saucepan, combine the Zinfandel, sugar, orange and lemon peels, cinnamon, water, and peppercorns. Bring to a boil over high heat, stirring to dissolve the sugar. Reduce the heat to medium and simmer, uncovered, for 20 minutes. Strain the liquid through a fine-mesh sieve into a bowl, discarding the solids. Let cool to room temperature. Add the raspberries to the bowl and let marinate for 30 minutes.

To serve, put a cookie on each plate. Spoon an equal amount of the raspberries onto each cookie and then a few tablespoons of the Zinfandel liquid. Place a dollop of chantilly cream on top and then finish with a second wafer. Serve immediately.

··· ❧ ···

PLANNING AHEAD

If the weather is not humid, the wafers may be made a day in advance. Store in an airtight container at room temperature. The Zinfandel liquid may be made 2 days in advance, covered, and refrigerated. You can marinate the raspberries the day of serving.

POPPYSEED SHORTCAKES WITH STRAWBERRIES

— SERVES 6 —

At Stars, we reworked this traditional American dessert in a variety of ways, but what counts in any version is a shortcake laden with fruit, cream, and sauce. For a real treat, cut each shortcake in half horizontally, butter the cut sides, and warm in the oven before serving.

POPPYSEED SHORTCAKES

2 CUPS ALL-PURPOSE FLOUR

6 TABLESPOONS PLUS ½ TEASPOON GRANULATED SUGAR

2 TEASPOONS POPPYSEEDS

2½ TEASPOONS BAKING POWDER

¼ TEASPOON KOSHER SALT

3 OUNCES (6 TABLESPOONS) COLD UNSALTED BUTTER, CUT INTO 1-INCH PIECES

¾ CUP PLUS 1 TABLESPOON HEAVY WHIPPING CREAM

1½ PINTS STRAWBERRIES (ABOUT 3 CUPS), HULLED AND QUARTERED LENGTHWISE

ABOUT 1 TABLESPOON GRANULATED SUGAR

1 RECIPE CHANTILLY CREAM (PAGE 276)

1 RECIPE BERRY SAUCE (PAGE 289) MADE WITH STRAWBERRIES

To make the shortcakes: Preheat the oven to 350°F. Line a baking sheet with parchment paper.

Stir together the flour, the 6 tablespoons sugar, poppyseeds, baking powder, and salt in the bowl of a stand mixer fitted with the paddle attachment. Scatter the butter pieces over the top and mix on low speed until the butter is the size of small peas. Slowly pour in the ¾ cup cream and continue to mix on low speed just until the dough comes together. (Alternatively, cut the butter into the dry ingredients with a pastry blender until the butter is the size of small peas and then slowly add the cream, stirring and tossing with a fork until the dough comes together.)

On a lightly floured work surface, pat or roll out the dough ¾ inch thick. Using a 2½-inch round cutter, cut the dough into 6 circles, cutting as close together as possible to minimize scraps. Place the shortcakes on the prepared baking sheet. Brush the tops with the remaining 1 tablespoon cream and sprinkle with the remaining ½ teaspoon sugar.

Bake until golden brown, about 25 minutes. Let cool on the baking sheet to room temperature.

To serve, in a bowl, gently toss the strawberries with sugar, sweetening the berries to taste. Cut the shortcakes in half horizontally, and place the bottom of each shortcake, cut-side up, on an individual plate. If desired, warm the shortcakes in a preheated oven (350°). Spoon an equal amount of the strawberries, the chantilly cream, and finally the berry sauce over each shortcake base. Put the tops in place and serve immediately.

··· ◯ ···

The shortcakes are best served the day they are baked. If you make them a day in advance, store them at room temperature and heat before serving. Sweeten the strawberries just before serving.

TARTS, PIES & PASTRIES

— CHAPTER 5 —

Tarts, pies, and puff pastries were a big part of the dessert lineup at Stars, and California's abundant—and delicious—fresh fruits were the driving force behind their popularity. Desserts with buttery crusts are a perfect way to show off a fruit's natural flavors. Sweet, juicy Bing cherries, fragrant peaches, or crisp fall apples need few added ingredients to turn them into a dessert that will have everyone asking for seconds.

But no matter how wonderful a filling may be, a homey pie, delicate tart, or sophisticated napoleon will be a disappointment if it does not have a crust that crunches and then melts in your mouth. Dough making is not hard to master, but you do need to pay attention to a few basic rules: make sure your butter is cold, never overmix the dough, and don't add too much liquid. Once you have made the puff pastry and pie and tart dough recipes a few times, you will become comfortable—and successful—putting them together, and your desserts will be the envy of everyone you know.

154
APRICOT CUSTARD TART

155
BING CHERRY TART

156
LEMON MASCARPONE TART WITH
FIGS AND RASPBERRIES

157
BLACKBERRY STREUSEL TART

158
CHOCOLATE TRUFFLE TART

159
MACAROON NUT TART

160
CRANBERRY LINZERTORTE

162
CARAMEL ALMOND TARTLETS WITH
WARM BLUEBERIES

164
WARM BITTERSWEET CHOCOLATE TARTLETS
WITH SPICED ALMONDS

165
FRENCH APPLE TARTLETS

166
PASSION FRUIT–MERINGUE TARTLETS

168
CORNMEAL TARTLETS WITH ORANGE CRÈME
FRAÎCHE AND STRAWBERRIES

170
BANANA NAPOLEONS WITH WARM
CARAMEL WALNUT SAUCE

172
PEAR NAPOLEONS WITH GINGER
PASTRY CREAM

173
KEY LIME PIE

174
PUMPKIN PIE

175
MAPLE PECAN PIE

176
BLUEBERRY PIE

177
PATRICK'S PEACH PIE

178
BANANA CREAM PIE

179
COCONUT CREAM PIE WITH MANGO AND
BLACKBERRY SAUCES

APRICOT CUSTARD TART

— SERVES 6 TO 8 —

This is a versatile summer dessert. You can substitute peaches, plums, or even berries for the apricots. It is ideal after a dinner of barbecued chicken, sliced tomatoes, and corn on the cob.

¾ POUND (ABOUT 5) RIPE APRICOTS

1 PREBAKED 9½-INCH TART CRUST (PAGE 292)

1 CUP GRANULATED SUGAR

2 LARGE EGG YOLKS

¾ CUP HEAVY WHIPPING CREAM

2 TABLESPOONS ALL-PURPOSE FLOUR

PINCH OF KOSHER SALT

¼ CUP (1 OUNCE) SLICED ALMONDS

Preheat the oven to 325°F.

Halve and pit the apricots, then cut into slices ¾ inch thick. Arrange the apricot slices in the tart crust in a decorative pattern. Set aside.

In a bowl, whisk together the sugar, egg yolks, and cream until blended. Stir in the flour and salt.

Carefully pour the cream mixture over the apricots. Sprinkle the almonds evenly over the top.

Bake until the custard is almost completely set, about 35 minutes. Let the tart cool until it can be handled, then remove the pan sides and place on a platter. Serve the tart slightly warm or at room temperature.

PLANNING AHEAD

The tart is best served the day it is made. Store at room temperature.

BING CHERRY TART

— SERVES 6 TO 8 —

Use summer cherries from a roadside stand or farmers' market for the best result. Be sure to buy extra cherries, so you have some to snack on while you are stemming and pitting. Readying the cherries for the tart is a bit laborious but worth the effort. Tell anyone who helps you that he or she will get the first and biggest slice.

CHERRY FILLING

3 POUNDS (ABOUT 5½ CUPS) BING CHERRIES

½ CUP GRANULATED SUGAR

2 TABLESPOONS TAPIOCA FLOUR OR CORNSTARCH

1 TEASPOON FRESHLY SQUEEZED LEMON JUICE

PINCH OF KOSHER SALT

1 PREBAKED 9½-INCH TART CRUST (PAGE 292) AND 1 LATTICE TOP (PAGE 291)

1 LARGE EGG, LIGHTLY BEATEN

1 TABLESPOON GRANULATED SUGAR

Preheat the oven to 350°F.

To make the filling: Stem and pit the cherries. There should be about 4 cups. Put the cherries in a heavy, nonreactive saucepan, cover, and place over medium-low heat. Cook the cherries until they begin to give off some of their juice, about 8 minutes. Uncover and add the sugar, tapioca flour, lemon juice, and salt. Continue to cook uncovered, stirring occasionally, just until the liquid starts to thicken, 3 to 5 minutes. Remove from the heat and let cool to room temperature.

Spread the cherries in the tart crust. Brush the beaten egg on the lattice strips and then sprinkle them with the sugar. Lay the strips over the top of the filled tart crust, forming a lattice pattern (see page 291).

Bake until the lattice is golden, 15 to 20 minutes. Let the tart cool until it can be handled, then remove the pan sides and place on a platter. Serve the tart warm or at room temperature.

PLANNING AHEAD

The tart is best served the day it is made. Store at room temperature. You may reheat the tart in a 325°F oven for 10 minutes.

LEMON MASCARPONE TART WITH FIGS AND RASPBERRIES

— SERVES 6 TO 8 —

I like to try to get nonbakers bitten by the baking bug. Two friends, Cassia and Cynthia, had done only a little baking before they came to my house for the weekend. They had a wonderful time preparing this tart and were astonished at how simple it was. Now they brag to all their friends about what accomplished bakers they are. During their visit, they discovered one of the secrets of baking: it isn't difficult. Tossing the fruit in cassis gives the tart a pretty glaze.

3 LARGE EGGS

6 TABLESPOONS HEAVY WHIPPING CREAM

3 OUNCES CREAM CHEESE, AT ROOM TEMPERATURE

¼ CUP MASCARPONE CHEESE

¼ CUP GRANULATED SUGAR

5 TABLESPOONS FRESHLY SQUEEZED LEMON JUICE

1 TEASPOON CHOPPED LEMON ZEST

PINCH OF KOSHER SALT

1 PREBAKED 9½-INCH TART CRUST (PAGE 290)

8 TO 10 BLACK MISSION FIGS, STEMS TRIMMED AND CUT LENGTHWISE INTO SLICES ½ INCH THICK

½ PINT RASPBERRIES (ABOUT 1 CUP)

2 TABLESPOONS CASSIS (OPTIONAL)

Preheat the oven to 325°F. Combine the eggs, cream, cream cheese, mascarpone, sugar, lemon juice, lemon zest, and salt in the bowl of a stand mixer fitted with the whip attachment and whip on medium speed until smooth. (A few small lumps are okay.) Pour the lemon cream into the tart crust.

Bake until set, 20 to 25 minutes. Let the tart cool to room temperature, then remove the pan sides and place on a platter.

In a bowl, combine the figs, raspberries, and cassis (if using) and mix gently. Arrange neatly on top of the tart. Serve at room temperature.

PLANNING AHEAD

The tart is best served the day it is made. Store at room temperature.

BLACKBERRY STREUSEL TART

— SERVES 6 TO 8 —

Select blackberries that are soft and juicy and not too tart or seedy.
I especially like olallieberries and marionberries, both varieties of
blackberries. Serve the tart with a big dollop of whipped cream. Or for
a double-berry hit, accompany the tart with black raspberry ice cream.

1½ PINTS BLACKBERRIES (ABOUT 3 CUPS)

½ CUP GRANULATED SUGAR

1 TABLESPOON CORNSTARCH OR TAPIOCA FLOUR

½ TEASPOON FRESHLY SQUEEZED LEMON JUICE

1 PREBAKED 9½-INCH TART CRUST (PAGE 290)

STREUSEL

¾ CUP ALL-PURPOSE FLOUR

⅓ CUP FIRMLY PACKED BROWN SUGAR

PINCH OF KOSHER SALT

3 OUNCES (6 TABLESPOONS) COLD UNSALTED
  BUTTER, CUT INTO ½-INCH PIECES

1 RECIPE CHANTILLY CREAM (PAGE 276)

Preheat the oven to 350°F. In a bowl, gently combine the blackberries, sugar, cornstarch, and lemon juice. Spread the blackberry mixture evenly in the tart crust.

To make the streusel: In a food processor, combine the flour, brown sugar, salt, and butter and pulse until the butter is the size of large peas. Sprinkle evenly over the blackberry filling.

Bake until the streusel is browned and the fruit is bubbling, about 25 minutes. Let the tart cool until it can be handled, then remove the pan sides and place on a platter. Serve warm or at room temperature, with chantilly cream on the side.

··· ···

PLANNING AHEAD

The streusel may be made 2 days in advance, covered, and refrigerated. The tart is best served the day it is made. Store at room temperature. You may reheat the tart in a 325°F oven for 10 minutes.

CHOCOLATE TRUFFLE TART

— SERVES 8 TO 10 —

This tart is incredibly rich, like truffles from two of my favorite
San Francisco chocolatiers, XOX and Recchiuti. Savor it in
small, heavenly slices.

½ CUP HEAVY WHIPPING CREAM

3½ OUNCES BITTERSWEET CHOCOLATE,
   FINELY CHOPPED

1 PREBAKED 9½-INCH TART CRUST (PAGE 290)

1 CUP PASTRY CREAM (PAGE 280)

¼ CUP COLD CARAMEL SAUCE (PAGE 285)

2 TABLESPOONS TOASTED, SKINNED, AND COARSELY
   CHOPPED HAZELNUTS (SEE PAGE 20)

In a small, heavy nonreactive saucepan, bring the
cream to a boil over medium heat. Remove from
the heat and add the chocolate. Let stand for
2 minutes and then whisk until smooth. Let cool to
lukewarm and then pour into the tart crust. Cover
and refrigerate until the chocolate cream is almost
set, about 30 minutes.

Spread the pastry cream over the choco-
late layer. In a small bowl, stir together the caramel
sauce and hazelnuts. Carefully spread the caramel sauce over the pastry cream. Refrigerate the tart
for at least 30 minutes.

Remove the tart from the refrigerator 15 minutes before serving. Remove the pan sides and place
on a platter to serve.

PLANNING AHEAD

The tart is best served the day it is made. Store
in the refrigerator for up to 8 hours, then let sit at
room temperature for 15 minutes before serving.

MACAROON NUT TART

— SERVES 6 TO 8 —

This tart was created for 690, Jeremiah's tropical restaurant just around the corner from Stars. The coconut, in both shredded and milk form, gives new sparkle to a traditional nut tart.

4 LARGE EGG YOLKS

½ CUP FIRMLY PACKED LIGHT BROWN SUGAR

⅓ CUP UNSWEETENED COCONUT MILK

PINCH OF KOSHER SALT

2½ OUNCES (5 TABLESPOONS) UNSALTED BUTTER, MELTED AND COOLED

1 CUP SWEETENED SHREDDED COCONUT, TOASTED (SEE PAGE 22)

¾ CUP (3 OUNCES) MACADAMIA NUTS, TOASTED (SEE PAGE 20) AND CUT IN HALF

1 CUP (4 OUNCES) PECANS, TOASTED (SEE PAGE 20)

1 PREBAKED 9½-INCH TART CRUST (PAGE 290)

1 RECIPE CHANTILLY CREAM (PAGE 276) OR ½ RECIPE CARAMEL ICE CREAM (PAGE 300)

Preheat the oven to 350°F.

In a large bowl, whisk together the egg yolks, brown sugar, coconut milk, and salt until blended. Whisk in the butter and then stir in the coconut, macadamia nuts, and pecans. Pour into the tart crust.

Bake until golden brown and just set, about 20 minutes. Let the tart cool until it can be handled, then remove the pan sides and place on a platter. Serve warm or at room temperature with the chantilly cream.

PLANNING AHEAD

The tart is best served the day it is made. Store at room temperature.

CRANBERRY LINZERTORTE

— SERVES 6 TO 8 —

Linzertorte, which originated in Linz, Austria, is traditionally made with raspberry jam. Here, I have substituted American cranberries. Fresh cranberries are available in the fall, so I make this dessert at Thanksgiving and put it on the buffet table alongside the pumpkin pie. A thin slice of the linzertorte with its sweet-tart cranberry filling and nutty crust is a good counterpoint to the creaminess of pumpkin pie.

CRUST

1   CUP ALL-PURPOSE FLOUR

6   TABLESPOONS GRANULATED SUGAR

PINCH OF GROUND CLOVES

½   TEASPOON GROUND CINNAMON

1   CUP (ABOUT 3½ OUNCES) SLICED ALMONDS, TOASTED (SEE PAGE 20) AND FINELY CHOPPED

1   LARGE EGG, HARD BOILED, WHITE RESERVED FOR ANOTHER USE, AND YOLK FINELY SIEVED

2   EGG YOLKS

1   TEASPOON VANILLA EXTRACT

¼   TEASPOON ALMOND EXTRACT

6   OUNCES (12 TABLESPOONS) UNSALTED BUTTER, AT ROOM TEMPERATURE

GRATED ZEST OF 1 LEMON

FILLING

5   CUPS (1 TO 1¼ POUNDS) CRANBERRIES

1   CUP PLUS 1 TABLESPOON GRANULATED SUGAR

GRATED ZEST OF 1 ORANGE

3   TABLESPOONS WATER

To make the crust: Combine the flour, sugar, cloves, cinnamon, almonds, and sieved egg yolk in the bowl of a stand mixer fitted with the paddle attachment and mix on medium-low speed until combined. Increase the speed to medium, add the egg yolks and the vanilla and almond extracts, and beat until blended. Add the butter and lemon zest and beat until a smooth dough forms.

Reserve one-third of the dough for the lattice top. Press the remaining dough evenly into the bottom and up the sides of a 9½-inch tart pan with a removable bottom. Divide the dough for the lattice into 8 equal portions. On a lightly floured work surface, use your palms to roll each piece into a 9¼-inch-long rod the width of a pencil. The dough is quite soft, so work gently and quickly, being careful not to press too hard. (If the dough is too soft to shape, refrigerate it for 30 minutes.) Place the dough rods on a baking sheet. Refrigerate the tart crust and the dough rods until firm, about 1 hour.

To make the filling: In a nonreactive saucepan, combine the cranberries, sugar, orange zest, and the water over medium heat. Cook, stirring occasionally, until the cranberries are soft, about 15 minutes. Let cool to room temperature.

Preheat the oven to 350°F. Fill the tart crust with the cooled filling. Arrange the rods of dough in a lattice pattern (see page 291) over the filling.

Bake until the lattice is golden brown and the filling is bubbly, 30 to 35 minutes. Let cool to room temperature. Remove the pan sides and place the linzertorte on a platter to serve.

··· ◌ ···

PLANNING AHEAD

The dough may be made 2 days in advance, wrapped, and refrigerated. Let stand at room temperature for 10 minutes before lining the tart pan and making the lattice top. The linzertorte may be baked 1 day in advance. Store at room temperature.

CARAMEL ALMOND TARTLETS WITH WARM BLUEBERRIES

— SERVES 6 —

My husband's three favorite dessert flavors—caramel, almonds, and berries—are in this recipe. The tartlets are good served warm or at room temperature. If you don't have tartlet pans, you can make a single 9½-inch tart, increasing the baking time to about 30 minutes. In winter, when blueberries are out of season, add a handful of chocolate chunks with the almonds.

2 CUPS (8 OUNCES) WHOLE NATURAL ALMONDS, TOASTED (SEE PAGE 20) AND COARSELY CHOPPED

6 PREBAKED 4-INCH TARTLET CRUSTS (PAGE 290)

1½ CUPS GRANULATED SUGAR

⅓ CUP WATER

1 CUP PLUS 2 TABLESPOONS HEAVY WHIPPING CREAM

1 LARGE EGG, LIGHTLY BEATEN

WARM BLUEBERRIES

1½ PINTS BLUEBERRIES (ABOUT 3 CUPS)

¼ CUP GRANULATED SUGAR

1 RECIPE CHANTILLY CREAM (PAGE 276)

Preheat the oven to 325°F. Scatter the almonds evenly in the bottoms of the tartlet crusts. Put the tartlet shells on a baking sheet.

In a heavy, nonreactive saucepan, stir the sugar and water together. Place over medium heat and cook, stirring occasionally, until the sugar dissolves and comes to a boil. Increase the heat to high and cook, without stirring, until the mixture becomes a golden amber. (See page 20 for tips on making caramel.)

Remove from the heat and let the bubbles subside for a few seconds. Stir in 2 tablespoons of the cream. Be careful as you stir, as the caramel will bubble up when you add the cream. Then slowly stir in the remaining 1 cup cream. Let cool for 5 minutes, then whisk in the egg.

Fill the tartlet crusts with the caramel cream. Bake until thick and bubbly, 15 to 20 minutes. Let the tartlets cool until they can be handled, then remove the pan sides.

To prepare the blueberries: In a large sauté pan, combine the blueberries and sugar over medium-high heat. Cook until the berries start to give off some of their juice, 2 to 3 minutes. Remove from the heat.

Place the tartlets on individual plates. Serve warm or at room temperature, topped with the chantilly cream and warm blueberries.

··· ⚜ ···

The tartlets are best served the day they are made. Store at room temperature. They may be reheated in a 325°F oven for 10 minutes. The berries may be prepared a day ahead, covered, and refrigerated. Reheat gently before serving.

WARM BITTERSWEET CHOCOLATE TARTLETS WITH SPICED ALMONDS

— SERVES 6 —

My sister always requests this dessert for her birthday "cake." I arrange the tartlets on a platter and write "Happy Birthday" in chocolate on the rim of the plate. This recipe, like the one for Caramel Almond Tartlets with Warm Blueberries (page 162), can be made as a single 9½-inch tart. Increase the baking time by 5 to 10 minutes.

2 OUNCES UNSWEETENED CHOCOLATE, CHOPPED

3 OUNCES (6 TABLESPOONS) UNSALTED BUTTER

3 LARGE EGGS

½ CUP GRANULATED SUGAR

⅛ TEASPOON KOSHER SALT

1 TABLESPOON LIGHT CORN SYRUP

2 TABLESPOONS MILK

½ TEASPOON VANILLA EXTRACT

1 TEASPOON COGNAC OR RUM (OPTIONAL)

⅓ CUP BITTERSWEET CHOCOLATE CHIPS

6 PREBAKED 4-INCH TARTLET CRUSTS (PAGE 290)

1 RECIPE CHANTILLY CREAM (PAGE 276)

½ RECIPE SPICED NUTS (PAGE 255) MADE WITH ALMONDS

Preheat the oven to 325°F. Melt the chocolate and butter together in a double boiler. (See page 19 for tips on melting chocolate.) Whisk until smooth and let cool until warm.

In a bowl, whisk together the eggs, sugar, and salt until blended. Whisk in the corn syrup until well mixed and then whisk in the milk, vanilla, and cognac (if using) until smooth. Stir in the melted chocolate mixture. Scatter the chocolate chips evenly over the bottoms of the tartlet crusts. Pour the chocolate mixture over the chocolate chips.

Bake until almost completely set, 20 to 25 minutes. Let the tartlets cool until they can be handled, then remove the pan sides. Place the tartlets on individual plates. Serve warm with a dollop of the chantilly cream and a sprinkling of the nuts. Serve the remaining cream and nuts on the side for guests to add as desired.

PLANNING AHEAD

The tartlets are best served the day they are made. Store at room temperature. You may reheat them in a 325°F oven for 10 minutes.

FRENCH APPLE TARTLETS

— SERVES 8 —

At the famed Poilâne bakery in Paris, you can buy the best apple tartlets, just out of the oven. They are baked at irregular intervals throughout the day, but the locals have a sixth sense for the schedule and queue up at the right time. These tartlets are modeled after the ones at Poilâne. Although they may be reheated, they taste best still warm from the oven.

1 RECIPE (1¾ POUNDS) PUFF PASTRY (PAGE 294)

7 FIRM, JUICY APPLES (ABOUT 3 POUNDS), PEELED, HALVED, CORED, AND SLICED ⅛ INCH THICK

¾ CUP GRANULATED SUGAR

2 OUNCES (4 TABLESPOONS) UNSALTED BUTTER

¼ TEASPOON KOSHER SALT

2 TABLESPOONS FRESHLY SQUEEZED LEMON JUICE

1 TABLESPOON CALVADOS (OPTIONAL)

1 CUP CRÈME FRAÎCHE, HOMEMADE (PAGE 279) OR PURCHASED

Line 2 baking sheets with parchment paper. On a lightly floured work surface, roll out the puff pastry into a 20-by-10-inch rectangle about ⅛ inch thick. Using a sharp knife, cut the pastry in half lengthwise and then into quarters crosswise to yield eight 5-inch squares. Carefully transfer the pastry squares to the baking sheets, making sure that they are not touching. Refrigerate for at least 30 minutes.

In a large saucepan, combine the apples, sugar, butter, salt, lemon juice, and Calvados (if using) over medium heat. Cook, stirring often, until the apples are soft, about 10 minutes. Transfer the apples to a bowl and let cool to room temperature. Preheat the oven to 375°F.

Place about ½ cup of the cooked apples in the middle of each square of puff pastry. Fold the 4 corners of the pastry toward the center of the square, covering the apples. (If the pastry does not bend easily and cracks, let it sit at room temperature for 5 minutes.) Pinch the edges of the puff pastry together at the corners to seal.

Bake until golden brown, about 30 minutes. Serve warm on individual plates with the crème fraîche.

PLANNING AHEAD

The apples may be prepared 3 days in advance, covered, and refrigerated. The day of serving, the tartlets may be assembled several hours in advance and refrigerated. You may reheat them in a 350°F oven for about 8 minutes.

PASSION FRUIT—MERINGUE TARTLETS

— SERVES 6 —

Ripe passion fruits are dimpled and rather ugly. Although they look like fruits past their prime, that is actually when they are at their best. To extract the juice from a passion fruit, cut it in half, scoop out the insides, purée them, and then strain the pulp. You will need about 5 passion fruits to yield ½ cup juice. If you cannot find fresh passion fruits, or don't feel like doing the work necessary to extract the juice, you can buy frozen passion fruit concentrate purée from The Perfect Purée of Napa Valley (www.perfectpuree.com). Passion fruits have more pucker power than lemons and pair well with the sweet meringue.

PASSION FRUIT CURD

4 LARGE EGG YOLKS

2 LARGE WHOLE EGGS

½ CUP GRANULATED SUGAR

½ CUP PASSION FRUIT JUICE

6 PREBAKED 4-INCH TARTLET CRUSTS (PAGE 290)

MERINGUE

4 LARGE EGG WHITES

1 CUP GRANULATED SUGAR

To make the curd: In a stainless-steel bowl, whisk together the egg yolks, whole eggs, and sugar until blended. Stir in the passion fruit juice. Place the bowl over a pan of simmering water, making sure the bottom of the bowl does not touch the water.

(See page 18 for tips on using and making a double boiler.) Whisking frequently, cook until almost as thick as mayonnaise, about 10 minutes. Remove the bowl from the pan and strain the curd through a medium-mesh sieve into a clean bowl. Cover with plastic wrap, pressing it directly on the surface, and refrigerate until cold, about 1 hour.

Fill the tartlet crusts with the curd. Set aside while you make the meringue.

Preheat the oven to 450°F.

To make the meringue: In the bowl of a stand mixer, whisk together the egg whites and sugar until blended. Place the bowl in a pan filled about one-third full of simmering water (in this case, the bottom of the bowl should be sitting in the water) and cook, whisking constantly, until hot, about 3 minutes. Remove from the water and place the bowl on the electric mixer fitted with the whip attachment. Whip on medium speed until stiff peaks form.

Spoon the meringue into a pastry bag fitted with a large decorative tip. Pipe the meringue on top of the tartlets, completely covering the curd. (Alternatively, you can spoon the meringue on top of the curd.)

Bake until the meringue is golden brown, about 8 minutes. Let cool to room temperature, then remove the pan sides. Serve the tartlets warm or at room temperature.

··· ⟨⟩ ···

PLANNING AHEAD
The curd may be made a day in advance. The tartlets are best served within 5 hours of baking. Store at room temperature.

CORNMEAL TARTLETS WITH ORANGE CRÈME FRAÎCHE AND STRAWBERRIES

— SERVES 6 —

Stone-ground cornmeal includes the germ and the bran of the corn kernel. It is not only better for you, but also provides greater texture and flavor in desserts than ordinary cornmeal does. Bob's Red Mill, located in Oregon and distributed nationally, makes a wonderful organic medium-grind stone-ground cornmeal.

CORNMEAL CRUSTS

1   CUP MEDIUM-GRIND YELLOW CORNMEAL,
    PREFERABLY STONE GROUND
1   CUP ALL-PURPOSE FLOUR
½   TEASPOON KOSHER SALT
3   TABLESPOONS GRANULATED SUGAR
2   TEASPOONS BAKING POWDER
3   OUNCES (6 TABLESPOONS) COLD UNSALTED
    BUTTER, CUT INTO 1-INCH PIECES
½   CUP HEAVY WHIPPING CREAM
FLOUR FOR DUSTING

ORANGE CRÈME FRAÎCHE

1   CUP CRÈME FRAÎCHE, HOMEMADE (PAGE 279)
    OR PURCHASED
GRATED ZEST OF 1 ORANGE
PINCH OF SALT
2   TABLESPOONS GRANULATED SUGAR

1½ PINTS STRAWBERRIES (ABOUT 3 CUPS), HULLED
    AND SLICED LENGTHWISE
1   TABLESPOON GRANULATED SUGAR, OR AS NEEDED
1   RECIPE BERRY SAUCE (PAGE 289) MADE WITH
    STRAWBERRIES

To make the cornmeal crusts: Preheat the oven to 325°F. Stir together the cornmeal, flour, salt, sugar, and baking powder in the bowl of a stand mixer fitted with the paddle attachment. Scatter the butter pieces over the top and mix on low speed until the butter is the size of small peas. Slowly pour in the cream and continue to mix on low speed until the dough comes together. (Alternatively, cut the butter into the dry ingredients with a pastry blender until the butter is the size of small peas and then slowly add the cream, stirring and tossing with a fork until the dough comes together.)

On a lightly floured work surface, roll out the dough ⅛ inch thick. Cut out as many 5-inch circles as possible. Gather together the scraps and reroll as necessary to get 6 circles total. Line six 4-inch tartlet pans with the dough circles, centering a dough circle over the pan and gently easing it into the bottom and up the sides. If necessary, trim the dough even with the pan rim. Refrigerate for at least 30 minutes.

Line the tartlet crusts with parchment paper and fill with pie weights, uncooked rice, or dried beans. (See page 292 for tips on prebaking crusts.) Place on a baking sheet and bake for 20 minutes. Remove the weights and parchment paper and bake until the crusts are light golden brown, about 10 minutes longer. Let cool completely, then remove the pan sides.

To make the orange crème fraîche: Combine the crème fraîche, orange zest, salt, and sugar in the bowl of a stand mixer fitted with the whip attachment and whip on medium-high speed until thick. Cover and refrigerate until serving.

To serve, put the strawberries in a bowl and gently mix in the 1 tablespoon sugar. Taste for sweetness and add more sugar if needed. Fill the prebaked crusts with orange crème fraîche and place on individual plates. Top with the strawberries and drizzle on some of the strawberry sauce.

PLANNING AHEAD

The tartlet crusts may be formed a day in advance, covered, and refrigerated. Bake the crusts the same day you serve the tartlets. Store at room temperature. The orange crème fraîche can be made a day in advance, covered, and refrigerated. Assemble the tartlets just before serving.

BANANA NAPOLEONS WITH WARM CARAMEL WALNUT SAUCE

— SERVES 6 —

I taught many baking classes during my years at Stars. This recipe was served at the restaurant and taught in classes from Seattle to New Jersey. It was a favorite on both coasts and in the middle of the country as well. Bananas are available all year, so you never have to wait for the proper season to enjoy this napoleon.

½ RECIPE (14 OUNCES) PUFF PASTRY (PAGE 294)

CARAMEL WALNUT SAUCE

3 OUNCES (6 TABLESPOONS) UNSALTED BUTTER

1 CUP FIRMLY PACKED DARK BROWN SUGAR

½ CUP GRANULATED SUGAR

⅔ CUP HEAVY WHIPPING CREAM

2 TEASPOONS VANILLA EXTRACT

1 CUP (4 OUNCES) WALNUTS, TOASTED (SEE PAGE 20) AND COARSELY CHOPPED

4 BANANAS, PEELED AND SLICED ON THE DIAGONAL ½ INCH THICK

1 TABLESPOON FRESHLY SQUEEZED LEMON JUICE

1 TABLESPOON DARK RUM (OPTIONAL)

1 RECIPE CHANTILLY CREAM (PAGE 276)

Line 2 baking sheets with parchment paper. On a lightly floured work surface, roll out the puff pastry into a 16-by 9-inch rectangle about ¹⁄₁₆ inch thick. With the tines of a fork, make holes about ⅛ inch apart all over the puff pastry. Using a sharp knife, cut the puff pastry into twelve 4-by-3-inch rectangles. Place the pastry rectangles on the prepared baking sheets, spacing them 1 inch apart. Place the baking sheets in the freezer for at least 30 minutes. Preheat the oven to 375°F.

Bake the puff pastry rectangles until golden brown, 10 to 15 minutes. Let cool on the baking sheets to room temperature.

To make the sauce: In a heavy saucepan, melt the butter over medium-low heat. Stir in the brown and granulated sugars and cook, stirring frequently, until the sugars are melted, about 5 minutes. Stir in the cream and vanilla and continue to cook until the sauce has thickened slightly, about 5 minutes. Remove from the heat and stir in the walnuts.

To assemble the napoleons: In a bowl, gently stir together the banana slices, lemon juice, and rum (if using). Place 1 pastry rectangle on each of 6 plates. Spoon some of the bananas on top of the pastry and then some chantilly cream. Drizzle the caramel walnut sauce over the cream and bananas. Place a second pastry rectangle on top. Serve immediately.

The caramel walnut sauce may be made 3 days ahead, covered, refrigerated, and then reheated gently just before serving. Do not add the walnuts until reheating, or they will become soggy. You may bake the pastry rectangles several hours in advance of serving, but keep them in an airtight container at room temperature so they remain crisp. Slice the bananas and assemble the napoleons just before serving.

PEAR NAPOLEONS WITH GINGER
PASTRY CREAM

— SERVES 6 —

At Stars, napoleons were always made to order. A napoleon sitting in a bakery case can be disappointing. If it sits too long, the pastry cream makes the pastry soggy, and you miss the experience of crispy and creamy in your mouth at the same time. Last-minute assembly ensures that these pear napoleons will be at their best.

4 RIPE PEARS (ABOUT 2 POUNDS), PEELED, HALVED, CORED, AND SLICED ⅓ INCH THICK

⅓ CUP SUGAR

1½ TEASPOONS FRESHLY SQUEEZED LEMON JUICE

2 TABLESPOONS BRANDY OR DARK RUM

PINCH OF SALT

½ RECIPE (14 OUNCES) PUFF PASTRY (PAGE 294)

½ RECIPE GINGER PASTRY CREAM (PAGE 280)

2 TABLESPOONS CONFECTIONERS' SUGAR

In a 12-inch sauté pan, combine the pears, sugar, lemon juice, brandy, and salt over medium-high heat. Cook, stirring occasionally, until the pears are soft but still retain their shape, about 10 minutes. Remove from the heat and let cool to room temperature.

Line 2 baking sheets with parchment paper. On a lightly floured work surface, roll out the puff pastry into a 16-by-9-inch rectangle about ¹⁄₁₆ inch thick. With the tines of a fork, make holes about ⅛ inch apart all over the puff pastry. Using a sharp knife, cut the pastry into twelve 4-by-3-inch rectangles. Place the pastry rectangles on the prepared baking sheets, spacing them 1 inch apart. Freeze the pastry for at least 30 minutes. Preheat the oven to 375°F.

Bake for 15 to 20 minutes, or until the pastry has puffed and is golden brown. Let cool on the baking sheets to room temperature.

Put 1 baked pastry rectangle on each of 6 plates. Spread a scant 3 tablespoons of the pastry cream on top of each rectangle. Divide the pears evenly among the cream-topped pastry. Dust the tops of the remaining 6 pastry rectangles with confectioners' sugar and place on top of the pears. Serve immediately.

PLANNING AHEAD

The pears may be cooked up to 2 days in advance, covered, and refrigerated. Bring to room temperature before serving. You may bake the pastry rectangles several hours in advance of serving but keep them in an airtight container at room temperature so they remain crisp. Assemble the napoleons just before serving.

KEY LIME PIE

— SERVES 8 —

This is how a Key lime pie should taste: simple and tart. I substituted ginger cookies for the graham crackers to give the crust a little zip. Most Floridians tell me that a true Key lime pie must have whipped cream topping, never meringue, but that is a matter of debate. The crust holds well, so this pie tastes just as good the next day.

GINGER CRUST

1 CUP FINELY GROUND GINGER COOKIES (ABOUT 9 COOKIES), FROM HOMEMADE (PAGE 218) OR PURCHASED CRISP GINGER COOKIES

2 OUNCES (4 TABLESPOONS) UNSALTED BUTTER, MELTED

FILLING

4 LARGE EGGS

1½ CUPS GRANULATED SUGAR

¾ CUP KEY LIME JUICE

2 OUNCES (4 TABLESPOONS) UNSALTED BUTTER, AT ROOM TEMPERATURE

TOPPING

¾ CUP HEAVY WHIPPING CREAM

2 TABLESPOONS GRANULATED SUGAR

To make the crust: Preheat the oven to 300°F. In a bowl, stir together the cookie crumbs and melted butter until the crumbs are evenly moistened. Press the crumbs into the bottom and up the sides of a 9½-inch pie pan. Bake until firm to the touch, about 15 minutes. Let cool to room temperature.

To make the filling: In a stainless-steel bowl, whisk together the eggs and the 1½ cups of sugar until blended. Whisk in the Key lime juice. Place the bowl over a pan of simmering water, making sure the bottom of the bowl does not touch the water. (See page 18 for tips on using and making a double boiler.) Whisking frequently, cook until almost as thick as mayonnaise, about 15 minutes. Remove the bowl from the pan and whisk in the butter until smooth. Spread the warm Key lime mixture into the prepared pie crust. Refrigerate until cold, about 1 hour.

To make the topping: In a bowl, whisk the cream with the 2 tablespoons sugar until soft peaks form. Pipe or spread the whipped cream over the top of the pie. Refrigerate until serving.

PLANNING AHEAD

The pie may be made a day in advance, covered, and refrigerated. Top the pie with the whipped cream the same day you serve it.

PUMPKIN PIE

— SERVES 8 —

Since everyone eats pumpkin pie on Thanksgiving, why not make it the best? The addition of rum and heavy cream is what makes this recipe, from Carolyn Weil, the first pastry chef at Stars, so special. Many pumpkin pie recipes don't call for prebaking the crust before pouring in the filling, which is a mistake. Prebaking is what prevents a soggy crust.

3 LARGE EGGS

½ CUP FIRMLY PACKED LIGHT BROWN SUGAR

½ CUP DARK CORN SYRUP

1½ CUPS HEAVY WHIPPING CREAM

1½ CUPS PUMPKIN PURÉE, HOMEMADE (PAGE 301) OR CANNED

1 TABLESPOON RUM

1 TEASPOON GROUND CINNAMON

¾ TEASPOON GROUND GINGER

½ TEASPOON SALT

1 PREBAKED 9½-INCH PIE CRUST (PAGE 290)

1 RECIPE CHANTILLY CREAM (PAGE 276)

Preheat the oven to 350°F.

In a large bowl, whisk together the eggs and brown sugar until blended. Add the corn syrup and whisk until smooth. Whisk in the cream, pumpkin purée, rum, cinnamon, ginger, and salt until well mixed. Pour into the prebaked pie crust.

Bake until the filling is set, about 30 minutes. Let cool to room temperature. Serve with the chantilly cream.

PLANNING AHEAD

The pie may be made a day in advance, covered, and refrigerated. Bring to room temperature before serving.

MAPLE PECAN PIE

— SERVES 8 —

Pecan pie is too often ordinary, but the use of maple syrup
turns this one into a classic Stars dessert, especially served warm
with your favorite coffee ice cream.

4 LARGE EGGS

⅔ CUP SUGAR

½ CUP PURE MAPLE SYRUP

½ CUP DARK CORN SYRUP

3 OUNCES (6 TABLESPOONS) UNSALTED BUTTER,
  MELTED

3 CUPS (10 OUNCES) PECANS, TOASTED
  (SEE PAGE 20) AND COARSELY CHOPPED

1 PREBAKED 9½-INCH PIE CRUST (PAGE 290)

1 PINT COFFEE ICE CREAM

Preheat the oven to 325°F.

In a large bowl, whisk together the eggs and
sugar until blended. Whisk in the maple and corn
syrups and then the melted butter until smooth.
Scatter the pecans evenly over the bottom of the pie
crust. Carefully pour in the syrup mixture.

Bake until the filling is just set, about 1 hour.
Serve warm or at room temperature with a scoop of
the ice cream alongside.

PLANNING AHEAD

The pie may be made a day in advance. Store at
room temperature. You may reheat the pie in a
325°F for 10 minutes.

BLUEBERRY PIE

— SERVES 8 —

From the end of July and into August, when blueberries are plump
and abundant, make this pie. Bake it in the morning when the weather
is cooler. As it sits on the countertop, you can look forward to its
juicy, sweet taste later in the day.

2½ PINTS BLUEBERRIES (ABOUT 5 CUPS)

½ CUP ALL-PURPOSE FLOUR

1 CUP PLUS 1 TEASPOON GRANULATED SUGAR

¼ TEASPOON KOSHER SALT

GRATED ZEST OF 1 LEMON

1 UNBAKED 9½-INCH PIE CRUST WITH OVERHANG
   AND 1 TOP CRUST (PAGE 290)

2 TABLESPOONS HEAVY WHIPPING CREAM

Preheat the oven to 375°F.

Place the berries in a large bowl. In a small
bowl, stir together the flour, 1 cup of the sugar,
the salt, and the lemon zest. Gently stir the dry
ingredients into the berries, coating evenly.

Spoon the blueberry mixture into the unbaked
pie crust. Lay the top crust over the blueberries.
Fold the edge of the top crust under the edge of
the bottom crust. Press the edges together firmly to
form a secure seal. With a fork, press a decorative
pattern into the pie edge. Cut four 1-inch slits in
the middle of the top of the pie. Brush the top of
the pie with the cream. Sprinkle the remaining
1 teaspoon sugar evenly over the top.

Bake until the crust starts to brown, about
40 minutes. Reduce the oven temperature to 350°F
and continue to bake until the crust is golden
brown and the blueberry mixture is thick and
bubbly, 45 minutes to 1 hour longer. Serve warm
or at room temperature.

PLANNING AHEAD

The pie is best served the day it is baked. Store
at room temperature. You may reheat the pie in a
325°F oven for 10 minutes.

PATRICK'S PEACH PIE

— SERVES 8 —

Patrick was a regular customer at Stars, and every year he would ask me when peaches would be available and if I would please make him a pie the moment they were. He was my peach barometer: when he started asking about peach pie, I knew the season was about to begin. Serve the pie with Chantilly Cream (page 276) or ice cream.

4 POUNDS RIPE PEACHES (ABOUT 7 LARGE), PEELED, PITTED, AND SLICED ¾ INCH THICK

¼ CUP FIRMLY PACKED BROWN SUGAR

¾ CUP PLUS 1 TABLESPOON GRANULATED SUGAR

⅓ CUP CORNSTARCH

¼ TEASPOON GROUND CINNAMON

PINCH OF KOSHER SALT

1 PREBAKED 9½-INCH PIE CRUST AND 1 LATTICE TOP (PAGE 290)

1 LARGE EGG, LIGHTLY BEATEN

Preheat the oven to 350°F.

Place the peaches in a large bowl. In a small bowl, stir together the brown sugar, ¾ cup of the granulated sugar, cornstarch, cinnamon, and salt. Gently stir the dry ingredients into the peaches, mixing evenly. Place the peaches in the pie crust. Brush the beaten egg on the lattice strips and then sprinkle them with the remaining 1 tablespoon sugar. Lay the strips over the top of the filled tart crust, forming a lattice pattern (see page 291).

Bake until the lattice is golden and the juices have thickened, about 1 hour and 10 minutes. If the lattice begins to get too brown before the pie has finished baking, cover the pie loosely with aluminum foil. Let cool to room temperature to serve.

··· ⌘ ···

PLANNING AHEAD

The pie is best served the day it is made. Store at room temperature.

BANANA CREAM PIE

— SERVES 8 TO 10 —

If apple is seen as the quintessential American pie, then banana is surely a close second. Chock-full of bananas, with just enough pastry cream to hold them together, banana cream pie has a prominent place in diners across the country. In *American Pie: Slices of Life (and Pie) from America's Back Roads*, Pascale Le Draoulec tells the captivating tale of her cross-country quest for great pies. For any lover of banana cream pie—or any flavor pie—it is a must read. Be sure to have a fresh pie like this one in the house when you sit down with the book. It makes you crave a piece.

5 MEDIUM BANANAS, PEELED AND SLICED ¼ INCH THICK

1 RECIPE BROWN SUGAR PASTRY CREAM (PAGE 280)

1 TEASPOON DARK RUM (OPTIONAL)

1 PREBAKED 9½-INCH PIE CRUST (PAGE 290)

½ CUP CRÈME FRAÎCHE, HOMEMADE (PAGE 279) OR PURCHASED

1 CUP SOUR CREAM

1 CUP CHOCOLATE SAUCE (PAGE 284), WARMED

In a bowl, fold together the bananas, pastry cream, and rum (if using). Spread into the pie crust.

Combine the crème fraîche and sour cream in the bowl of a stand mixer fitted with the whip attachment and whip on high speed until thick. Using a spatula, spread the cream over the banana filling.

Refrigerate the pie until ready to serve. Serve with warm chocolate sauce drizzled over each slice.

PLANNING AHEAD

This pie is best served the day it is made. Keep refrigerated until serving.

COCONUT CREAM PIE WITH MANGO AND BLACKBERRY SAUCES

— SERVES 8 —

On the menu at Stars, we put sophisticated desserts, like soufflés and napoleons, next to homey desserts, like pies and crisps. Mixing styles was never out of place, since each dessert was always the best it could be. In this recipe, an old-fashioned coconut cream pie was given the Stars touch by the addition of blackberry and mango sauces, a garnish that sends it off the flavor charts.

8 LARGE EGG YOLKS

½ CUP GRANULATED SUGAR

3 TABLESPOONS CORNSTARCH

⅛ TEASPOON KOSHER SALT

2½ CUPS MILK

2 CUPS SWEETENED SHREDDED COCONUT,
   TOASTED (SEE PAGE 22)

1 OUNCE (2 TABLESPOONS) UNSALTED BUTTER,
   AT ROOM TEMPERATURE

½ TEASPOON VANILLA EXTRACT

1 PREBAKED 9½-INCH PIE CRUST (PAGE 290)

1½ CUPS CRÈME FRAÎCHE, HOMEMADE (PAGE 279)
   OR PURCHASED

1 CUP MANGO SAUCE (PAGE 289)

1 CUP BERRY SAUCE (PAGE 289) MADE WITH
   BLACKBERRIES

In a bowl, whisk together the egg yolks, sugar, cornstarch, and salt until blended.

Put the milk in a heavy, nonreactive saucepan and place over medium heat until small bubbles appear around the edges of the pan, then remove from the heat. While whisking constantly, pour the milk into the egg mixture in a slow, steady stream. Stir in 1½ cups of the toasted coconut. Pour the mixture back into the pan, place over medium heat, and cook, stirring constantly and making sure to scrape the bottom of the pan, until thick, about 8 minutes. Remove from the heat and whisk in the butter and vanilla extract. Pour the mixture into a clean bowl. Cover with plastic wrap, pressing it directly onto the surface. Refrigerate until cold, about 1 hour.

Spread the cold coconut filling into the pie crust. In a bowl, whisk the crème fraîche until thick. Using a spatula, spread it evenly over the coconut filling. Sprinkle the remaining coconut on top.

To serve, spoon some of the sauces on each plate. Place a piece of pie on top.

··· ❧ ···

PLANNING AHEAD

The coconut filling may be made a day in advance. Assemble the pie the day you serve it. Refrigerate until serving.

CAKES

— CHAPTER 6 —

The term "cake" often brings to mind two white or yellow layers covered with frosting. But traditional layer cakes are only a small part of the cake repertoire. In this chapter, you will find cheesecake, cream cake, miniature cakes, upside-down cake, gingerbread, pound cake, angel food cake, and more. Many of them are simple-to-make cakes that can be easily transformed into a dinner-party dessert with a scoop of ice cream or a dollop of cream and a drizzle of sauce.

184
ESPRESSO–CHOCOLATE CHIP
ANGEL FOOD CAKE

186
BLUEBERRY LEMON CHEESECAKE WITH
A CORNMEAL CRUST

188
GOAT CHEESE CAKE WITH MIXED BERRIES

189
PUMPKIN CHEESECAKE

190
GINGER MASCARPONE CHEESECAKE WITH
A CHOCOLATE CRUST

192
CHOCOLATE-HAZELNUT POUND CAKE WITH
ESPRESSO-CINNAMON CREAM

194
CORNMEAL POUND CAKE WITH BLACKBERRIES
AND DOUBLE CREAM

195
TORTA REGINA

196
ORANGE SPICE CAKE WITH BERRIES

198
PLUM-CARDAMOM UPSIDE-DOWN CAKE

200
FRENCH SILK

202
BUTTER ALMOND CAKE WITH STRAWBERRIES
AND CARAMEL CREAM

203
TUSCAN CREAM CAKE

204
DRUNKEN CHOCOLATE CAKE

206
GINGERBREAD WITH WARM APPLES AND
CIDER SABAYON

208
GRANDMOTHERS' CHOCOLATE CAKE

210
LEMON CURD CAKE

ESPRESSO–CHOCOLATE CHIP ANGEL FOOD CAKE

— SERVES 10 TO 12 —

Angel food cake usually needs to be served with fruit or a sauce
to liven it up. But not this one. The espresso and chocolate chips
contribute enough flavor for it to stand on its own. When you are in a
hurry, a slice of this cake and a cup of coffee are both quick and satisfying.
To transform it into a dinner-party dessert, serve it with warm
Chocolate Caramel Sauce (page 288) and any kind of ice cream
that strikes your fancy.

2 TEASPOONS INSTANT ESPRESSO POWDER

1⅓ CUPS CAKE FLOUR, SIFTED

⅛ TEASPOON KOSHER SALT

1¾ CUPS (ABOUT 12 LARGE) EGG WHITES

1 TEASPOON CREAM OF TARTAR

1¾ CUPS GRANULATED SUGAR

1½ TEASPOONS VANILLA EXTRACT

1¼ TEASPOONS FRESHLY SQUEEZED LEMON JUICE

¾ CUP BITTERSWEET CHOCOLATE CHIPS,
   COARSELY CHOPPED

Preheat the oven to 350°F. Have ready an ungreased
10-inch nonstick angel food cake pan.

Sift together the espresso powder and flour
onto a piece of parchment paper or into a bowl.
Add the salt and set aside.

Put the egg whites in the large bowl of a stand
mixer fitted with the whip attachment and whip on
medium speed until frothy. Add the cream of tartar,

increase the speed to high, and continue whipping
while slowly pouring in the sugar until the whites
are firm and satiny, about 3 minutes.

Reduce the speed to low, add the vanilla and
lemon juice and then add the dry ingredients.
When the flour mixture is almost completely
incorporated, remove the bowl from the mixer
stand and fold in the chocolate chips with a
spatula. Make sure that the chips are spread evenly
throughout the batter and that the flour mixture is
evenly incorporated. But be careful not to overmix,
or you will deflate the batter and the cake will not
rise fully in the oven.

Pour the batter into the cake pan. Cut through
the batter a few times with a table knife to break
up any air pockets. Bake until a skewer inserted
into the center comes out clean, 40 to 45 minutes.
Invert the cake and let cool completely upside down
in the pan. (If the pan does not have feet, balance

the inverted pan on the neck of a bottle or rest the edge of the pan rim on 3 or 4 ramekins.)

To unmold the cake, run a long knife around the inside edge of the pan. Then, holding the center tube, free the cake from the pan sides. Slip a knife between the cake and the bottom of the pan to loosen the cake and gently flip the cake over, letting it fall onto a platter. (If the pan does not have a removable bottom, release the sides with the knife, then place a platter on top of the cake. Gently invert the platter and the cake together. Lift off the pan.) To serve, cut into slices with a serrated knife, using a gentle sawing motion.

··· ⟬⟬⟬ ···

PLANNING AHEAD
The cake may be made a day in advance. Wrap in plastic wrap and store at room temperature.

BLUEBERRY LEMON CHEESECAKE WITH A CORNMEAL CRUST

— SERVES 8 TO 10 —

I lived in New York City for five years before moving to California and going to work at Stars. A true fan of the Big Apple, I am in awe of many things I found in the city, including the efficiency of the subway, the idea of a neighborhood as a microcosm, and, of course, the cheesecake. Yielding a cheesecake as dense and rich as it can be, this recipe is what all cheesecake recipes should be, regardless of their flavor. It is irrelevant that one slice carries the equivalent of half the recommended daily adult calories. It is worth every moment you will need to spend in the gym.

CORNMEAL CRUST

4 OUNCES (8 TABLESPOONS) UNSALTED BUTTER, AT ROOM TEMPERATURE

¼ CUP GRANULATED SUGAR

½ CUP ALL-PURPOSE FLOUR

½ CUP MEDIUM-GRIND YELLOW CORNMEAL, PREFERABLY STONE GROUND (SEE CORNMEAL TARTLETS WITH ORANGE CRÈME FRAÎCHE AND STRAWBERRIES, PAGE 168, FOR INFORMATION ON CORNMEAL)

PINCH OF KOSHER SALT

LEMON FILLING

2 POUNDS CREAM CHEESE, AT ROOM TEMPERATURE

1 CUP MASCARPONE CHEESE, AT ROOM TEMPERATURE

1½ CUPS GRANULATED SUGAR

2 LARGE EGGS

GRATED ZEST OF 2 LEMONS

3 TABLESPOONS FRESHLY SQUEEZED LEMON JUICE

BLUEBERRY TOPPING

1½ PINTS BLUEBERRIES (ABOUT 3 CUPS)

½ CUP GRANULATED SUGAR

1 TABLESPOON WATER

2 TEASPOONS FRESHLY SQUEEZED LEMON JUICE

To make the crust: Preheat the oven to 350°F. Wrap the bottom and sides of a 9-inch round springform pan in a double thickness of aluminum foil.

Put the butter and sugar in the bowl of a stand mixer fitted with the paddle attachment and beat on medium speed until smooth. Reduce the speed to low and mix in the flour, cornmeal, and salt.

Press the cornmeal mixture evenly into the bottom of the prepared pan. Bake until light brown, about 20 minutes. Let cool while you make the filling. Reduce the oven temperature to 325°F.

To make the filling: Combine the cream cheese, mascarpone, and sugar in a large mixer bowl and beat with the paddle attachment on medium speed until smooth. Add the eggs, lemon zest, and lemon juice and mix until incorporated. Spread the filling over the crust.

Bake until all but the very center of the cake is set, about 1 hour. Remove the cheesecake from the oven. Using a knife, loosen the edges of the cheesecake from the pan sides. (This will help prevent cracks from forming in the middle of the cake.) Let cool for 30 minutes and then cover and refrigerate until cold, about 6 hours.

To make the blueberry topping: In a small, heavy saucepan, combine the blueberries, sugar, water, and lemon juice over medium-low heat. Cook, stirring occasionally, until the mixture is thick, 5 to 10 minutes. Remove from the heat and let cool to room temperature. Cover and refrigerate until cold.

To serve, run a knife around the inside edge of the pan to loosen the cake, then remove the pan sides and set the cheesecake on a platter. Spoon the blueberry topping evenly over the top. Cut the cheesecake with a hot, dry knife (see page 22).

··· ∞ ···

PLANNING AHEAD

The cheesecake and the blueberry topping may be made 2 days in advance and kept refrigerated. Spread the topping on the cheesecake just before serving.

GOAT CHEESE CAKE WITH MIXED BERRIES

— SERVES 6 TO 8 —

I first served this cake at a brunch in New York City in 1993, at the first annual convention of Women Chefs and Restaurateurs (WCR). It was a cathartic event, with founders Barbara Tropp, Lidia Bastianich, Barbara Lazaroff, Joyce Goldstein, Anne Rosenzweig, Johanne Killeen, Mary Sue Milliken, and Elka Gilmore bringing everyone together to promote women in restaurants. Today, WCR has an impressive scholarship program and is a significant voice for women in the food industry.

BUTTER AND GRANULATED SUGAR FOR
  THE CAKE PAN
11 OUNCES FRESH GOAT CHEESE, AT ROOM
  TEMPERATURE
¾ CUP GRANULATED SUGAR
1 TEASPOON VANILLA EXTRACT
GRATED ZEST OF 1 LEMON
1 TEASPOON FRESHLY SQUEEZED LEMON JUICE
6 LARGE EGGS, SEPARATED
3 TABLESPOONS ALL-PURPOSE FLOUR
½ PINT BLACKBERRIES (ABOUT 1 CUP)
1 PINT RASPBERRIES (ABOUT 2 CUPS)

Preheat the oven to 350°F. Butter a 9-inch round cake pan and dust with granulated sugar, tapping out the excess.

Put the goat cheese, sugar, vanilla, lemon zest, and lemon juice in the bowl of a stand mixer fitted with the paddle attachment and beat until smooth. Stir in the egg yolks two at a time, mixing well after each addition. Mix in the flour until incorporated.

Put the egg whites in another mixer bowl, fit the mixer with the whip attachment, and whip on medium speed until soft peaks form. Using a spatula, gently fold the egg whites into the goat cheese mixture. Spread the batter into the prepared pan.

Bake until a skewer inserted into the center comes out clean, 25 to 30 minutes. Let cool to room temperature.

To serve, run a knife around the inside edge of the pan to loosen the cake, invert a platter on top of the pan, and then invert the plate and pan together. Lift off the pan. Top with the berries and serve.

PLANNING AHEAD

The cake may be made a day ahead and kept refrigerated. Place the berries on top of the cake just before serving.

PUMPKIN CHEESECAKE

— SERVES 10 TO 12 —

This cheesecake is so delicious that you shouldn't limit it to fall, when jack-o'-lanterns are on doorsteps. If you want to dress it up, drizzle it with a little Chocolate Sauce (page 284) and top it with Spiced Nuts (page 255) made with pecans for crunch.

GINGER CRUST

ABOUT 18 CRISP GINGER COOKIES, HOMEMADE
   (PAGE 218) OR PURCHASED
1½ OUNCES (3 TABLESPOONS) UNSALTED BUTTER,
   MELTED

PUMPKIN FILLING

1 POUND 13 OUNCES CREAM CHEESE, AT ROOM
   TEMPERATURE
1 CUP MASCARPONE CHEESE, AT ROOM TEMPERATURE
1 CUP PLUS 2 TABLESPOONS GRANULATED SUGAR
PINCH OF KOSHER SALT
2 LARGE EGGS
¼ TEASPOON GROUND GINGER
½ TEASPOON GROUND CINNAMON
1¾ CUPS PUMPKIN PURÉE, HOMEMADE (PAGE 301)
   OR PURCHASED

To make the crust: Preheat the oven to 300°F. In a food processor, finely grind the cookies. You should have about 2 cups. Put the crumbs in a bowl and stir in the melted butter until the crumbs are evenly moistened. Press the mixture evenly into the bottom of a 9-inch round springform pan. Bake until firm to the touch, about 10 minutes. Let cool to room temperature.

To make the filling: Put the cream cheese and mascarpone in the bowl of a stand mixer fitted with the paddle attachment and beat on medium speed until smooth. Continue to beat while slowly adding the sugar and salt. When the mixture is smooth, add the eggs one at a time, mixing well after each addition. Finally, add the ginger, cinnamon, and pumpkin purée and beat until all the ingredients are evenly incorporated and the batter is smooth. Spread the filling over the crust.

Bake until all but the very center of the cake is set, about 1½ hours. Remove the cheesecake from the oven. Using a knife, loosen the edges of the cheesecake from the pan sides. (This will help prevent cracks from forming in the middle of the cake.) Let cool for 30 minutes and then cover and refrigerate until cold, about 6 hours.

Run a knife around the inside edge of the pan again to loosen the cake, then remove the pan sides and set the cheesecake on a platter. Cut with a hot, dry knife (see page 22).

PLANNING AHEAD

The cheesecake may be made a day ahead and kept refrigerated.

GINGER MASCARPONE CHEESECAKE WITH A CHOCOLATE CRUST

— SERVES 10 TO 12 —

Barbara Tropp got me hooked on the combination of ginger and chocolate at China Moon, her San Francisco restaurant, where she served a brilliant ginger ice cream with bittersweet chocolate sauce. I used the pairing as an inspiration for many desserts at Stars. This was one of them. Both Barbara and China Moon are no longer with us, but I think of her every time I make this cheesecake.

CRUST

4 OUNCES (8 TABLESPOONS) UNSALTED BUTTER, CHILLED, CUT INTO ½-INCH PIECES

¼ CUP GRANULATED SUGAR

¾ CUP ALL-PURPOSE FLOUR

¼ CUP UNSWEETENED COCOA POWDER

PINCH OF KOSHER SALT

FLOUR FOR DUSTING

FILLING

2 POUNDS CREAM CHEESE, AT ROOM TEMPERATURE

1 CUP MASCARPONE CHEESE, AT ROOM TEMPERATURE

1½ CUPS GRANULATED SUGAR

2 LARGE EGGS

1 TABLESPOON PEELED AND GRATED FRESH GINGER

To make the crust: Combine the butter and sugar in the bowl of a stand mixer fitted with the paddle attachment and mix on low speed until the butter and sugar begin to incorporate, about 15 seconds. Add the flour, cocoa powder, and salt and continue to mix on low speed until the dough comes together, about 3 minutes.

On a lightly floured work surface, roll out the dough into a 9-inch circle. Place the dough circle in the bottom of a 9-inch round springform pan. Make sure it fills the bottom of the pan, pressing it into the edges if necessary. Refrigerate the crust for at least 1 hour or overnight.

Preheat the oven to 300°F. Bake until the surface no longer looks wet, 30 to 35 minutes. Let cool to room temperature.

To make the filling: Combine the cream cheese and mascarpone in a bowl of the stand mixer and beat with the paddle attachment on medium speed until smooth. Continue to beat while slowly adding the sugar. When the mixture is smooth, beat in the eggs one at a time, mixing well after each addition. Finally, beat in the grated ginger. Spread the filling over the crust.

Bake until the cheesecake is evenly set throughout when you gently shake the pan, about 55 minutes. Remove the cheesecake from the oven. Using a knife, loosen the edges of the cheesecake from the pan sides. (This will help prevent cracks from forming in the middle of the cake.) Let cool for 30 minutes and then cover and refrigerate until cold, about 6 hours.

Run a knife around the inside edge of the pan again to loosen the cake, then remove the pan sides and set the cheesecake on a platter. Cut with a hot, dry knife (see page 22).

PLANNING AHEAD

The cheesecake may be made a day in advance and kept refrigerated.

CHOCOLATE-HAZELNUT POUND CAKE WITH ESPRESSO-CINNAMON CREAM

— SERVES 10 —

Of all the recipes I have created, this one is probably the most versatile. You can make it, as here, in a Bundt pan and serve it as the main attraction with espresso-cinnamon cream. It is also used, minus the hazelnuts, in Chocolate Caramel Bread Pudding (page 64). Once you taste it, you will discover how good it is and will think up new ways to serve it.

POUND CAKE

BUTTER FOR THE PAN

1 CUP ALL-PURPOSE FLOUR

¾ CUP UNSWEETENED COCOA POWDER

¼ TEASPOON BAKING POWDER

½ TEASPOON KOSHER SALT

½ CUP MILK

½ TEASPOON FRESHLY SQUEEZED LEMON JUICE

1 TEASPOON VANILLA EXTRACT

2 TABLESPOONS WATER

6 OUNCES (12 TABLESPOONS) UNSALTED BUTTER, AT ROOM TEMPERATURE

1½ CUPS GRANULATED SUGAR

3 LARGE EGGS

1 CUP (4 OUNCES) HAZELNUTS, TOASTED AND SKINNED (SEE PAGE 20) AND THEN COARSELY CHOPPED

ESPRESSO-CINNAMON CREAM

8 OUNCES MASCARPONE CHEESE

2 CUPS HEAVY WHIPPING CREAM

½ TEASPOON VANILLA EXTRACT

2 TEASPOONS INSTANT ESPRESSO POWDER

¼ TEASPOON GROUND CINNAMON

2 TABLESPOONS SUGAR

PINCH OF KOSHER SALT

1 RECIPE VANILLA CUSTARD SAUCE (PAGE 282)

To make the cake: Preheat the oven to 350°F. Butter a 10-inch Bundt pan.

Sift together the flour, cocoa powder, and baking powder onto a piece of parchment paper or into a bowl. Add the salt and set aside. In a small bowl or measuring cup, stir together the milk, lemon juice, vanilla, and water and set aside.

Combine the butter and sugar in the bowl of a stand mixer fitted with the paddle attachment and beat on medium-high speed until light and fluffy, about 2 minutes. Add the eggs one at a time, mixing well after each addition. Reduce the speed to low and add the dry ingredients in 3 additions alternately with the milk mixture in 2 additions, beginning and ending with the dry ingredients and mixing well after each addition. Stir in the hazelnuts. Spread the batter into the prepared pan.

Bake until a skewer inserted into the center comes out clean, about 50 minutes. Let cool to room temperature.

To make the espresso-cinnamon cream: In a bowl, combine the mascarpone, cream, vanilla, espresso powder, cinnamon, sugar, and salt. Whisk until soft peaks form.

To serve, run a knife around the inside edge of the pan to loosen the cake, invert a platter on top of the pan, and then invert the plate and pan together. Lift off the pan. Spoon some custard sauce on individual plates and set a slice of cake on the sauce. Top the cake with a dollop of the espresso-cinnamon cream.

PLANNING AHEAD

The cake may be made a day in advance. Wrap in plastic wrap and store at room temperature. The espresso-cinnamon cream may be made several hours in advance, covered, and refrigerated. It may need to be lightly rewhipped before serving.

CORNMEAL POUND CAKE WITH BLACKBERRIES AND DOUBLE CREAM

— SERVES 8 —

Sliced, toasted, and served with honey for breakfast, cornmeal pound cake is divine. But toasted and served with blackberries and rich cream, it is transcendent.

BUTTER FOR THE PAN

1¼ CUPS ALL-PURPOSE FLOUR

1½ TEASPOONS BAKING POWDER

1 CUP MEDIUM-GRIND YELLOW CORNMEAL, PREFERABLY STONE GROUND (SEE CORNMEAL TARTLETS WITH ORANGE CRÈME FRAÎCHE AND STRAWBERRIES, PAGE 168, FOR INFORMATION ON CORNMEAL)

PINCH OF KOSHER SALT

3 OUNCES (6 TABLESPOONS) UNSALTED BUTTER, AT ROOM TEMPERATURE

1 CUP FIRMLY PACKED DARK BROWN SUGAR

½ CUP GRANULATED SUGAR

5 LARGE EGGS

¾ CUP SOUR CREAM

½ TEASPOON VANILLA EXTRACT

2 PINTS BLACKBERRIES (ABOUT 4 CUPS)

1 RECIPE DOUBLE CREAM (PAGE 278)

Preheat the oven to 350°F. Butter an 8½-by-4½-by-2¾-inch loaf pan.

Sift together the flour and baking powder into a bowl. Stir in the cornmeal and salt. Set aside.

Combine the butter, brown sugar, and granulated sugar in the bowl of a stand mixer fitted with the paddle attachment and beat on medium-high speed until light and fluffy, about 2 minutes. Add the eggs one at a time, mixing well after each addition. Reduce the speed to medium-low and beat in the sour cream and vanilla until well mixed. Reduce the speed to low, add the dry ingredients, and mix until combined. Pour the batter into the prepared pan.

Bake until a skewer inserted into the center comes out almost completely clean, about 1 hour. Let cool to room temperature. Run a knife around the inside edge of the pan to loosen the cake. Invert a platter on top of the pan and then invert the plate and pan together. Lift off the pan.

Preheat the broiler. Cut the pound cake into 8 slices, lay them on a baking sheet, slip under the broiler, and broil until toasted. Serve immediately, topped with the blackberries and double cream.

PLANNING AHEAD

The cake may be made up to 2 days in advance. Wrap in plastic wrap and store at room temperature.

TORTA REGINA

This flavorful cake is very light, so it can easily handle the addition of both ice cream (caramel or vanilla, pages 300 and 299, respectively) and Orange Custard Sauce (page 283). It is also luscious eaten plain with an espresso in the late afternoon.

1⅓ CUPS (5½ OUNCES) HAZELNUTS, TOASTED
    AND SKINNED (SEE PAGE 20)

5½ OUNCES BITTERSWEET CHOCOLATE,
    FINELY CHOPPED

GRATED ZEST OF 1 LEMON

GRATED ZEST OF 1 ORANGE

6 LARGE EGGS, SEPARATED

½ CUP GRANULATED SUGAR

Preheat the oven to 350°F. Line the bottom of a 9-inch round cake pan with parchment paper.

In a food processor, combine the hazelnuts, chocolate, and lemon and orange zests and pulse to grind finely. Set aside.

Combine the egg yolks and ¼ cup of the sugar in the bowl of a stand mixer fitted with the whip attachment and whip on high speed until slightly increased in volume, about 2 minutes. Reduce the speed to low, add the ground nut mixture, and mix until blended. The batter will be very stiff.

Wash and dry the whip attachment. Put the egg whites in a clean mixer bowl, fit the mixer with the clean whip, and whip on medium speed until frothy. Increase the speed to high and whip until soft peaks form, about 1 minute. Reduce the speed to medium and add the remaining ¼ cup sugar in a steady stream. Once it has all been added, increase the speed to high and whip until stiff peaks form.

Using a spatula, fold half the egg whites into the batter. When they are almost completely incorporated, fold in the remaining egg whites just until no white streaks remain. Gently spread the batter into the prepared pan.

Bake until a skewer inserted into the center comes out clean, about 25 minutes. Let cool to room temperature. Run a knife around the inside edge of the pan to loosen the cake, invert a platter on top of the pan, and invert the plate and pan and together. Lift off the pan and carefully remove the parchment.

Cool to room temperature and serve.

··· ❧ ···

PLANNING AHEAD

The cake may be made a day ahead. Wrap in plastic wrap and store at room temperature.

ORANGE SPICE CAKE WITH BERRIES

— SERVES 10 —

A generous amount of citrus and spices gives this cake character. My friends call it my "shower cake" because I frequently take it to wedding and baby showers. If you are the lucky recipient of the party, you will find it easy to nibble on a slice while you are opening presents. Everyone else can enjoy the cake with the berries and cream while they watch you at work.

CAKE

BUTTER FOR THE PAN

3 TABLESPOONS FINE DRIED BREAD CRUMBS

3 CUPS ALL-PURPOSE FLOUR

½ TEASPOON GROUND WHITE PEPPER

¾ TEASPOON GROUND CINNAMON

¾ TEASPOON GROUND CARDAMOM

¾ TEASPOON BAKING SODA

¾ TEASPOON BAKING POWDER

¾ TEASPOON KOSHER SALT

1 CUP MILK

2 TABLESPOONS FRESHLY SQUEEZED LEMON JUICE

GRATED ZEST OF 2 ORANGES

¾ TEASPOON PEELED AND GRATED FRESH GINGER

8 OUNCES (16 TABLESPOONS) UNSALTED BUTTER,
   AT ROOM TEMPERATURE

1½ CUPS GRANULATED SUGAR

3 LARGE EGGS

GLAZE

½ CUP GRANULATED SUGAR

¼ CUP FRESHLY SQUEEZED ORANGE JUICE

1½ TEASPOONS FRESHLY SQUEEZED LEMON JUICE

1 PINT RASPBERRIES (ABOUT 2 CUPS)

1 PINT BLUEBERRIES (ABOUT 2 CUPS)

1 RECIPE CHANTILLY CREAM (PAGE 276)

To make the cake: Preheat the oven to 350°F. Butter a 10-inch Bundt pan and dust with the bread crumbs, tapping out the excess.

Sift together the flour, white pepper, cinnamon, cardamom, baking soda, and baking powder onto a piece of parchment paper or into a bowl. Add the salt and set aside. In a small bowl or measuring cup, stir together the milk, lemon juice, orange zest, and ginger and set aside.

Combine the butter and sugar in the bowl of a stand mixer fitted with the paddle attachment and beat on medium-high speed until light and fluffy, about 3 minutes. Add the eggs one at a time, mixing well after each addition. Reduce the speed to low and add the dry ingredients in 3 additions alternating with the milk mixture in 2 additions, beginning and ending with the dry ingredients and mixing well after each addition. Spread the batter into the prepared pan.

Bake the cake until a skewer inserted into the center comes out clean, about 40 minutes. Let cool for 15 minutes. Invert a platter on top of the pan and then invert the plate and pan together. Lift off the pan.

To make the glaze: In a small saucepan, combine the sugar, orange juice, and lemon juice over low heat, stirring to dissolve the sugar. Brush the glaze on the cake. It will seem like a lot of glaze, but the cake will absorb it. Let the cake cool to room temperature.

Slice the cake and serve with the raspberries, blueberries, and chantilly cream.

PLANNING AHEAD
The cake may be made a day ahead. Wrap in plastic wrap and store at room temperature.

PLUM-CARDAMOM UPSIDE-DOWN CAKE

— SERVES 10 —

You don't need to limit your upside-down cake to pineapple. Other fruits taste just as good, if not better. Over the years at Stars, I put many different fruits upside down. This version was one of the favorites of the diners and the kitchen staff alike. I learned the method for mixing the cake from dessert expert Rose Levy Beranbaum.

PLUM SYRUP

6 OUNCES (12 TABLESPOONS) UNSALTED BUTTER

1 CUP FIRMLY PACKED BROWN SUGAR

1¾ POUNDS (ABOUT 6) PLUMS, PITTED AND SLICED
  ½ INCH THICK

CAKE

1½ CUPS CAKE FLOUR

2 TEASPOONS BAKING POWDER

¾ TEASPOON GROUND CARDAMOM

¼ TEASPOON KOSHER SALT

½ CUP PLUS 1 TABLESPOON MILK

1 TEASPOON VANILLA EXTRACT

2 OUNCES (4 TABLESPOONS) UNSALTED BUTTER,
  AT ROOM TEMPERATURE

1 CUP GRANULATED SUGAR

2 LARGE EGGS

1 RECIPE VANILLA CUSTARD SAUCE (PAGE 282)

To make the plum syrup: Line the bottom of a 9-inch square baking pan with parchment paper. In a small saucepan, melt the butter over medium heat. Whisk in the brown sugar until the sugar dissolves. Remove from the heat and whisk until smooth. Pour the syrup into the bottom of the prepared pan.

Arrange the plum slices, slightly overlapping them, in 3 rows, completely covering the bottom of the pan.

To make the cake: Preheat the oven to 350°F. Sift together the cake flour, baking powder, and cardamom onto a piece of parchment paper or into a bowl. Add the salt and set aside. In a small bowl or measuring cup, stir together the milk and vanilla and set aside.

Combine the butter and sugar in the bowl of a stand mixer fitted with the paddle attachment and beat on medium-high speed until creamy, about

1 minute. Reduce the speed to low and add the dry ingredients in 3 additions, alternating with the milk mixture in 2 additions, beginning and ending with the dry ingredients and mixing well after each addition. Increase the speed to medium and beat until smooth, about 1 minute. Add the eggs one at a time, mixing well after each addition, then continue to beat for 1 minute. Spread the batter on top of the plums.

Bake until a skewer inserted into the center comes out clean, about 45 minutes. Let cool for 15 minutes. Run a knife around the inside edge of the pan to loosen the cake, invert a platter on top of the pan, and then invert the plate and pan together. Lift off the pan and carefully remove the parchment paper.

Slice the cake and serve warm or at room temperature with the custard sauce.

PLANNING AHEAD

The cake is best served the day it is made. Wrap in plastic wrap and store at room temperature.

FRENCH SILK

— SERVES 12 —

This fudgelike mousse cake pushes the opulence barometer right to the edge, stopping just short of excess. It is for serious chocoholics only. Use pasteurized eggs if you are concerned about eating uncooked eggs.

CRUST

¾ CUP (3 OUNCES) WALNUTS, TOASTED (SEE PAGE 20)

1 CUP (4 OUNCES) PECANS, TOASTED (SEE PAGE 20)

½ CUP FIRMLY PACKED BROWN SUGAR

PINCH OF GROUND CINNAMON

4 OUNCES (8 TABLESPOONS) UNSALTED BUTTER, MELTED

FILLING

1¼ POUNDS BITTERSWEET CHOCOLATE, CHOPPED

6 OUNCES (12 TABLESPOONS) UNSALTED BUTTER, AT ROOM TEMPERATURE

¾ CUP GRANULATED SUGAR

6 LARGE EGGS

¼ CUP HEAVY WHIPPING CREAM

½ TEASPOON VANILLA EXTRACT

TOPPING

1 CUP HEAVY WHIPPING CREAM

2 TABLESPOONS GRANULATED SUGAR

To make the crust: In a food processor, combine the walnuts, pecans, brown sugar, and cinnamon and pulse until the nuts are coarsely chopped.

Pour the nuts into a bowl, add the butter, and stir until the nuts are evenly moistened. Press the nut mixture evenly onto the bottom of a 9-inch round springform pan. Refrigerate for 30 minutes.

To make the filling: Melt the chocolate in a double boiler. (See page 19 for tips on melting chocolate.) While the chocolate is melting, combine the butter and sugar in the bowl of a stand mixer fitted with the paddle attachment and beat on medium speed until smooth, about 1 minute. Switch to the whip attachment and add the eggs two at a time, mixing well after each addition. Scrape down the sides of the bowl, increase the speed to medium-high, and whip until well blended, about 2 minutes. The mixture will look curdled.

Remove the melted chocolate from the heat and stir until smooth and warm but not hot. With the mixer on low speed, add the chocolate to the egg mixture. Scrape the sides and along the bottom of the bowl and then continue to mix on low speed until the chocolate is fully incorporated. Add the cream and vanilla and mix until blended. Spread the filling over the crust. Refrigerate until firm, about 3 hours.

To make the topping: In a bowl, whisk together the cream and sugar until soft peaks form. Cover and refrigerate until serving.

Using a spatula, spread the topping over the top of the cake. Run a hot, dry knife (see page 22) around the inside edge of the pan to loosen the cake, then remove the pan sides and set the cake on a serving platter. Slice the cake with a hot, dry knife and serve chilled.

··· ᚲᚲᚲᚲᚲ ···

PLANNING AHEAD

The cake may be made 2 days in advance and kept in the refrigerator. The topping can be made up to 4 hours in advance, covered, and refrigerated. It may need to be lightly rewhipped before using. You may put the topping on the cake up to 2 hours before serving and keep the cake in the refrigerator. If storing foods with strong odors, such as shrimp, invert a large bowl over the cake to protect it from them.

BUTTER ALMOND CAKE WITH STRAWBERRIES AND CARAMEL CREAM

— SERVES 8 TO 10 —

Created in the student kitchen of our talented Stars sous chef Hollyce Snyder, this dessert is what got Hollyce her job at Stars. We worked together for many years. She is over six feet tall and I am five feet two inches. We often joked that we should open a business and sell doughnuts out the front door and tall and petite clothes out the back!

BUTTER FOR THE PAN

1 CUP CAKE FLOUR

½ TEASPOON BAKING POWDER

PINCH OF KOSHER SALT

10 OUNCES ALMOND PASTE

GRATED ZEST OF 2 ORANGES

1¼ CUPS GRANULATED SUGAR, PLUS MORE IF NEEDED FOR SWEETENING BERRIES

8 OUNCES (16 TABLESPOONS) UNSALTED BUTTER, AT ROOM TEMPERATURE

6 LARGE EGGS

2 PINTS STRAWBERRIES (ABOUT 4 CUPS), HULLED AND QUARTERED LENGTHWISE

½ RECIPE CARAMEL CREAM (PAGE 277)

Preheat the oven to 350°F. Butter a 10-inch Bundt pan.

Sift together the cake flour and baking powder onto a piece of parchment paper or into a bowl. Add the salt and set aside.

Put the almond paste and orange zest in the bowl of a stand mixer fitted with the paddle attachment and beat on medium speed until smooth and malleable, about 2 minutes. Slowly add the 1¼ cups sugar and beat until incorporated. Add the butter and beat until creamy. Add the eggs one at a time, mixing well after each addition. Continue to beat until the mixture is well blended and has increased slightly in volume, about 1 minute. Using a spatula, fold in the flour mixture. Spread the batter into the prepared pan.

Bake until a skewer inserted into the center comes out clean, 35 to 40 minutes. Let cool to room temperature. Invert a platter on top of the pan and invert the plate and pan together. Lift off the pan.

Slice the cake into wedges. If the strawberries need sweetening, gently stir in sugar to taste. Spoon some strawberries and dollop some caramel cream on top of each piece of cake.

PLANNING AHEAD

The cake may be made a day in advance. Wrap in plastic wrap and store at room temperature.

TUSCAN CREAM CAKE

— SERVES 10 —

The Saturday before Easter, my husband's family and I go shopping
in North Beach, San Francisco's traditional Italian neighborhood.
Strolling from store to store, we buy focaccia, ravioli, cold cuts, cheeses,
bread sticks, wine, espresso-roast coffee beans, and cookies. We take it all
home, spread it on the table, and enjoy a huge feast. The meal ends
with thick slices of sacripantina, bought at the Stella bakery on Columbus
Avenue. This sponge cake layered with zabaglione cream is an
adaptation of Stella's famed cake.

2 RECIPES SPONGE CAKE (PAGE 296)

2 RECIPES ZABAGLIONE (PAGE 281)

1½ CUPS HEAVY WHIPPING CREAM

¼ CUP SUGAR

1 CUP CHOCOLATE SHAVINGS (SEE PAGE 21)

¾ CUP CRUSHED AMARETTI OR BISCOTTI

Against a short end of one of the sponge cakes, cut a 9-inch circle. With the remainder of the sponge cake, cut half of a 9-inch circle. Repeat with the second sheet of sponge cake. Cut each circle and each half circle in half horizontally, so you will have a total of 4 circles and 4 half circles. (You will need all the circles and 2 of the half circles, so freeze the extra half circles and any scrap pieces for making trifles.)

Put a cake layer in the bottom of a 9-inch springform pan. Top with a generous ¾ cup of the zabaglione. Top with a second cake layer, and then with another generous ¾ cup of the zabaglione. For the third cake layer, fit two half circles side by side on the zabaglione. Repeat with more zabaglione and end with the fourth full cake circle. You will have 5 cake layers and 4 zabaglione layers. Refrigerate until cold, about 2 hours.

In a bowl, combine the cream and sugar and whisk until soft peaks form. Cover and refrigerate until serving.

Run a knife around the inside edge of the pan, and then remove the pan sides and set the cake on a platter. Frost the sides and top of the cake with the whipped cream. Decorate the top with the chocolate shavings and the sides with the crushed amaretti. Cut into wedges to serve.

··· ⟲ ···

PLANNING AHEAD

The cake may be made a day in advance, but frost the cake and decorate with the chocolate shavings and cookie crumbs the day you serve it. Keep refrigerated until serving.

DRUNKEN CHOCOLATE CAKE

— SERVES 8 TO 10 —

This cake is an adaptation of a cake that originated with Bjorn Olson, a good cook turned architect and a friend of Jeremiah's. It is aptly named because of the amount of rum in it.

CHOCOLATE CAKE

4½ OUNCES BITTERSWEET CHOCOLATE,
    COARSELY CHOPPED

3 OUNCES (6 TABLESPOONS) UNSALTED BUTTER

½ CUP DARK RUM

3 LARGE EGGS, SEPARATED

½ PLUS ⅓ CUP GRANULATED SUGAR

¾ CUP ALL-PURPOSE FLOUR

PINCH OF KOSHER SALT

CHOCOLATE GLAZE

¾ CUP HEAVY WHIPPING CREAM

6 OUNCES BITTERSWEET CHOCOLATE, CHOPPED

1 RECIPE CHANTILLY CREAM (PAGE 276)

To make the cake: Preheat the oven to 350°F. Line the bottom of a 9-inch round cake pan with parchment paper.

Melt the chocolate, butter, and rum together in a double boiler. (See page 19 for tips on melting chocolate.) Whisk until smooth and set aside to cool to lukewarm.

Combine the egg yolks and ½ cup of the sugar in the bowl of a stand mixer fitted with the whip attachment and whip on high speed until thick, about 3 minutes. Reduce the speed to medium-low and mix in the chocolate mixture until blended. Add the flour and salt and mix until blended.

Wash and dry the whip attachment. Put the egg whites in a clean mixer bowl, fit the mixer with the clean whip, and beat on medium speed until frothy. Increase the speed to high and whip until soft peaks form. Slowly add the remaining ⅓ cup sugar and whip until stiff peaks form.

Using a spatula, fold half of the egg whites into the chocolate batter. When they are almost completely incorporated, fold in the remaining egg whites just until no white streaks remain. Gently spread the batter into the prepared pan.

Bake until a skewer inserted into the center comes out clean, about 35 minutes. Let cool to room temperature. Line a baking sheet with parchment paper. Run a knife around the inside edge of the cake pan to loosen the cake, invert a wire rack on top of the cake, and invert the pan and rack together. Lift off the pan. Place the rack on the prepared baking sheet.

To make the chocolate glaze: In a small, heavy saucepan, bring the cream to a boil over high heat. Remove from the heat, add the chocolate, and whisk until smooth. Let the glaze cool until it thickens slightly but is still pourable, 30 to 60 minutes.

Slowly pour the glaze evenly over the top of the cake, allowing it to run down the sides. When the glaze stops dripping, use a large metal spatula to transfer the cake to a platter. Let the glaze continue to set before serving, about 1 hour.

Cut the cake with a hot, dry knife (see page 22). Serve with the chantilly cream.

··· ⌒ ···

PLANNING AHEAD

The cake may be made a day in advance. Cover it with a cake cover or invert a large bowl over it (plastic wrap will stick to the glaze) and store at room temperature. If the weather is hot, keep refrigerated and bring to room temperature before serving.

GINGERBREAD WITH WARM APPLES AND CIDER SABAYON

— SERVES 6 —

Of all the recipes in *Stars Desserts* and *Four Star Desserts*, this is the one I make the most often, and also the one people tell me they make again and again. Dessert doesn't get much better than this.

GINGERBREAD

BUTTER FOR THE PAN

1½ CUPS WATER *[handwritten: 2 ¼]*

1 CUP MOLASSES *[handwritten: 1 ½]*

1 TEASPOON BAKING SODA *[handwritten: 1 ½]*

2½ CUPS ALL-PURPOSE FLOUR *[handwritten: 3¾]*

2 TEASPOONS GROUND GINGER *[handwritten: 3]*

1¼ TEASPOONS GROUND CINNAMON *[handwritten: 2]*

PINCH OF GROUND CLOVES *[handwritten: 1/2]*

1 TABLESPOON BAKING POWDER *[handwritten: 1 ½]*

½ TEASPOON KOSHER SALT *[handwritten: 1]*

4 OUNCES (8 TABLESPOONS) UNSALTED BUTTER, *[handwritten: 6]*
   AT ROOM TEMPERATURE

1 CUP BROWN SUGAR *[handwritten: 1/2]*

1 LARGE EGG *[handwritten: 2]*

WARM APPLES

1 OUNCE (2 TABLESPOONS) UNSALTED BUTTER

7 FIRM, JUICY APPLES (ABOUT 7 POUNDS), PEELED, HALVED, CORED, AND SLICED ³⁄₁₆ INCH THICK

½ CUP GRANULATED SUGAR

2 TABLESPOONS APPLE JUICE OR CALVADOS

2 TABLESPOONS FRESHLY SQUEEZED LEMON JUICE

PINCH OF KOSHER SALT

1 RECIPE CIDER SABAYON (PAGE 281)

To make the gingerbread: Preheat the oven to 350°F. Butter a 9-inch square baking pan.

In a small saucepan, bring the water to a boil. Remove from the heat and stir in the molasses and baking soda. Set aside to cool to lukewarm. Sift together the flour, ginger, cinnamon, cloves, and baking powder onto a piece of parchment paper or into a bowl. Add the salt and set aside.

Combine the butter and sugar in the bowl of a stand mixer fitted with the paddle attachment and beat on medium-high speed until light and fluffy, about 2 minutes. Add the egg and beat until incorporated. Reduce the speed to low and add the dry ingredients in 3 additions, alternating with the cooled molasses mixture in 2 additions, beginning and ending with the dry ingredients and mixing well after each addition. Spread the batter into the prepared pan.

Bake until a skewer inserted into the center comes out clean, 30 to 35 minutes. Let cool to room temperature.

To prepare the apples: In a large sauté pan, combine the butter, apples, sugar, apple juice, lemon juice, and salt and cook, stirring occasionally, until the apples are soft but still retain their shape, about 10 minutes.

Cut the gingerbread into pieces. Top with the warm apples and the cider sabayon.

··· ⌒~⌒ ···

PLANNING AHEAD
The gingerbread may be made a day in advance. Wrap in plastic wrap and store at room temperature. The apples may be cooked 2 days in advance, covered, and refrigerated. Reheat before serving.

GRANDMOTHERS' CHOCOLATE CAKE

— SERVES 10 TO 12 —

Half of this cake comes from my grandmother, and the other half from my husband's grandmother. I grew up eating the chocolate frosting and my husband grew up eating the cake. Put the components together and all that is missing is a tall glass of milk.

CHOCOLATE CAKE

BUTTER FOR THE PANS

1½ CUPS UNSWEETENED COCOA POWDER

1¼ CUPS BOILING WATER

1½ CUPS CAKE FLOUR

1½ CUPS ALL-PURPOSE FLOUR

1¼ TEASPOONS BAKING POWDER

1¼ TEASPOONS BAKING SODA

1¼ CUPS BUTTERMILK

1¼ TEASPOONS VANILLA EXTRACT

5 OUNCES (10 TABLESPOONS) UNSALTED BUTTER,
AT ROOM TEMPERATURE

2¾ CUPS FIRMLY PACKED BROWN SUGAR

3 LARGE EGGS

BITTERSWEET CHOCOLATE FROSTING

4 OUNCES BITTERSWEET CHOCOLATE,
COARSELY CHOPPED

8 OUNCES UNSWEETENED CHOCOLATE,
COARSELY CHOPPED

8 OUNCES (16 TABLESPOONS) UNSALTED BUTTER

3 CUPS CONFECTIONERS' SUGAR

PINCH OF KOSHER SALT

¾ CUP PLUS 2 TABLESPOONS MILK

2 TEASPOONS VANILLA EXTRACT

To make the cake: Preheat the oven to 350°F. Butter three 9-inch round cake pans and line the bottoms with parchment paper.

In a small heatproof bowl, whisk together the cocoa and the boiling water to make a smooth paste. Sift together the cake flour, all-purpose flour, baking powder, and baking soda onto a piece of parchment paper or into a bowl. In a small bowl or measuring cup, stir together the buttermilk and vanilla. Set aside separately.

Combine the butter and brown sugar in the bowl of a stand mixer fitted with the paddle attachment and beat on medium-high speed until light and smooth, about 2 minutes. Add the eggs one at a time, mixing well after each addition. Reduce the speed to low and add the dry ingredients in 3 additions, alternating with the buttermilk mixture in 2 additions, beginning and ending with the dry ingredients and mixing well after each addition. Add the cocoa paste and mix until combined. Divide the batter evenly among the 3 prepared pans.

Bake until a skewer inserted into the center comes out clean, about 25 minutes. Let cool to room temperature. Run a knife around the inside edge of each pan to loosen the cake. Working with 1 cake at a time, invert a platter on top of the pan and invert the plate and pan together. Lift off the pan. Carefully remove the parchment paper and set the layer aside.

To make the frosting: Melt the bittersweet and unsweetened chocolates and butter together in a double boiler. (See page 19 for tips on melting chocolate.) Remove from the heat, whisk until smooth, and set aside to cool to lukewarm.

Sift the confectioners' sugar into a large bowl and stir in the salt. Whisk the milk and then the vanilla into the confectioners' sugar. Add the melted chocolate mixture and stir until smooth. The frosting should be thick enough to be spreadable.

If it is too thin, let it sit for 10 to 15 minutes at room temperature.

Place a cake layer on a platter. Using an icing spatula, spread frosting on top, creating a layer about ⅜ inch thick. Top with a second cake layer and again spread with frosting about ⅜ inch thick. Place the third cake layer on top and frost the top and sides of the cake with the remaining frosting. Cut into wedges to serve.

PLANNING AHEAD

The cake may be made a day in advance. Once the frosting has set, cover loosely with plastic wrap and store at room temperature.

LEMON CURD CAKE

— SERVES 8 TO 10 —

This cake is moist and lemony. It is full of flavor on its own, but garnishing it with a scattering of juicy organic raspberries is an addition with which no one will argue.

4 LARGE EGG YOLKS

2 LARGE WHOLE EGGS

2¾ CUPS GRANULATED SUGAR

½ CUP PLUS 3 TABLESPOONS FRESHLY SQUEEZED
  LEMON JUICE

BUTTER AND FLOUR FOR THE PAN

2 CUPS SIFTED CAKE FLOUR

1 TABLESPOON BAKING POWDER

½ TEASPOON KOSHER SALT

2 OUNCES (4 TABLESPOONS) UNSALTED BUTTER,
  AT ROOM TEMPERATURE

2 TEASPOONS FINELY CHOPPED LEMON ZEST

6 LARGE EGG WHITES

1 TABLESPOON CONFECTIONERS' SUGAR

In a stainless-steel bowl, whisk together the egg yolks, whole eggs, and ½ cup of the granulated sugar. Whisk in ½ cup of the lemon juice. Place the bowl over a pan of simmering water, making sure the bottom of the bowl does not touch the water, and heat, stirring occasionally, until the mixture is thick, about 5 minutes. (See page 18 for tips on using and making a double boiler.) Remove from the heat and strain through a fine-mesh sieve into a clean bowl. Cover with plastic wrap, pressing it directly on the surface, and refrigerate until cold, about 1 hour.

Preheat the oven to 325°F. Butter a 9-inch round springform pan and dust with flour, tapping out the excess.

Sift together the cake flour, ¾ cup of the sugar, and the baking powder onto a piece of parchment paper or into a bowl. Add the salt and set aside. In a large bowl, stir together the cold lemon curd, butter, lemon zest, and the remaining 3 tablespoons lemon juice. Stir in the dry ingredients until well blended.

Put the egg whites in the bowl of a stand mixer fitted with the whip attachment and whip on medium speed until frothy. Increase the speed to high, slowly add the remaining 1½ cups granulated sugar, and whip until soft peaks form. Using a spatula, fold the egg whites into the batter. Spread the cake batter into the prepared pan.

Bake until a skewer inserted into the center comes out clean, 50 to 55 minutes. Let cool to room temperature. Run a knife around the inside edge of the pan to loosen the cake, then remove the pan sides. Invert a platter on top of the cake and invert the plate and pan together. Lift off the pan bottom. Using a large metal spatula, turn the cake right-side up on a serving plate.

Dust the top of the cake with the confectioners' sugar and serve.

··· ◡◠◯ ···

The cake may be made a day in advance. Wrap in plastic wrap and store at room temperature. Dust with sugar just before serving.

COOKIES & CANDIES

— CHAPTER 7 —

At Stars, we often changed the cookies on our cookie plate but several always had to be there. Our customers would have staged a revolt if we omitted the Stareos, Ginger Cookies, or Lemon Squares. Some regulars would request a cookie plate with only a single type, and we would see them wrapping what they did not eat in a cocktail napkin and slipping the napkin into their coat pockets for a treat later.

Cookies and candies are the rubies and emeralds of desserts. They can stand on their own, free of garnishes, and be as satisfying as any plated dessert. You can also enjoy them all day long. Dip biscotti in your morning coffee, nibble on a macaroon for a pick-me-up in mid-afternoon, or treat yourself to a mint-scented chocolate truffle after dinner. At any moment of the day, these jewels of the dessert repertoire are there to deliver the small, sweet bite you crave.

216
CHOCOLATE CHIP COOKIES

217
CINNAMON SUGAR COOKIES

218
GINGER COOKIES

220
SHORTBREAD COOKIES

222
CHINESE ALMOND COOKIES

223
RUSSIAN TEA CAKES

224
CHOCOLATE MERINGUE COOKIES

225
COCONUT MACAROONS

226
COCONUT HAYSTACKS

227
COCONUT SESAME COOKIES

228
BROWN BUTTER MADELEINES

230
MARMALADE WINDOW COOKIES

231
MACADAMIA NUT BISCOTTI

232
ALMOND BISCOTTI

234
DOUBLE-CHOCOLATE BISCOTTI

236
THREE-CHOCOLATE BROWNIES

237
CHOCOLATE-PEPPERMINT BROWNIES

238
BLACK-AND-WHITE BROWNIES

239
STAREOS

249
LEMON SQUARES

250
DATE BARS

251
CHOCOLATE ALMOND BARK

252
WHITE CHOCOLATE–MINT TRUFFLES

254
COFFEE TOFFEE

255
SPICED NUTS

CHOCOLATE CHIP COOKIES

— MAKES ABOUT 36 COOKIES —

There are an infinite number of chocolate chip cookie recipes, but this one is among the best. Big and full of chips and not too sweet, these cookies are loyal to the Toll House tradition. Usually I find light and dark brown sugars interchangeable, but in this case I like to use both.

2½ CUPS ALL-PURPOSE FLOUR

1 TEASPOON BAKING SODA

1 TEASPOON KOSHER SALT

8 OUNCES (16 TABLESPOONS) UNSALTED BUTTER, AT ROOM TEMPERATURE

1 CUP FIRMLY PACKED LIGHT BROWN SUGAR

1 CUP FIRMLY PACKED DARK BROWN SUGAR

2 LARGE EGGS

1 TEASPOON VANILLA EXTRACT

2½ CUPS BITTERSWEET CHOCOLATE CHIPS

Preheat the oven to 350°F. Line 2 baking sheets with parchment paper.

In a bowl, stir together the flour, baking soda, and salt. Set aside.

Put the butter in the bowl of a stand mixer fitted with the paddle attachment and beat on medium speed until smooth, about 30 seconds. Slowly add the brown sugars and again beat until smooth, about 1 minute. Add the eggs one at a time, mixing well after each addition. Mix in the vanilla until incorporated. Remove the bowl from the mixer stand and, using a spatula, fold in the dry ingredients just until combined. Fold in the chocolate chips, distributing them evenly.

To shape each cookie, using a spoon or ice-cream scoop, scoop up a spoonful of the dough and roll between your palms into a 1½-inch ball. As the balls are formed, place on the prepared baking sheets, spacing them 2½ inches apart. If you want the baked cookies to be taller, refrigerate the dough for 1 hour. If you don't mind them a little flatter, you can bake them right away.

Bake until golden brown, about 14 minutes. At the midway point, switch the baking sheets between the racks and rotate them 180 degrees to ensure even baking. Let cool on the baking sheets for 5 minutes. You may then transfer them to wire racks or leave then on the pans to cool further. Serve warm or at room temperature.

PLANNING AHEAD

The dough may be made up to a week in advance and kept in the refrigerator. The cookies are best warm, but they may be made a day ahead and stored in an airtight container at room temperature.

CINNAMON SUGAR COOKIES

— MAKES ABOUT 36 COOKIES —

I remember these cookies, affectionately called snickerdoodles, from my childhood. They were among the few cookies that could compete against the popular chocolate chip. Slightly underbaking them will result in a soft, chewy texture, while leaving them in the oven for the full amount of time will yield crisp cookies.

1⅓ CUPS ALL-PURPOSE FLOUR

1 TEASPOON CREAM OF TARTAR

½ TEASPOON BAKING SODA

PINCH OF KOSHER SALT

4 OUNCES (8 TABLESPOONS) UNSALTED BUTTER, AT ROOM TEMPERATURE

¾ CUP PLUS 1½ TABLESPOONS SUGAR

1 LARGE EGG

½ TEASPOON VANILLA EXTRACT

1 TEASPOON GROUND CINNAMON

Preheat the oven to 350°F. Line 2 baking sheets with parchment paper.

In a bowl, stir together the flour, cream of tartar, baking soda, and salt. Set aside.

Combine the butter and ¾ cup of the sugar in the bowl of a stand mixer fitted with the paddle attachment and beat on medium-high speed until light and fluffy, about 1 minute. Add the egg and vanilla and beat until smooth. Reduce the speed to low and mix in the dry ingredients until combined.

In a small, shallow bowl, stir together the remaining 1½ tablespoons sugar and the cinnamon. To shape each cookie, using a small spoon or ice-cream scoop, scoop up a spoonful of the dough and then roll between your palms into a 1-inch ball. As the balls are formed, roll them in the cinnamon sugar, coating evenly, and then place on the prepared baking sheets, spacing them 2 inches apart.

Bake until golden brown, about 12 minutes. At the midway point, switch the baking sheets between the racks and rotate them 180 degrees to ensure even baking. Let cool on the baking sheets to room temperature.

PLANNING AHEAD

The cookies may be made a day in advance. Store them in an airtight container at room temperature.

GINGER COOKIES

In the Grill Room, the private dining room at Stars, we served these cookies hot from the oven with coffee. The gentle ginger flavor rounded off guests' taste buds at the end of a multicourse meal. They were also a staff favorite, so I always made extra for the waiters to nibble on while they cleaned up after the parties ended. The baking time given here is for soft cookies. For crispier cookies or to use the cookies for a crumb crust, bake for 14 minutes.

2 ¼ CUPS ALL-PURPOSE FLOUR

2 TEASPOONS BAKING SODA

2 TEASPOONS GROUND GINGER

1 TEASPOON GROUND CINNAMON

½ TEASPOON GROUND ALLSPICE

½ TEASPOON KOSHER SALT

¼ TEASPOON GROUND WHITE PEPPER

¾ CUP GRANULATED SUGAR

½ CUP FIRMLY PACKED LIGHT BROWN SUGAR

8 OUNCES (16 TABLESPOONS) UNSALTED BUTTER, AT ROOM TEMPERATURE

1 LARGE EGG

⅓ CUP LIGHT OR DARK MOLASSES

In a bowl, stir together the flour, baking soda, ginger, cinnamon, allspice, salt, and pepper. Set aside.

Combine ½ cup of the granulated sugar, the brown sugar, and the butter in the bowl of a stand mixer fitted with the paddle attachment and beat on medium speed until smooth, about 1 minute. Add the egg and beat until mixed, then beat in the molasses until blended. Reduce the speed to low, add the dry ingredients, and mix until incorporated. Refrigerate the dough for 30 minutes.

Preheat the oven to 325°F. Line 2 baking sheets with parchment paper.

Spread the remaining ¼ cup granulated sugar in a small, shallow bowl. To shape each cookie, using a small spoon or ice-cream scoop, scoop up a spoonful of the dough and roll between your palms into a ¾-inch ball. As the balls are formed, roll them in the sugar, coating evenly, and then place on the prepared baking sheets, spacing them 2 to 3 inches apart. Flatten the balls slightly with 2 fingers.

Bake until golden brown and set around the edges but still soft inside, about 12 minutes. At the midway point, switch the baking sheets between the racks and rotate them 180 degrees to ensure even baking. Let cool on the baking sheets to room temperature.

PLANNING AHEAD
The dough may be made up to a week in advance and kept in the refrigerator. The cookies may be baked a day ahead. Store in an airtight container at room temperature.

SHORTBREAD COOKIES

— MAKES 24 COOKIES —

We baked shortbread at Stars every day. For a Meals on Wheels gala in New York, I made thirty-five hundred shortbread cookies, packed them between layers of bubble wrap, and took them as my carry-on luggage on my flight to the East Coast. I stared at the overhead bin for the entire ride, making sure no one jostled them. At Rockefeller Center, I served the cookies with berries and cream. You can freeze the cutout unbaked cookies and slip them into the oven straight from the freezer. Over the years, we created many variations, but we could never decide which one we liked best. There's no need to pick your favorite—you can make them all. Here is a master recipe with four variations.

8 OUNCES (16 TABLESPOONS) COLD UNSALTED
BUTTER, CUT INTO ½-INCH PIECES

½ CUP GRANULATED SUGAR

2 CUPS ALL-PURPOSE FLOUR

PINCH OF KOSHER SALT

FLOUR FOR DUSTING

Combine the butter and sugar in the bowl of a stand mixer fitted with the paddle attachment and beat on low speed until the butter and sugar begin to incorporate, about 15 seconds. Add the flour and salt and continue to mix until the dough comes together, about 3 minutes. It will look dry just before it comes together.

Line 2 baking sheets with parchment paper. On a lightly floured work surface, roll out the dough ¼ inch thick. Using a 2-inch star cutter or other shaped cutter, cut out as many cookies as possible. Gather together the scraps, reroll, and cut out more cookies. You should have about 24 cookies. Place the cookies on the prepared baking sheets, spacing them 1 inch apart. Refrigerate until firm, at least 1 hour.

Preheat the oven to 300°F.

Bake the shortbread until firm, about 35 minutes. At the midway point, switch the baking sheets between the racks and rotate them 180 degrees to ensure even baking. Let cool on the baking sheets to room temperature.

Hazelnut Shortbread: In a food processor, pulse ½ cup (about 2 ounces) toasted and skinned hazelnuts (see page 20) until finely ground. Add the ground nuts with the flour. Proceed as directed.

Espresso Shortbread: Reduce the flour to 1¾ cups and add ¼ cup espresso-grind (extrafine) coffee with the flour. Proceed as directed.

Orange Shortbread: Add the grated zest of 2 oranges with the butter and sugar. Proceed as directed.

Cinnamon Shortbread: Add ½ teaspoon ground cinnamon with the flour. Proceed as directed.

··· ✺ ···

The shortbread dough may be made and cut out a week in advance. Wrap tightly and refrigerate or freeze. The cookies may be baked 2 days in advance. Store in an airtight container at room temperature.

CHINESE ALMOND COOKIES

— MAKES 36 COOKIES —

Katherine, a cook at Restaurant 690, which Jeremiah opened
near Stars, created these cookies. They are similar to those found in
Chinatowns everywhere and were a favorite at both Stars and the
Peak Café in Hong Kong.

1 TABLESPOON WATER

1 TEASPOON BAKING POWDER

½ TEASPOON BAKING SODA

8 OUNCES (16 TABLESPOONS) UNSALTED BUTTER,
AT ROOM TEMPERATURE

2 CUPS CONFECTIONERS' SUGAR

2 LARGE EGGS

¾ TEASPOON ALMOND EXTRACT

2 CUPS ALL-PURPOSE FLOUR

⅓ CUP (ABOUT 1 OUNCE) SLICED ALMONDS,
TOASTED (SEE PAGE 20)

FLOUR FOR DUSTING

36 WHOLE NATURAL ALMONDS,
TOASTED (SEE PAGE 20)

In a small bowl, stir together the water, baking
powder, and baking soda. Set aside.

Put the butter in the bowl of a stand mixer fitted
with the paddle attachment and beat on medium
speed until smooth, about 1 minute. Slowly add the
sugar, again beating until smooth, about 30 seconds.
Add the water mixture and beat until combined, and
then beat in 1 egg and the almond extract. Reduce
the speed to low, add the flour and sliced almonds,
and mix until the dough comes together, about

15 seconds. Cover the dough and refrigerate until
firm, about 1 hour.

Preheat the oven to 325°F. Line 2 baking
sheets with parchment paper.

On a lightly floured work surface, divide the
dough in half. Shape each half into a log about
9 inches long and 1 inch in diameter. Cut each log
crosswise into slices ½ inch thick. (If the cookies do
not stay round when you cut them, the dough is too
soft. Refrigerate until firm enough to slice, about
30 minutes.) Place the cookies on the prepared
baking sheets, spacing them about 2 inches apart.
Press a whole almond into the middle of each cookie.
In a small bowl or cup, lightly beat the remaining
egg. Brush the cookies with the beaten egg.

Bake until golden brown, about 10 minutes.
At the midway point, switch the baking sheets
between the racks and rotate them 180 degrees to
ensure even baking. Let cool on the baking sheets
to room temperature.

PLANNING AHEAD

The cookies may be made up to 2 days in advance.
Store in an airtight container at room temperature.

RUSSIAN TEA CAKES

— MAKES ABOUT 48 COOKIES —

Bakers in many eastern European countries make a version of this cookie. This is the favorite recipe of Yugoslavian-born Denise Hale, who lives in San Francisco and commissioned the recipe so that she would have the cookies for weekends at her ranch and for her luncheons at Stars. You can substitute hazelnuts or walnuts for the pecans or use a mixture of all three.

1¾ CUPS (6 OUNCES) PECANS, TOASTED (SEE PAGE 20)

6 TABLESPOONS GRANULATED SUGAR

8 OUNCES (16 TABLESPOONS) UNSALTED BUTTER, AT ROOM TEMPERATURE

½ TEASPOON VANILLA EXTRACT

2 CUPS ALL-PURPOSE FLOUR

½ TEASPOON KOSHER SALT

¼ CUP CONFECTIONERS' SUGAR

Preheat the oven to 325°F. Line 2 baking sheets with parchment paper.

In a food processor, combine the pecans and 2 tablespoons of the granulated sugar and process until the nuts are finely ground. Set aside.

Combine the butter and the remaining 4 tablespoons granulated sugar in the bowl of a stand mixer fitted with the paddle attachment and beat on medium-high speed until light and fluffy, about 1 minute. Add the vanilla and beat until combined. Reduce the speed to low, add the flour, salt, and ground nuts, and mix until incorporated.

To shape each cookie, using a small spoon or ice-cream scoop, scoop up a spoonful of the dough and then roll between your palms into a 1-inch ball. As the balls are formed, place on the prepared baking sheets, spacing them 1 inch apart.

Bake until light brown, about 20 minutes. At the midway point, switch the baking sheets between the racks and rotate them 180 degrees to ensure even baking. Remove the cookies from the oven and, while they are still hot, dust them with the confectioners' sugar. Let cool on the baking sheets to room temperature.

PLANNING AHEAD
The cookies may be made 2 days ahead. Store in an airtight container at room temperature.

CHOCOLATE MERINGUE COOKIES

— MAKES ABOUT 24 COOKIES —

Made without butter, these appealingly rough-looking cookies are ideal when you crave something chocolate and sweet but you don't want something too rich or indulgent.

3 EGG WHITES

½ CUP GRANULATED SUGAR

¾ CUP BITTERSWEET CHOCOLATE CHIPS

1 TABLESPOON UNSWEETENED COCOA POWDER

¼ TEASPOON VANILLA EXTRACT

Preheat the oven to 300°F. Line 2 baking sheets with parchment paper.

Put the egg whites in the bowl of a stand mixer fitted with the whip attachment and whip on medium speed until frothy. Increase the speed to medium-high and whip until soft peaks form. Slowly add the sugar in a steady stream and continue to whip until firm, satiny peaks form.

Using a spatula, fold in the chocolate chips, cocoa powder, and vanilla. Do not overmix. The batter should have some brown and white streaks. To form the cookies, drop the batter by the heaping tablespoonful onto the prepared baking sheets, spacing them about 2 inches apart.

Bake until dry on the outside but still soft inside, about 25 minutes. At the midway point, switch the baking sheets between the racks and rotate them 180 degrees to ensure even baking. Let cool on the baking sheets to room temperature.

PLANNING AHEAD

The cookies may be made a day ahead. Store in an airtight container at room temperature.

COCONUT MACAROONS

— MAKES 36 COOKIES —

You can vary the taste of macaroons by using different kinds of honey. California wildflower, French lavender, or Australian blue gum honey produces equally good but quite different results. I like these macaroons crusty on the outside and soft inside. If you like them soft inside and out, bake at 300°F for 20 minutes.

½ CUP (ABOUT 4) LARGE EGG WHITES

1¼ CUPS GRANULATED SUGAR

1 TABLESPOON HONEY

½ TEASPOON VANILLA EXTRACT

2⅔ CUPS UNSWEETENED SHREDDED COCONUT

½ CUP PLUS 2 TABLESPOONS CAKE FLOUR

4 OUNCES BITTERSWEET CHOCOLATE, COARSELY CHOPPED

In a stainless-steel bowl, whisk together the egg whites, sugar, honey, and vanilla until blended. Place over a pan of simmering water and cook, whisking occasionally, until hot, about 2 minutes. (See page 18 for tips on using and making a double boiler.) Remove the bowl from the heat and stir in the coconut and flour until incorporated. Refrigerate the dough until firm, about 1 hour.

Preheat the oven to 325°F. Line 2 baking sheets with parchment paper.

To shape each cookie, using a small spoon or ice-cream scoop, scoop up the dough into 1-inch balls. As the cookies are formed, place them on the prepared baking sheets, spacing them about 2 inches apart.

Bake until golden brown, about 15 minutes. At the midway point, switch the baking sheets between the racks and rotate them 180 degrees to ensure even baking. Let cool on the baking sheets to room temperature.

Melt the chocolate in a double boiler. (See page 19 for tips on melting chocolate.) Whisk until smooth and let cool until warm. Line a baking sheet with fresh parchment paper. With a table knife or small icing spatula, spread a thin layer of chocolate on the bottom of each macaroon. Place the cookies, chocolate-side down, on the prepared baking sheet. Let stand until the chocolate is set, about 1 hour.

PLANNING AHEAD

The macaroons may be made 2 days ahead. Store in an airtight container at room temperature.

COCONUT HAYSTACKS

— MAKES ABOUT 18 —

These simple-to-make chocolate-covered stacks of coconut look like little piles of hay. You can add ¼ cup coarsely chopped dried cranberries or cherries to increase your fruit intake for the day.

8 OUNCES BITTERSWEET CHOCOLATE,
FINELY CHOPPED

1 CUP SWEETENED FLAKED COCONUT, TOASTED
(SEE PAGE 22)

Line a baking sheet with parchment paper. Melt the chocolate in a double boiler just until melted but not hot. (See page 19 for tips on melting chocolate.) Remove from the heat and stir until smooth. Stir in the coconut.

Using 2 small spoons, a small ice-cream scoop, or your fingers, form the chocolate-and-coconut mixture into mounds about 1½ inches tall (about 1 tablespoon each) and place them on the prepared baking sheet about ½ inch apart. Refrigerate until set, about 1 hour.

··· ◦◦◦ ···

PLANNING AHEAD

The coconut haystacks are best served the day they are made. They may be made a day ahead and stored in an airtight container at room temperature, but because the chocolate is not tempered, they may bloom (get a speckled appearance). Being careful not to overheat the chocolate will help prevent this from happening. Don't worry if the chocolate does discolor, as the taste will not be affected.

COCONUT SESAME COOKIES

— MAKES 36 COOKIES —

This recipe comes from Joyce Orenstein, the mother of my friend (and fellow pastry chef) Julia Orenstein. When the cookies brown, the sugar caramelizes, giving them a rich flavor and crisp texture. The cookies are incredible served with a simple tropical fruit compote of pineapples, papaya, mangoes, and bananas.

7 OUNCES (14 TABLESPOONS) UNSALTED BUTTER, AT ROOM TEMPERATURE

⅔ CUP GRANULATED SUGAR

1¼ CUPS ALL-PURPOSE FLOUR

⅓ CUP PLUS 2 TEASPOONS SESAME SEEDS

¾ CUP SWEETENED SHREDDED COCONUT

¼ CUP (ABOUT 1 OUNCE) SLICED ALMONDS, TOASTED (SEE PAGE 20)

FLOUR FOR DUSTING

Combine the butter and sugar in the bowl of a stand mixer fitted with the paddle attachment and beat on medium speed until smooth, about 30 seconds. Reduce the speed to low, add the flour, ⅓ cup of the sesame seeds, the coconut, and the almonds, and mix just until incorporated.

On a lightly floured board, divide the dough in half. Shape each half into a log about 9 inches long. Wrap the logs separately in plastic wrap and refrigerate until firm, about 1 hour.

Preheat the oven to 350°F. Line 2 baking sheets with parchment paper.

Cut each log crosswise into rounds about ⅜ inch thick, and place the rounds on the prepared baking sheets, spacing them about 2 inches apart. Sprinkle the remaining sesame seeds on top of the cookies.

Bake until golden brown, about 20 minutes. At the midway point, switch the baking sheets between the racks and rotate them 180 degrees to ensure even baking. Let cool on the sheets.

··· ⌾ ···

PLANNING AHEAD

The cookies may be made several days in advance. Store in an airtight container at room temperature.

BROWN BUTTER MADELEINES

— MAKES 24 COOKIES —

Traditional tea cakes of Proustian fame, madeleines are good
with a cup of hot tea or an espresso. They are particularly good when
made with European-style butter, which has a higher butterfat
content than regular butter and thus delivers greater richness, while
browning the butter adds a distinctive flavor. Use butter to coat
the madeleine molds, not nonstick spray. The madeleines will release
from the pan much easier.

BUTTER AND FLOUR FOR THE MOLDS

6 OUNCES (12 TABLESPOONS) UNSALTED BUTTER

4 LARGE EGGS

PINCH OF KOSHER SALT

⅔ CUP GRANULATED SUGAR

1 TEASPOON GRATED LEMON ZEST

1 TEASPOON VANILLA EXTRACT

¾ CUP ALL-PURPOSE FLOUR

CONFECTIONERS' SUGAR FOR DUSTING

Preheat the oven to 350°F. Butter twenty-four 3-inch madeleine molds and coat with flour, tapping out the excess.

In a small saucepan, melt the butter over medium heat and cook until it is golden brown and gives off a nutty aroma, about 3 minutes.

Strain through a fine-mesh sieve placed over a small bowl. Discard the brown pieces. Let cool to room temperature.

Combine the eggs and salt in the bowl of a stand mixer fitted with the whip attachment and whip on high speed until thick, about 3 minutes. Reduce the speed to medium and slowly add the sugar in a steady stream. Increase the speed to high and whip for 3 minutes. The mixture should be thick enough so that when you lift a bit of it with the whip, it falls slowly back into the bowl in a ribbon that dissolves on the surface. Reduce the speed to low and mix in the lemon zest and vanilla.

Using a spatula, alternately fold in the flour and butter in 3 additions each, beginning with the flour and making sure each addition is fully incorporated before adding the next one. Spoon batter into each of the prepared molds.

Bake until the madeleines are golden brown and spring back when lightly touched, 12 to 15 minutes. Remove from the oven and unmold them immediately by tapping the edge of the pan on the counter. You may have to tap it a couple of times to release them all. Let cool to room temperature on a wire rack. Dust with the confectioners' sugar.

··· ⌒ ···

PLANNING AHEAD

The madeleines are best eaten the day they are made. Store covered at room temperature.

MARMALADE WINDOW COOKIES

— MAKES ABOUT 24 COOKIES —

A straightforward sandwich cookie is dressed up by cutting out a decorative shape in the center of the top cookie. When I present sweets with fillings, I like to give people a hint of what is inside.

8 OUNCES (16 TABLESPOONS) UNSALTED BUTTER,
    AT ROOM TEMPERATURE

1 CUP GRANULATED SUGAR

GRATED ZEST OF 1 LEMON

2 LARGE EGGS

½ TEASPOON VANILLA EXTRACT

4 CUPS ALL-PURPOSE FLOUR

ABOUT 1 CUP GOOD-QUALITY ORANGE MARMALADE,
    PREFERABLY WITHOUT LARGE FRUIT CHUNKS

Preheat the oven to 350°F. Line 2 baking sheets with parchment paper.

Combine the butter, sugar, and lemon zest in the bowl of a stand mixer fitted with the paddle attachment and beat on medium speed until smooth and creamy, about 30 seconds. Add the eggs and vanilla and mix well. Reduce the speed to low, add the flour, and mix just until incorporated. Form the dough into a ball, wrap in plastic wrap, and refrigerate until firm but not so hard that it cannot be rolled, about 1 hour.

On a lightly floured work surface, roll out the dough ⅛ inch thick. Using a fluted pastry wheel,

cut the dough into 2-inch squares. Gather together the scraps, reroll, and continue cutting out 2-inch squares until you have 48 squares. With a small decorative cutter, cut out the center from 24 of the squares. Place the cookie squares ¼ inch apart on the prepared baking sheets.

Bake until golden brown around the edges, about 15 minutes. At the midway point, switch the baking sheets between the racks and rotate them 180 degrees to ensure even baking. (If you like, bake the decorative cutouts along with the cookie squares. Enjoy them as mini cookies for nibbling.) Let cool on the baking sheets to room temperature.

Place 2 teaspoons marmalade in the center of each solid cookie square. Gently press the cutout cookies on top of the marmalade.

PLANNING AHEAD

The cookies may be made a day ahead. Store in an airtight container at room temperature.

MACADAMIA NUT BISCOTTI

— MAKES ABOUT 36 COOKIES —

These delicate, crumbly biscotti are just as delicious, though not as firm, as the Almond Biscotti on page 232.

1 CUP (4 OUNCES) MACADAMIA NUTS, TOASTED (SEE PAGE 20)

1½ CUPS ALL-PURPOSE FLOUR

1½ TEASPOONS BAKING POWDER

¼ TEASPOON KOSHER SALT

4 OUNCES (8 TABLESPOONS) UNSALTED BUTTER, AT ROOM TEMPERATURE

6 TABLESPOONS GRANULATED SUGAR

1 LARGE EGG

¼ TEASPOON VANILLA EXTRACT

FLOUR FOR DUSTING

Preheat the oven to 350°F. Line a baking sheet with parchment paper.

In a food processor, combine the nuts, flour, baking powder, and salt and pulse until the nuts are ground medium-fine. Set aside.

Combine the butter and sugar in the bowl of a stand mixer fitted with the paddle attachment and beat on medium speed until smooth. Add the egg and vanilla and mix until incorporated.

Add the nut-flour mixture and mix on low speed until smooth.

On a lightly floured work surface, divide the dough in half. Shape each half into a log 12 inches long. Place the logs on the prepared baking sheet, spacing them about 1½ inches apart.

Bake until the logs are lightly golden, about 20 minutes. Let cool on the baking sheet to room temperature. Reduce the oven temperature to 300°F.

Transfer the logs to a cutting board and, using a serrated knife, slice crosswise on a slight diagonal ½ inch thick. Place the slices cut-side up on the baking sheet and return to the oven. Bake until golden brown and dry on top, about 10 minutes. Let cool completely on the baking sheet.

PLANNING AHEAD

The biscotti may be made up to 1 week in advance. Store in an airtight container at room temperature.

ALMOND BISCOTTI

— MAKES ABOUT 36 COOKIES —

This recipe was developed by Jules Vranian, one of the first pastry chefs at Stars. Just like me, twenty years later, she is still baking professionally. Once you get your hands in sugar and flour, you don't want to stop. These traditional Italian biscotti are great dipped in coffee or a glass of vin santo. If desired, dip one cut side in melted chocolate, lay the cookies, chocolate-side down, on a parchment paper–lined baking sheet, until set.

3 LARGE WHOLE EGGS

3 LARGE EGG YOLKS

1 TEASPOON VANILLA EXTRACT

2¾ CUPS ALL-PURPOSE FLOUR

1⅔ CUPS GRANULATED SUGAR

1 TEASPOON BAKING POWDER

½ TEASPOON KOSHER SALT

1 TEASPOON ANISEEDS

GRATED ZEST OF 1 LEMON

GRATED ZEST OF 1 LIME

GRATED ZEST OF 1 ORANGE

1⅔ CUPS (7 OUNCES) WHOLE NATURAL ALMONDS,
    TOASTED (SEE PAGE 20)

FLOUR FOR DUSTING

Preheat the oven to 325°F. Line 2 baking sheets with parchment paper.

In a bowl, lightly whisk together the whole eggs, egg yolks, and vanilla. Set aside.

Combine the flour, sugar, baking powder, salt, aniseeds, and the citrus zests in the bowl of a stand mixer fitted with the paddle attachment. Beat on low speed until mixed. Add the egg mixture and continue to mix until almost completely incorporated, about 15 seconds. Add the almonds and mix until the dough comes together.

On a lightly floured work surface, divide the dough into thirds. Shape each third into a log about 10 inches long. Place 2 logs on a prepared baking sheet, spacing them about 3 inches apart. Place the third log on the second baking sheet.

Bake until light brown, about 20 minutes. Let cool on the baking sheets to room temperature. Reduce the oven temperature to 300°F.

Transfer the logs to a cutting board and, using a serrated knife, slice crosswise on a slight diagonal ¾ inch thick. Place the slices, cut-side up, on 1 baking sheet. Bake until golden brown and dry, about 15 minutes. Let cool to room temperature.

DOUBLE-CHOCOLATE BISCOTTI

— MAKES ABOUT 32 COOKIES —

It is hard to imagine that there was a time in the United States when only Italians and foodies were familiar with biscotti. Now these crunchy treats are everywhere, from bakeries to gas-station quick stops. Like anything that brings pleasure into your life, you wonder how you ever got along without biscotti.

3 LARGE EGGS

¾ TEASPOON VANILLA EXTRACT

1⅓ CUPS ALL-PURPOSE FLOUR

1 CUP GRANULATED SUGAR

½ CUP UNSWEETENED COCOA POWDER

2¼ TEASPOONS INSTANT ESPRESSO POWDER

1½ TEASPOONS BAKING SODA

⅛ TEASPOON KOSHER SALT

⅔ CUP BITTERSWEET CHOCOLATE CHIPS

1 CUP (4 OUNCES) HAZELNUTS, TOASTED AND SKINNED (SEE PAGE 20)

FLOUR FOR DUSTING

7 OUNCES WHITE CHOCOLATE, FINELY CHOPPED

Preheat the oven to 325°F. Line a baking sheet with parchment paper.

In a bowl, lightly whisk together the eggs and vanilla. Set aside.

Combine the flour, sugar, cocoa powder, espresso powder, baking soda, salt, chocolate chips, and hazelnuts in the bowl of a stand mixer fitted with the paddle attachment and beat on low speed until evenly mixed. Add the egg mixture and mix until the dough comes together.

On a lightly floured work surface, divide the dough in half. Roll each half into a log about 12 inches long. Place the logs on the prepared baking sheet, spacing them about 3 inches apart.

Bake until the sides are firm and the tops are cracked and no longer wet looking, about 25 minutes. Let cool on the pan to room temperature. Reduce the oven temperature to 300°F.

Transfer the logs to a cutting board and, using a serrated knife, slice crosswise on a slight diagonal ¾ inch thick. Place the slices, cut-side up, on the baking sheet. Bake until dry and firm, about 25 minutes. Let cool to room temperature.

Melt the white chocolate in a double boiler. (See page 19 for tips on melting chocolate.) Whisk until smooth. Line the baking sheet with fresh parchment paper. With a table knife or small icing spatula, spread a thin layer of the white chocolate on a cut side of each cookie. Place the biscotti, chocolate-side down, on the prepared baking sheet. Let stand until the chocolate is set, about 30 minutes.

··· ༄ ···

PLANNING AHEAD

The biscotti may be made a week in advance. Store in an airtight container at room temperature.

THREE-CHOCOLATE BROWNIES

— MAKES 16 BROWNIES —

Everyone has an opinion about what makes a good brownie: cakelike or fudgy, with or without nuts. I like them fudgy. But there is one thing that everyone agrees on: the more chocolate the better. The addition of three different types of chocolate chunks to these brownies takes care of that requirement. Now, everyone can just argue over the nuts.

BUTTER FOR THE PAN

4 OUNCES UNSWEETENED CHOCOLATE,
   FINELY CHOPPED

4 OUNCES (8 TABLESPOONS) UNSALTED BUTTER,
   AT ROOM TEMPERATURE

1½ CUPS GRANULATED SUGAR

4 LARGE EGGS

1 TEASPOON VANILLA EXTRACT

2 OUNCES WHITE CHOCOLATE, CHOPPED INTO
   ¼-INCH PIECES

2 OUNCES BITTERSWEET CHOCOLATE, CHOPPED
   INTO ¼-INCH PIECES

2 OUNCES MILK CHOCOLATE, CHOPPED INTO
   ¼-INCH PIECES

¾ CUP ALL-PURPOSE FLOUR

2 TABLESPOONS UNSWEETENED COCOA POWDER

¼ TEASPOON KOSHER SALT

½ CUP (4 OUNCES) WALNUTS, TOASTED
   (SEE PAGE 20), OPTIONAL

Preheat the oven to 325°F. Butter a 9-inch square baking pan.

Melt the unsweetened chocolate in a double boiler just until melted but not hot. (See page 19 for tips on melting chocolate.) Remove from the heat and whisk until smooth.

Put the butter and sugar in the bowl of a stand mixer fitted with the paddle attachment and beat on medium speed until smooth, about 1 minute. Add the eggs two at a time, mixing well after each addition. Add the melted chocolate and the vanilla and mix until incorporated. Reduce the speed to low; add the white, bittersweet, and milk chocolate pieces and mix to distribute evenly. Mix in the flour, cocoa powder, salt, and walnuts (if using). Spread the batter into the prepared pan.

Bake until a skewer inserted into the center comes out with a moist crumb, about 30 minutes. Let cool to room temperature. Cut into 16 brownies, each about 2¼ inches square.

PLANNING AHEAD

These brownies may be made a day ahead. Store in an airtight container at room temperature.

CHOCOLATE-PEPPERMINT BROWNIES

— MAKES 24 BROWNIES —

These brownies are adapted from a cookie recipe by my grandmother, after whom I am named. I prefer to use the batter for brownies, because they come out moister than the cookies. If you don't have loose tea, slit open a few tea bags.

BROWNIES

BUTTER AND FLOUR FOR THE PAN

12 OUNCES UNSWEETENED CHOCOLATE,
   FINELY CHOPPED

12 OUNCES (24 TABLESPOONS) UNSALTED BUTTER

1 TABLESPOON PEPPERMINT TEA LEAVES

3 CUPS GRANULATED SUGAR

6 LARGE EGGS

1½ CUPS ALL-PURPOSE FLOUR

PINCH OF KOSHER SALT

GLAZE

6 OUNCES BITTERSWEET CHOCOLATE,
   FINELY CHOPPED

1½ OUNCES (3 TABLESPOONS) UNSALTED BUTTER

To make the brownies: Preheat the oven to 350°F. Butter a 9-by-13-inch baking pan and coat with flour, tapping out the excess.

Melt the chocolate and butter together in a double boiler. (See page 19 for tips on melting chocolate.) Whisk until smooth and let cool until warm. In a food processor, combine the tea leaves and sugar and process to grind finely.

In a bowl, whisk together the eggs and the sugar mixture until well combined. Stir in the melted chocolate mixture and then stir in the flour and salt. Spread the batter into the prepared pan.

Bake until a skewer inserted into the center comes out with a moist crumb, about 30 minutes. Let cool to room temperature.

To make the glaze: Melt the chocolate and butter together in a double boiler. Whisk until smooth and let cool to warm. Pour the glaze over the brownies. Let the glaze set, about 30 minutes. Cut into 24 brownies, each about 2¼ inches square.

PLANNING AHEAD

These brownies may be made a day ahead. Cover with plastic wrap and store at room temperature.

BLACK-AND-WHITE BROWNIES

— MAKES 24 BROWNIES —

In the mid-afternoon, neighborhood office workers regularly stopped by StarMart, our take-out shop, for these brownies. Don't let the addition of the cream cheese lead you to believe that these are wimpy brownies. They are intense, just as a proper brownie should be.

BUTTER FOR THE PAN

5 OUNCES BITTERSWEET CHOCOLATE,
    COARSELY CHOPPED

2 OUNCES UNSWEETENED CHOCOLATE,
    COARSELY CHOPPED

7 OUNCES (14 TABLESPOONS) UNSALTED BUTTER,
    AT ROOM TEMPERATURE

2 CUPS GRANULATED SUGAR

5 LARGE EGGS

¾ CUP ALL-PURPOSE FLOUR

PINCH OF KOSHER SALT

1¼ POUNDS CREAM CHEESE, AT
    ROOM TEMPERATURE

1 TEASPOON VANILLA EXTRACT

Preheat the oven to 325°F. Butter a 9-by-13-inch baking pan.

Melt the chocolates together in a double boiler. (See page 19 for tips on melting chocolate.) Whisk until smooth and let cool until warm.

Combine the butter and 1¼ cups of the sugar in the bowl of a stand mixer fitted with the paddle attachment and beat on medium speed until smooth, about 30 seconds. Add 3 of the eggs one at a time, mixing well after each addition. Reduce the speed to low, add the melted chocolate, and mix until smooth. Mix in the flour and salt. Measure out about 1 cup of the chocolate batter and set aside. Spread the remaining batter in the prepared pan.

Combine the cream cheese and the remaining ¾ cup sugar in a clean mixer bowl and beat on medium speed until smooth. Add the remaining 2 eggs and the vanilla and again beat until smooth. Spread the cream cheese mixture in an even layer over the chocolate batter. Scatter spoonfuls of the reserved chocolate batter over the cream cheese layer. With a knife, swirl the chocolate batter into the cream cheese layer to create a marbled effect.

Bake until a skewer inserted into the center comes out with a moist crumb, about 50 minutes. Let cool for at least 30 minutes. (The brownies are easier to cut when completely cool.) Cut into 24 brownies, each about 2¼ inches square.

··· ❧ ···

PLANNING AHEAD
The brownies may be made a day in advance. Cover with plastic wrap and store at room temperature.

STAREOS

— MAKES 18 COOKIES —

Frequently, waiters would come into the kitchen at Stars and say, "The people on table 44 want all Stareos on the cookie plate. Is that okay?" Not only was it okay, I got a kick out of the fact that customers knew exactly what they wanted and weren't shy about asking for it. These cookies are "gourmet" Oreos, a mascarpone filling sandwiched between chocolate shortbread. We cut the cookies into stars—hence their name—but you can make them whatever shape you wish.

CHOCOLATE SHORTBREAD

1½ CUPS ALL-PURPOSE FLOUR

PINCH OF KOSHER SALT

½ CUP UNSWEETENED COCOA POWDER, SIFTED

8 OUNCES (16 TABLESPOONS) COLD UNSALTED
     BUTTER, CUT INTO ½-INCH PIECES

½ CUP GRANULATED SUGAR

FLOUR FOR DUSTING

FILLING

1 CUP MASCARPONE CHEESE

1 TABLESPOON GRANULATED SUGAR

¼ TEASPOON VANILLA EXTRACT

To make the chocolate shortbread: In a bowl, stir together the flour, salt, and cocoa powder and set aside. Combine the butter and sugar in the bowl of a stand mixer fitted with the paddle attachment and beat on low speed until the butter and sugar begin to incorporate, about 15 seconds. Add the dry ingredients and continue to mix until the dough comes together, about 3 minutes. It will look dry just before it comes together.

Line 2 baking sheets with parchment paper. On a lightly floured work surface, roll out the dough ¼ inch thick. Using a 2-inch star cutter, cut out as many cookies as possible. Gather together the scraps, reroll, and continuing cutting out cookies until you have 36 cookies. Place the cookies on the prepared baking sheets, spacing them 1 inch apart. Refrigerate until firm, at least 1 hour.

Preheat the oven to 300°F. Bake the shortbread until firm, about 35 minutes. At the midway point, switch the baking sheets between the racks and rotate them 180 degrees to ensure even baking. Let cool on the baking sheets to room temperature.

CONTINUED...

CONTINUED...

To make the filling: In a small bowl, stir together the mascarpone, sugar, and vanilla until smooth.

Turn 18 of the cookies bottom-side up on a work surface. Using a table knife or small icing spatula, spread about 1 tablespoon of the filling on the bottom of each cookie. Top with the remaining cookies, bottom-side down.

··· ⌒ ···

PLANNING AHEAD

The shortbread dough may be made and cut out a week in advance. Wrap tightly and refrigerate or freeze. The cookies may be baked 2 days in advance. Store in an airtight container at room temperature. The mascarpone cream may also be made 2 days ahead. Cover and refrigerate, but bring to room temperature before assembling the sandwiches. The cookies should be assembled the day you are going to serve them and covered and refrigerated until serving.

>> STAREOS

BANANA NAPOLEONS WITH WARM CARAMEL WALNUT SAUCE ··· PAGE 170

<< GOAT CHEESE CAKE WITH MIXED BERRIES ··· PAGE 188

GINGERBREAD WITH APPLES AND CIDER SABAYON ··· PAGE 206

>> FRENCH SILK ··· PAGE 200

TORTA REGINA ··· PAGE 195

<< ESPRESSO–CHOCOLATE CHIP ANGEL FOOD CAKE ··· PAGE 184

LEMON SQUARES

— MAKES 24 SQUARES —

Lemon square aficionados swear by this recipe. I have received letters from complete strangers saying they have tried numerous lemon square recipes, and this one is the most lemony of them all. For easier cutting, let the bars sit for several hours after baking.

CRUST

1½ CUPS ALL-PURPOSE FLOUR

½ CUP CONFECTIONERS' SUGAR

6 OUNCES (12 TABLESPOONS) COLD UNSALTED
    BUTTER, CUT INTO ½-INCH PIECES

FILLING

6 LARGE EGGS

3 CUPS GRANULATED SUGAR

1 CUP PLUS 2 TABLESPOONS FRESHLY SQUEEZED
    LEMON JUICE

½ CUP ALL-PURPOSE FLOUR

ABOUT 3 TABLESPOONS CONFECTIONERS' SUGAR

To make the crust: Preheat the oven to 325°F. Combine the flour and confectioners' sugar in the bowl of a stand mixer fitted with the paddle attachment and beat on low speed until mixed. Add the butter and continue to mix until the butter is the size of small peas, about 30 seconds. The mixture will be very dry. Gently press the mixture evenly onto the bottom of a 9-by-13-inch baking pan.

Bake until golden brown, 20 to 25 minutes. Let cool to room temperature. Reduce the oven temperature to 300°F.

To make the filling: In a large bowl, whisk together the eggs and granulated sugar until smooth. Stir in the lemon juice and then the flour. Pour the filling on top of the crust.

Bake until the lemon filling is set, about 40 minutes. Let cool to room temperature and then put in the refrigerator for 1 hour or keep at room temperature for 3 hours before cutting. Cut into squares measuring about 2¼ inches and dust the tops with the confectioners' sugar.

PLANNING AHEAD

The squares may be made a day in advance, covered, and refrigerated. Bring to room temperature before serving.

<< LEMON SQUARES

DATE BARS

— MAKES 36 BARS —

These are delicious eaten on the go, but if you have a plate and spoon, they are wonderful with a big scoop of vanilla ice cream.

BUTTER FOR THE PAN

2 CUPS (12 OUNCES) FRESH DATES, PITTED

2 CUPS ALL-PURPOSE FLOUR

2 TEASPOONS BAKING POWDER

⅛ TEASPOON SALT

½ TEASPOON GROUND CINNAMON

3 OUNCES (6 TABLESPOONS) UNSALTED BUTTER,
    AT ROOM TEMPERATURE

1½ CUPS FIRMLY PACKED BROWN SUGAR

3 LARGE EGGS

¼ CUP FRESHLY SQUEEZED ORANGE JUICE

½ TEASPOON VANILLA EXTRACT

¾ CUP PECANS, TOASTED (SEE PAGE 20) AND
    COARSELY CHOPPED

Preheat the oven to 350°F. Butter a 9-inch-by-13-inch baking pan.

In a food processor, combine the dates and flour and pulse until the dates are reduced to about ½-inch pieces. Transfer to a bowl and stir in the baking powder, salt, and cinnamon.

Combine the butter and brown sugar in the bowl of a stand mixer fitted with the paddle attachment and beat on medium-high speed until smooth, about 1 minute. Add the eggs one at a time, mixing well after each addition. Reduce the speed to low, add the orange juice and vanilla, and beat until well mixed. Add the date-flour mixture and pecans and mix just until incorporated. Spread the batter into the prepared pan.

Bake until a skewer inserted into the center comes out clean, about 25 minutes. Let cool to room temperature. Cut into bars about 1½ by 2 inches.

PLANNING AHEAD

The bars may be made a day in advance. Store in an airtight container at room temperature.

CHOCOLATE ALMOND BARK

— MAKES ABOUT 1 POUND —

Chocolate bark may be made with any combination of chocolate and nuts. I like to make several kinds and put them together on a platter, creating contrasting colors, textures, and tastes. My favorite combinations are white chocolate and pistachio, bittersweet chocolate and almond, and milk chocolate and hazelnut.

8 OUNCES BITTERSWEET, MILK, OR WHITE
  CHOCOLATE, COARSELY CHOPPED
1½ CUPS (6 OUNCES) WHOLE NATURAL ALMONDS,
  PISTACHIOS, OR HAZELNUTS, TOASTED (SEE PAGE 20)

Line a baking sheet with parchment paper or a nonstick baking liner. Melt the chocolate in a double boiler just until melted but not hot. (See page 19 for tips on melting chocolate.) Remove from the heat and stir until smooth. Stir in the nuts.

Pour the chocolate-and-nut mixture onto the prepared baking sheet and spread it into a layer ¼ inch thick with an offset spatula. Let stand at room temperature until hardened, about 6 hours.

Break the bark into pieces, making them various sizes and shapes.

··· ∽ ···

PLANNING AHEAD

The bark is best eaten the day it is made. It may be made a day ahead and stored in an airtight container at room temperature, but because the chocolate is not tempered, it may bloom (get a speckled appearance). Being careful not to overheat the chocolate will help prevent this from happening. Don't worry if the chocolate does discolor, as the taste will not be affected.

WHITE CHOCOLATE—MINT TRUFFLES

— MAKES ABOUT FIFTY 1-INCH TRUFFLES —

When you are presented with a box of assorted truffles, it is difficult
to pick just one or two. I am one of those obnoxious people who likes to
cut a truffle in half, eat one of the halves, and put the remaining half
back in the box. I know it ruins it for the next person, but I can't resist
trying as many different ones as possible. White chocolate and mint
is one of my favorite mixes. Use El Rey, Valrhona, Lindt, or Callebaut
white chocolate. These brands melt thinner than others, giving you
a thinner coating and a more delicate filling. I use a mini ice-cream
scoop to form the truffles.

1 POUND 10 OUNCES WHITE CHOCOLATE,
  FINELY CHOPPED
1 CUP HEAVY WHIPPING CREAM
¼ CUP LOOSELY PACKED FRESH MINT LEAVES
1½ OUNCES BITTERSWEET CHOCOLATE,
  FINELY CHOPPED

Place 1 pound of the white chocolate in a bowl.
In a small, heavy nonreactive saucepan, heat the
cream over medium-high heat until small bubbles
appear around the edges of the pan. Remove from
the heat, add the mint leaves, cover, and let steep
for 15 minutes.

Strain the cream through a fine-mesh sieve
held over the white chocolate, discarding the
mint. Whisk together the chocolate and cream
until smooth. Cover and refrigerate until firm,
2 to 3 hours.

Line a large tray or baking sheet with parchment paper. To form each truffle, use a small
ice-cream scoop or spoon to scoop up about 1 teaspoon of the white chocolate mixture, then roll it
between your palms into a ball about 1 inch in
diameter. As the truffles are formed, place them
on the prepared tray. If the chocolate gets soft,
refrigerate again until firm, about 30 minutes.

Line 2 baking sheets with parchment paper.
Melt the remaining 10 ounces white chocolate in
a double boiler just until melted but not hot. (See
page 19 for tips on melting chocolate.) Remove

from the heat and whisk until smooth. One or two at a time, place the balls in the melted white chocolate, coating them evenly, then remove them with 2 forks, allowing any excess chocolate to drip off. Place the coated truffles on the prepared baking sheets. Refrigerate until firm, about 30 minutes.

Melt the bittersweet chocolate in a double boiler or a microwave oven. Whisk until smooth. With the tines of a fork, drizzle the bittersweet chocolate over the white chocolate truffles. Let stand until the bittersweet chocolate is hardened, about 30 minutes.

··· ❧ ···

PLANNING AHEAD

The truffles may be made up to 3 days in advance. Store in an airtight container in the refrigerator and bring to room temperature before serving.

COFFEE TOFFEE

The addition of coffee to toffee is welcome, because it gives the toffee a bitter edge, reducing the sweetness. You will need a candy thermometer and a nonstick baking liner, like Silpat, to make this candy. The liners work better than parchment paper because they allow you to spread the toffee thin and easily remove it from the pan.

2 TEASPOONS INSTANT ESPRESSO OR
   COFFEE POWDER
½ TEASPOON GROUND CINNAMON
¼ TEASPOON KOSHER SALT
1 CUP GRANULATED SUGAR
6 TABLESPOONS FIRMLY PACKED DARK
   BROWN SUGAR
6 TABLESPOONS WATER
1 TABLESPOON LIGHT OR DARK MOLASSES
8 OUNCES (16 TABLESPOONS) UNSALTED BUTTER,
   CUT INTO 1-INCH PIECES
4 OUNCES BITTERSWEET CHOCOLATE,
   FINELY CHOPPED
2 OUNCES WHITE CHOCOLATE, FINELY CHOPPED

Line a baking sheet with a nonstick baking liner. In a small bowl, stir together the espresso powder, cinnamon, and salt.

In a heavy, nonreactive saucepan, stir together the granulated sugar, brown sugar, water, and molasses and bring to a boil over medium heat. Stir in the butter until incorporated. Cook, without stirring, until the mixture is thick and reaches 298°F on a candy thermometer. Stir in the espresso mixture and remove from the heat.

Pour the mixture onto the prepared baking sheet and spread into a thin layer with an offset spatula. Let stand at room temperature until hardened, about 20 minutes.

Melt each chocolate separately just until melted but not hot. (See page 19 for tips on melting chocolate.) Whisk each chocolate until smooth. Using the offset spatula, spread the bittersweet chocolate evenly over the toffee. Drizzle the white chocolate evenly over the bittersweet chocolate. Using a toothpick or a fork, cut through the chocolates to create a marbled effect. Let the chocolates stand at room temperature until hardened, about 2 hours.

Break the toffee into pieces about 1½ by 2 inches.

PLANNING AHEAD

The toffee may be made up to 1 week in advance. Store in an airtight container at room temperature.

SPICED NUTS

— MAKES 4½ CUPS —

I make these with pecan halves, wrap them in festive bags, and
give them as holiday gifts. You may also prepare them with almonds and
serve them as a garnish on the bittersweet chocolate tartlets on
page 164. You need only a half recipe for the tartlets, but I like to make
a full one. That way, there is sure to be enough to nibble
on for a couple of days.

1 LARGE EGG WHITE

2 TEASPOONS VANILLA EXTRACT

½ CUP FIRMLY PACKED LIGHT BROWN SUGAR

2 TABLESPOONS GROUND CINNAMON

4⅓ CUPS (14 TO 16 OUNCES) PECAN HALVES OR
    WHOLE NATURAL ALMONDS

Preheat the oven to 300°F.

In a bowl, whisk together the egg white and
vanilla until frothy. Stir in the brown sugar, cinnamon, and pecans until the nuts are evenly coated.
Spread the pecans evenly on a baking sheet.

Toast, stirring every 10 minutes, until the nuts
are dry, about 30 minutes. Remove from the oven
and let cool to room temperature.

··· ⟋⟍ ···

PLANNING AHEAD

These nuts may be made 2 weeks in advance. Store
in an airtight container at room temperature.

BREAKFAST

CHAPTER 8

The aroma of fresh hot coffee is a good way to get yourself out of bed in the morning. Add some homemade pastries just out of the oven and your family will scramble into the kitchen, ready to take on the day. Breakfast should not be an afterthought, a time when you eat bland or processed foods just because they are quick and convenient. A cinnamon-laced roll, a gingery pear muffin, or a toasted slice of banana bread is better than a bagel any day. The treats in this chapter will turn everyone in your house into a morning person.

260
CINNAMON ROLLS

262
WALNUT ROLL

264
BANANA PECAN BREAD

265
PEACH STREUSEL COFFEE CAKE

266
HOLLYCE'S OATMEAL SCONES

267
PEAR GINGER MUFFINS

268
BLUEBERRY CORNMEAL MUFFINS

269
BLACKBERRY–SOUR CREAM MUFFINS

270
APPLE TURNOVERS

CINNAMON ROLLS

— MAKES 12 ROLLS —

At most airports, you can smell the cinnamon rolls as soon as you step off of the plane. The aroma is intoxicating, but commercial versions are practically as big as your head and made with preservatives and trans fats. The rolls we made at Stars used only natural ingredients and were presented in a more reasonable size. For fans of sticky buns, I have included a variation for them.

DOUGH

1 TABLESPOON ACTIVE DRY YEAST

3 TABLESPOONS MILK, WARMED

2¾ CUPS ALL-PURPOSE FLOUR

2 TABLESPOONS GRANULATED SUGAR

½ TEASPOON KOSHER SALT

3 LARGE EGGS, AT ROOM TEMPERATURE

6 OUNCES (12 TABLESPOONS) UNSALTED BUTTER,
   AT ROOM TEMPERATURE

FLOUR FOR DUSTING

CINNAMON BUTTER

8 OUNCES (16 TABLESPOONS) UNSALTED BUTTER,
   AT ROOM TEMPERATURE

2¼ TEASPOONS GROUND CINNAMON

¾ CUP FIRMLY PACKED BROWN SUGAR

BUTTER FOR THE PAN

3 OUNCES (¾ CUP) PECANS, TOASTED (SEE PAGE 20)
   AND COARSELY GROUND

ROYAL ICING

1 CUP CONFECTIONERS' SUGAR

1½ TABLESPOONS WATER

To make the dough: In a small bowl, dissolve the yeast in the milk and let stand for about 5 minutes until foamy. In a medium bowl, stir together the flour, granulated sugar, and salt.

Put the eggs and the yeast-milk mixture in the bowl of a stand mixer fitted with the paddle attachment and beat on medium-low speed until incorporated. Add the dry ingredients and mix until blended. Add the butter and beat, scraping the sides of the bowl as necessary until incorporated and the mixture comes together in a dough.

Transfer the dough to a lightly floured work surface and knead until smooth and satiny, about 5 minutes. Place the dough in a large bowl, cover the bowl with a kitchen towel, and let the dough rise in a warm place until doubled in bulk, 1 to 2 hours.

Make the cinnamon butter: While the dough is rising, put the butter, cinnamon, and brown sugar in another bowl of the stand mixer and beat on medium speed until creamy, about 15 seconds. Set aside at room temperature.

Lightly butter a 9-by-13-inch baking pan. On a lightly floured work surface, roll out the dough into an 18-by-11-inch rectangle. Spread the cinnamon butter evenly over the dough. Sprinkle the ground pecans evenly over the cinnamon butter. Starting from a long side, roll up the dough. Pinch the seam of the roll to seal it. Cut the log crosswise into 12 equal pieces. Place the rolls with a cut side up in the prepared pan.

Cover the pan with plastic wrap and let the rolls rise in a warm place until doubled in bulk, about 2 hours.

Preheat the oven to 350°F. Bake the rolls until golden brown, about 35 minutes. Let cool for 5 minutes, then invert the pan onto a cutting board and lift off the pan. Turn the cinnamon rolls right-side up.

To make the royal icing: In a small bowl, whisk together the confectioners' sugar and water until smooth. Drizzle the icing over the warm or room-temperature cinnamon rolls and serve.

VARIATION

Sticky Buns: Make the rolls as directed. Before you put the rolls in the baking pan, in a bowl, whisk together 1 cup dark corn syrup, 1½ cups cold Caramel Sauce (page 285), and 1½ cups (6 ounces) pecan halves, toasted (see page 20). Pour the mixture into the bottom of the pan and place the rolls on top. Bake as directed. Omit the icing.

PLANNING AHEAD

The rolls may be formed a day ahead, arranged in the baking pan, and then put in the refrigerator to rise overnight. The next day, transfer them directly from the refrigerator to the preheated oven. Serve them the day you bake them. They may be reheated in a 350°F for 5 minutes.

WALNUT ROLL

— SERVES 8 TO 10 —

The Yugoslavian name for this recipe is *povitica* (pronounced poh-va-teet-sa), and it has been passed down through the generations of my husband's family. I also make smaller rolls and give them out to family members on Christmas Eve, so they can indulge the next morning when they are opening presents. The slices are delicious served plain or toasted.

DOUGH

3½ CUPS ALL-PURPOSE FLOUR

¼ CUP GRANULATED SUGAR

1 TEASPOON KOSHER SALT

2½ TEASPOONS (1 ENVELOPE) ACTIVE DRY YEAST

½ CUP WATER

½ CUP MILK

4 OUNCES (8 TABLESPOONS) UNSALTED BUTTER,
   AT ROOM TEMPERATURE

1 LARGE EGG

FLOUR FOR DUSTING

BUTTER FOR THE BOWL

WALNUT FILLING

3 CUPS (10 OUNCES) WALNUTS, TOASTED
   (SEE PAGE 20)

4 OUNCES (8 TABLESPOONS) UNSALTED BUTTER,
   AT ROOM TEMPERATURE

½ CUP FIRMLY PACKED BROWN SUGAR

1 LARGE EGG

½ TEASPOON VANILLA EXTRACT

1 TEASPOON GROUND CINNAMON

1 LARGE EGG, LIGHTLY BEATEN

To make the dough: Stir together 1 cup of the flour, the granulated sugar, salt, and yeast in the bowl of a stand mixer fitted with the paddle attachment.

In a small saucepan, place the water, milk, and butter over low heat until the butter melts and the liquid is warm, about 120°F on an instant-read thermometer. Remove from the heat.

With the mixer on medium speed, gradually pour the milk mixture into the dry ingredients and beat until incorporated, about 1 minute. Increase the speed to medium-high, add the egg and ½ cup of the remaining flour, and beat for 2 minutes. Reduce the speed to low, add the remaining 2 cups flour, and beat until incorporated and the mixture comes together in a dough.

Transfer the dough to a lightly floured work surface and knead until smooth and satiny, about 10 minutes. Place the dough in a large buttered bowl, cover the bowl with a kitchen towel, and let the dough rise in a warm place until doubled in bulk, about 1½ hours.

To make the walnut filling: In a food processor, pulse the walnuts until finely ground. In a bowl, using a stand mixer or by hand, beat together the butter and brown sugar until smooth. Stir in the egg, vanilla, and cinnamon until incorporated. Add the ground walnuts and mix until evenly distributed.

Line a baking sheet with parchment paper. On a lightly floured work surface, roll out the dough into a 20-by-15-inch rectangle. Spread the walnut filling evenly over the dough. Starting from a long side, roll up the dough, pinching the ends of the roll to seal them. Gently pull the dough to a length of 25 inches and then twist it into a snail shape. Place it on the prepared baking sheet. Let rise, uncovered, in a warm place until doubled in bulk, about 1½ hours.

Preheat the oven to 325°F. Brush the beaten egg over the shaped dough. Bake until dark golden brown, 40 to 45 minutes. Let cool for at least 10 to 15 minutes on the baking sheet before cutting into pieces. Serve warm or at room temperature. The pieces are also delicious toasted.

PLANNING AHEAD
The roll may be made a day in advance. Cover it loosely with plastic wrap and store at room temperature.

BANANA PECAN BREAD

— MAKES 1 LOAF —

The advantage of this bread is that it improves with a day or so of aging. It is even better toasted or warmed and then spread with butter. Loaf pans come in many sizes. If you have a loaf pan close to the size mentioned here, use it. It isn't necessary to go out and buy a new one. If you have a smaller pan, fill it two-thirds full of batter and make muffins or mini-loaves out of the remaining batter. If you have a larger pan, the recipe will still work fine. The baking time will vary depending on what pan or pans you use, so rely on the skewer test for knowing when the bread is done.

BUTTER FOR THE PAN

1¾ CUPS ALL-PURPOSE FLOUR

1 TEASPOON BAKING POWDER

¼ TEASPOON KOSHER SALT

6 OUNCES (12 TABLESPOONS) UNSALTED BUTTER,
AT ROOM TEMPERATURE

1 CUP FIRMLY PACKED LIGHT BROWN SUGAR

3 LARGE EGGS

2 VERY RIPE BANANAS, PEELED

½ CUP (2 OUNCES) PECANS OR WALNUTS, TOASTED
(SEE PAGE 20) AND COARSELY CHOPPED

Preheat the oven to 350°F. Butter an 8½-by-4½-by-2¾-inch loaf pan.

In a bowl, stir together the flour, baking powder, and salt. Set aside.

Combine the butter and brown sugar in the bowl of a stand mixer fitted with the paddle attachment and beat on medium speed until light and creamy, about 1 minute. Add the eggs one at a time, mixing well after each addition. Reduce the speed to medium-low, add the bananas, and mix until incorporated. Reduce the speed to low, add the dry ingredients and nuts, and mix just until incorporated. Spread the batter into the prepared pan.

Bake until a skewer inserted into the center comes out clean, about 1 hour. Let cool in the pan for 30 minutes. Invert the pan onto a cutting board, lift off the pan, and let the bread cool on the board to room temperature.

PLANNING AHEAD

The bread may be made up to 2 days ahead. Wrap it in plastic and store at room temperature.

PEACH STREUSEL COFFEE CAKE

— SERVES 8 TO 10 —

This recipe comes from my seventh-grade home economics class.
I had no interest in cutting out a skirt pattern and using a needle and
thread to sew the hem, but the cooking part didn't feel like school.
For our final project, we made this coffee cake. I am sure my teacher,
Mrs. Hallahan, would approve of the changes I have made since then.

STREUSEL

1 CUP FIRMLY PACKED BROWN SUGAR

1 TABLESPOON GROUND CINNAMON

4 OUNCES (8 TABLESPOONS) UNSALTED BUTTER,
   MELTED

½ CUP ALL-PURPOSE FLOUR

CAKE

BUTTER FOR THE PAN

3 CUPS ALL-PURPOSE FLOUR

4 TEASPOONS BAKING POWDER

1 TEASPOON KOSHER SALT

4 OUNCES (8 TABLESPOONS) UNSALTED BUTTER,
   AT ROOM TEMPERATURE

1½ CUPS GRANULATED SUGAR

2 LARGE EGGS

1 CUP MILK

2 CUPS PEELED AND COARSELY CHOPPED
   (½-INCH PIECES) PEACHES (ABOUT
   4 MEDIUM PEACHES)

To make the streusel: In a bowl, stir together the brown sugar, cinnamon, butter, and flour. Set the mixture aside.

To make the cake: Preheat the oven to 350°F. Butter a 9-by-13-inch baking pan.

In a bowl, stir together the flour, baking powder, and salt. Set aside.

Combine the butter and sugar in the bowl of a stand mixer fitted with the paddle attachment and beat on medium-high speed until light and fluffy, 1 to 2 minutes. Add the eggs and mix until incorporated. Reduce the speed to low and add the dry ingedients in 2 additions, alternating with the milk, 2 additions, mixing well after each addition.

Spread half of the batter into the prepared pan. Sprinkle half of the streusel on top and spread the remaining batter over it. Distribute the peaches evenly across the pan and then gently press them into the batter. Scatter the remaining streusel on top.

Bake until a skewer inserted into the center comes out clean, 40 to 45 minutes. Let cool for 15 minutes before serving.

··· ❧ ···

PLANNING AHEAD

The coffee cake may be made a day in advance. Wrap in plastic wrap and store at room temperature.

HOLLYCE'S OATMEAL SCONES

— MAKES 10 SCONES —

Developed for the opening of Stars Café, these scones took the neighborhood by storm. For a decadent treat, eat them with jam and Double Cream (page 278).

3 CUPS PLUS 2 TABLESPOONS ALL-PURPOSE FLOUR

½ CUP PLUS 2 TABLESPOONS GRANULATED SUGAR

1¼ TEASPOONS KOSHER SALT

1¼ TEASPOONS BAKING SODA

2½ TEASPOONS BAKING POWDER

10 OUNCES (20 TABLESPOONS) COLD UNSALTED
    BUTTER, CUT INTO 1-INCH PIECES

2 CUPS OLD-FASHIONED ROLLED OATS

1 CUP DRIED CURRANTS

GRATED ZEST OF 2 ORANGES

¾ CUP BUTTERMILK

FLOUR FOR DUSTING

Preheat the oven to 350°F. Line a baking sheet with parchment paper.

Combine the flour, sugar, salt, baking soda, and baking powder in the bowl of a stand mixer fitted with the paddle attachment and mix on low speed until combined. Scatter the butter pieces over the top and mix on low speed until the butter is the size of small peas. Add the oats, currants, and orange zest and mix until incorporated. Slowly pour in the buttermilk and continue to mix on low speed until the dough comes together, about 30 seconds.

On a lightly floured work surface, roll or pat out the dough ¾ inch thick. Cut out 10 circles each 3½ inches in diameter. Place the circles on the prepared baking sheet.

Bake until golden brown, about 20 minutes. Serve warm or at room temperature.

PLANNING AHEAD

The scones may be baked a day ahead, but they taste best fresh from the oven. You may make the dough, cut out the scones, cover, and refrigerate overnight, and then bake them in the morning.

PEAR GINGER MUFFINS

— MAKES 18 MUFFINS —

One weekend, out of blueberries and with a houseful of unexpected
guests, I searched in the back of the refrigerator for ingredients
to put into muffins. I discovered some fresh ginger and pears and
a new recipe was born.

BUTTER FOR THE PAN

2½ CUPS ALL-PURPOSE FLOUR

1½ TEASPOONS BAKING POWDER

PINCH OF KOSHER SALT

7 OUNCES (14 TABLESPOONS) UNSALTED BUTTER,
   AT ROOM TEMPERATURE

¾ CUP FIRMLY PACKED BROWN SUGAR

6 TABLESPOONS GRANULATED SUGAR

2 LARGE EGGS

¼ CUP MILK

1 TEASPOON VANILLA EXTRACT

1 TABLESPOON PEELED AND GRATED FRESH GINGER

2 RIPE PEARS (ABOUT 15 OUNCES), PEELED, HALVED,
   CORED, AND COARSELY CHOPPED

Preheat the oven to 325°F. Butter 18 standard
muffin-pan wells or line with paper liners.

In a bowl, stir together the flour, baking powder, and salt. Set aside.

Combine the butter, brown sugar, and granulated sugar in the bowl of a stand mixer fitted
with the paddle attachment and beat on medium
speed until light and creamy, about 1 minute. Add
the eggs and beat until incorporated. Reduce the
speed to medium-low, add the milk and vanilla,
and beat until combined. On low speed, add the
dry ingredients and mix just until incorporated.
Add the ginger and pears and mix just until evenly
distributed. Do not overmix. Spoon the batter into
the prepared muffin-pan wells, filling them three-
fourths full.

Bake until a skewer inserted into the center of a
muffin comes out clean, about 30 minutes. Let cool
for 10 minutes and then remove the muffins from
the pans. Serve warm or at room temperature.

··· ···

PLANNING AHEAD

The muffins may be made a day in advance, but
they are best eaten the same day they are baked. If
making ahead, cover with plastic wrap and store at
room temperature.

BLUEBERRY CORNMEAL MUFFINS

— MAKES 12 MUFFINS —

Plump fresh blueberries are always preferred over their frozen
counterparts for making muffins, but you can make respectable
muffins with frozen blueberries. Don't thaw them before adding them,
or they will turn your muffins blue. Also, instead of mixing them
into the batter, put half the batter in the muffin cups, sprinkle in some
berries, and then put more batter on top. When I eat these muffins,
I like to split them in half, toast them under the broiler, and
then drizzle on some honey.

BUTTER FOR THE PAN

1 CUP MEDIUM-GRIND YELLOW CORNMEAL,
  PREFERABLY STONE GROUND (SEE CORNMEAL
  TARTLETS WITH ORANGE CRÈME FRAÎCHE AND
  STRAWBERRIES, PAGE 168, FOR INFORMATION
  ON CORNMEAL)

1 CUP ALL-PURPOSE FLOUR

⅓ CUP SUGAR

2 TEASPOONS BAKING POWDER

1 TEASPOON BAKING SODA

½ TEASPOON KOSHER SALT

¼ CUP MILK

2 LARGE EGGS

2 OUNCES (4 TABLESPOONS) UNSALTED BUTTER,
  MELTED

1 CUP SOUR CREAM

1 PINT BLUEBERRIES (ABOUT 2 CUPS)

Preheat the oven to 350°F. Butter 12 standard
muffin-pan wells or line with paper liners.

In a large bowl, stir together the cornmeal,
flour, sugar, baking powder, baking soda, and salt.
In a medium bowl, whisk together the milk, eggs,
butter, and sour cream. Stir the egg-milk mixture
into the dry ingredients. When the mixtures are
almost completely combined, gently stir in the
blueberries. Do not overmix. Spoon the batter into
the prepared muffin-pan wells, filling them three-
fourths full.

Bake until a skewer inserted into the center of
a muffin comes out clean, 20 to 25 minutes. Let
cool for 10 minutes and then remove them from the
pans. Serve warm or at room temperature.

PLANNING AHEAD

The muffins may be made a day in advance, but
they are best eaten the same day they are baked. If
making ahead, cover with plastic wrap and store at
room temperature.

BLACKBERRY—SOUR CREAM MUFFINS

— MAKES 12 MUFFINS —

These muffins are easy to make, and with wild blackberries and a large dollop of maple butter (maple syrup whisked into butter), they are divine.

BUTTER FOR THE PAN

1 CUP MILK

½ CUP SOUR CREAM

2 LARGE EGGS

3 CUPS FLOUR

¾ CUP GRANULATED SUGAR

1½ TABLESPOONS BAKING POWDER

½ TEASPOON KOSHER SALT

6 OUNCES (12 TABLESPOONS) COLD UNSALTED BUTTER, CUT INTO ½-INCH PIECES

½ PINT BLACKBERRIES (ABOUT 1 CUP)

2 TABLESPOONS FIRMLY PACKED LIGHT BROWN SUGAR

Preheat the oven to 375°F. Butter 12 standard muffin-pan wells or line with paper liners.

In a bowl, whisk together the milk, sour cream, and eggs. Set aside.

Combine the flour, granulated sugar, baking powder, and salt in the bowl of a stand mixer fitted with the paddle attachment and mix on low speed until combined. Scatter the butter pieces over the top and mix until the butter is the size of small peas. Add the sour cream mixture and mix until the batter comes together, about 15 seconds. Using a spatula, gently fold in the blackberries. Spoon the batter into the prepared muffin-pan wells, filling them three-fourths full. Sprinkle the brown sugar on top.

Bake until a skewer inserted into the center of a muffin comes out clean, about 30 minutes. Let cool for 10 minutes and then remove them from the pans. Serve warm or at room temperature.

PLANNING AHEAD

The muffins may be made a day in advance, but they are best eaten the same day they are baked. If making ahead, cover with plastic wrap and store at room temperature.

APPLE TURNOVERS

— MAKES 8 TURNOVERS —

My New Hampshire nieces and nephew like me to make these turnovers when I visit them. They are the perfect thing for them to grab as they run out the door to catch the school bus. They always take an extra one for the driver.

DOUGH

8 OUNCES CREAM CHEESE, AT ROOM TEMPERATURE

8 OUNCES (16 TABLESPOONS) UNSALTED BUTTER, AT ROOM TEMPERATURE

2 TABLESPOONS GRANULATED SUGAR

¼ CUP HEAVY WHIPPING CREAM

2½ CUPS ALL-PURPOSE FLOUR

PINCH OF KOSHER SALT

APPLE FILLING

8 FIRM, JUICY APPLES (ABOUT 3½ POUNDS), PEELED, HALVED, CORED, AND SLICED 3/16 INCH THICK

¾ CUP GRANULATED SUGAR

2 OUNCES (4 TABLESPOONS) UNSALTED BUTTER

¼ TEASPOON KOSHER SALT

2 TABLESPOONS FRESHLY SQUEEZED LEMON JUICE

1 TABLESPOON SUGAR

1 TEASPOON GROUND CINNAMON

FLOUR FOR DUSTING

1 LARGE EGG, LIGHTLY BEATEN

To make the dough: Combine the cream cheese, butter, and sugar in the bowl of a stand mixer fitted with the paddle attachment and beat on medium speed until smooth, about 30 seconds. Reduce the speed to medium-low, add the cream, flour, and salt, and beat until incorporated and the mixture comes together in a dough. Cover the dough and refrigerate for 1 hour.

To make the filling: In a large sauté pan, combine the apples, sugar, butter, salt, and lemon juice over medium heat. Cook, stirring occasionally, until the apples are soft but still retain their shape, about 10 minutes. Remove from the heat and let cool to room temperature. You should have about 2⅔ cups.

Preheat the oven to 350°F. Line a baking sheet with parchment paper. In a small bowl, stir together the sugar and cinnamon and set aside.

On a lightly floured work surface, roll out the dough ⅛ inch thick. (If the dough is difficult to roll, let it sit at room temperature for 10 minutes.) Cut out 8 circles each about 6 inches in diameter.

To form each turnover, place about ⅓ cup of the apple filling off center on a dough circle. Brush the outer ¼-inch edge of the circle with beaten egg and fold the circle in half, forming a half circle. Press the edges together and then fold the edge over to seal securely. Cut 3 air slits, each about ¼ inch long, in the top of the turnover. As the turnovers are formed, place them on the prepared baking sheet. Brush the tops with the beaten egg and sprinkle with the cinnamon sugar.

Bake until golden brown, about 25 minutes. Serve warm.

··· ⟳ ···

PLANNING AHEAD

The dough and the apples may be prepared a day ahead and refrigerated overnight. Assemble and bake the turnovers the next morning just before serving.

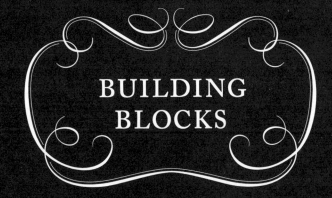

BUILDING BLOCKS

— CHAPTER 9 —

The sauces, pastry doughs, ice creams, and other recipes in this chapter are called for in many of the desserts in this book. If possible, keep some of these basic components on hand in your freezer or refrigerator, so that you create last-minute desserts for unexpected company or for when you crave something sweet. Also, use your imagination when using these recipes. No rules apply when pairing sauces with cakes or ice creams with tarts. The combinations that work are what you find delicious.

276
CHANTILLY CREAM

277
CARAMEL CREAM

278
DOUBLE CREAM

279
CRÈME FRAÎCHE

280
PASTRY CREAM

281
CHAMPAGNE SABAYON

282
VANILLA CUSTARD SAUCE

284
CHOCOLATE SAUCE

285
CARAMEL SAUCE

286
PLUM CARAMEL SAUCE

287
APPLE CARAMEL SAUCE

288
ESPRESSO CARAMEL SAUCE

288
CHOCOLATE CARAMEL SAUCE

289
BERRY SAUCE

289
MANGO SAUCE

290
TART AND PIE DOUGH

293
BRIOCHE

294
PUFF PASTRY

296
SPONGE CAKE

297
CRÊPES

298
CHOCOLATE CRÊPES

299
VANILLA ICE CREAM

300
CARAMEL ICE CREAM

301
PUMPKIN PURÉE

302
ALMOND PRALINE

CHANTILLY CREAM

— MAKES ABOUT 2¼ CUPS —

Chantilly cream should be velvety and just hold its shape. Some cooks argue that it has the best flavor and texture when whipped by hand, rather than with a mixer. I do it both ways. Also, I have discovered that if you overwhip the cream by mistake, you can fold in a few spoonfuls of unwhipped cream to rescue it. For the best volume and flavor, look for cream that is not ultrapasteurized. Also, I don't use confectioners' sugar to sweeten the cream. The cornstarch in the sugar gives it a chalky taste. If you like big dollops of whipped cream on your desserts, this recipe doubles well.

1 CUP HEAVY WHIPPING CREAM

½ TEASPOON VANILLA EXTRACT

1 TABLESPOON GRANULATED SUGAR

Put the cream, vanilla, and sugar in a bowl and whip by hand with a whisk or with an electric mixer on medium speed until soft peaks begin to form. The cream should hold its shape but still be very smooth.

Cover and refrigerate until serving.

··· ◦꩜◦ ···

PLANNING AHEAD

You can whip the cream an hour or two in advance, cover, and refrigerate it. If it sits longer than that, it will start to thin out and you will need to rewhip it lightly before using. A few quick stirs with a whisk will do the trick.

CARAMEL CREAM

Superbly simple, but be sure to make enough. Everyone always wants another spoonful.

½ CUP MASCARPONE CHEESE

1½ CUPS HEAVY WHIPPING CREAM

½ CUP COLD CARAMEL SAUCE (PAGE 285)

PINCH OF KOSHER SALT

In a large bowl, combine the mascarpone, cream, caramel sauce, and salt. Whisk until the mixture holds its shape.

Cover and refrigerate until serving.

··· ❧ ···

PLANNING AHEAD

The cream may be made up to 8 hours ahead and kept refrigerated. If it is made more than an hour ahead, it may need to be lightly rewhipped before using.

DOUBLE CREAM

It is a shame that English double Devon cream is difficult to find in the United States. I created this recipe as a substitute.

¾ CUP MASCARPONE CHEESE

1½ CUPS HEAVY WHIPPING CREAM

½ TEASPOON VANILLA EXTRACT

2 TABLESPOONS GRANULATED SUGAR

SMALL PINCH OF KOSHER SALT

In a large bowl, combine the mascarpone, cream, vanilla, sugar, and salt. Whisk until the mixture holds its shape.

Cover and refrigerate until serving.

··· ◦≫ ···

PLANNING AHEAD

The cream may be made up to 8 hours ahead and kept refrigerated. If it is made more than an hour ahead, it may need to be lightly rewhipped before using.

CRÈME FRAÎCHE

— MAKES 6 CUPS —

The tangy flavor of crème fraîche pairs well with sweets. If it is unavailable in your area, here is how to make your own. The method is adapted from a recipe by Sadie Kendall, of Kendall Farms in Atascadero, California. She makes crème fraîche commercially and supplied it to Stars. You can make crème fraîche with sour cream or buttermilk. Each imparts a slightly different flavor.

4 CUPS HEAVY WHIPPING CREAM
(NOT ULTRAPASTEURIZED)
¼ CUP FULL-FAT BUTTERMILK OR SOUR CREAM

In a stainless-steel or glass bowl, whisk together the cream and buttermilk until blended. Transfer to a plastic or glass container with an airtight lid and cover the container. Let the cream stand at room temperature (about 68°F) until it thickens.

This will take 24 to 48 hours. Once it is ready, store in the refrigerator.

··· ⌇ ···

PLANNING AHEAD
The crème fraîche will keep for several weeks in the refrigerator. As it ages, it will give off some watery liquid. Spoon it off and discard it to keep the crème fraîche thick.

PASTRY CREAM

— MAKES ABOUT 2 CUPS —

Pastry cream is a staple of the baking repertoire, used in tarts, pies, and napoleons. Over the years I have had both many wonderful and many not-so-wonderful versions. The trick is to use enough thickener, either cornstarch or flour, to make a thick cream, but not so much that you end up with a pasty taste. Whisking in a little butter at the end helps give the cream a smooth texture.

6 LARGE EGG YOLKS

⅓ CUP GRANULATED SUGAR

PINCH OF KOSHER SALT

¼ CUP CORNSTARCH

2 CUPS MILK

¾ TEASPOON VANILLA EXTRACT

½ OUNCE (1 TABLESPOON) UNSALTED BUTTER

In a bowl, whisk together the egg yolks, sugar, and salt until blended. Whisk in the cornstarch.

In a heavy, nonreactive saucepan, heat the milk over medium heat until small bubbles appear around the edges of the pan. Remove from the heat and, while whisking constantly, pour the milk into the egg mixture in a slow, steady stream. Pour the mixture back into the pan and cook over medium-low heat, stirring constantly with a heat-resistant spatula, until thickened, about 8 minutes.

Strain through a medium-mesh sieve into a clean bowl. Stir in the vanilla and butter. Cover with plastic wrap, pressing it directly onto the surface.

Refrigerate until cold, for at least 1 hour, before using in another recipe.

VARIATIONS

Cinnamon Pastry Cream: Add ¼ teaspoon ground cinnamon and ½ cinnamon stick to the milk before heating.

Brown Sugar Pastry Cream: Substitute ⅓ cup firmly packed brown sugar for the granulated sugar.

Espresso Pastry Cream: Add 2 tablespoons instant espresso powder to the milk before heating.

Ginger Pastry Cream: Add a 1-inch piece of fresh ginger, roughly chopped, to the milk before heating.

PLANNING AHEAD

The pastry cream may be made up to 3 days in advance and kept refrigerated.

CHAMPAGNE SABAYON

— MAKES ABOUT 1½ CUPS —

Sabayon was a Stars staple. Its velvety thick consistency makes it
the best dessert sauce there is. I find it difficult to write a dessert menu
and not include it at least once. At Stars, we always had several
flavors on hand, to be used on a moment's notice. Many of the trifles call
for 2 recipes of Sabayon; you can double the recipe or make it twice.

4 LARGE EGG YOLKS

¼ CUP GRANULATED SUGAR

SMALL PINCH OF KOSHER SALT

6 TABLESPOONS CHAMPAGNE

½ CUP HEAVY WHIPPING CREAM

Prepare an ice bath. (See page 18 for tips on using
an ice bath). In a stainless-steel bowl, whisk together
the egg yolks, sugar, and salt until blended. Whisk
in the Champagne.

Place the bowl over a pan of simmering water,
making sure the bottom of the bowl does not touch
the water. (See page 18 for tips on using and making
a double boiler.) Cook, whisking constantly, until
it is thick and there are no air bubbles, 3 to 4 minutes. The mixture should mound slightly when
dropped from the whisk.

Remove the bowl from the pan and place
it in the ice bath. Let cool to room temperature,
whisking occasionally.

Whisk the cream until soft peaks form. Using a
spatula, fold the cream into the cooled sabayon just
until combined.

Cover and refrigerate until serving.

VARIATIONS

Cider Sabayon: Substitute 6 tablespoons sparkling
apple cider (hard or nonalcoholic) or 5 tablespoons
apple juice and 1 tablespoon Calvados (apple brandy)
for the Champagne.

Grand Marnier Sabayon: Substitute ¼ cup freshly
squeezed orange juice and 2 tablespoons Grand
Marnier for the Champagne.

Riesling Sabayon: Substitute 6 tablespoons dry
Riesling for the Champagne. Increase the cream to
½ cup plus 2 tablespoons.

Zabaglione: Substitute ¼ cup Marsala and 2 tablespoons sherry for the Champagne. Increase the
cream to ¾ cup.

PLANNING AHEAD

The sabayon may be made a day ahead and kept
refrigerated.

VANILLA CUSTARD SAUCE

— MAKES ABOUT 1½ CUPS —

Also known as crème anglaise, this sauce is one of the most
versatile of all the dessert sauces. It can be superb by itself
(remember, when frozen, it is ice cream) and there is hardly
a fruit, cake, pudding, or cobbler that is not enhanced by
a spoonful of it. This is the basic vanilla-flavored custard sauce.
Variations for other flavors follow.

4 LARGE EGG YOLKS

3 TABLESPOONS GRANULATED SUGAR

PINCH OF KOSHER SALT

1½ CUPS MILK

ONE 1-INCH PIECE VANILLA BEAN, SPLIT

    LENGTHWISE, OR ½ TEASPOON VANILLA EXTRACT

Prepare an ice bath. (See page 18 for tips on using an ice bath.) In a bowl, whisk together the egg yolks, sugar, and salt until blended.

Pour the milk into a heavy, nonreactive saucepan. If using the vanilla bean, use the blade of a knife to scrape the seeds from the pod halves into the milk and then add the pod halves. If using vanilla extract, reserve to add later. Place over medium heat until small bubbles appear around the edges of the pan.

Remove from the heat and, while whisking constantly, pour the milk into the egg mixture in a slow, steady stream. Pour the mixture back into the pan and cook over medium-low heat, stirring constantly with a heat-resistant spatula, until it has thickened slightly and coats the spatula, about 5 minutes. Pour into a clean bowl and place the bowl in the ice bath. Let cool to room temperature, stirring occasionally. Stir in the vanilla extract, if using.

Pour through a fine-mesh sieve into a clean bowl, cover, and refrigerate until serving.

Coffee Custard Sauce: Add 1 tablespoon ground dark roast coffee to the milk before heating.

Orange Custard Sauce: Add the peel of ½ orange to the milk before heating.

Chocolate Custard Sauce: Just before you whisk the milk into the egg yolk mixture, whisk 1 ounce bittersweet chocolate, finely chopped, into the hot milk until melted.

Cinnamon Custard Sauce: Add ⅛ teaspoon ground cinnamon and ½ cinnamon stick to the milk before heating.

Rum Custard Sauce: Stir 1½ tablespoons dark rum into the strained sauce.

··· ⌇⊚ ···

The sauce may be made 2 days ahead and kept refrigerated.

CHOCOLATE SAUCE

— MAKES ABOUT 1½ CUPS —

At Stars, we served this sauce over ice cream and on selected desserts. It wasn't unusual for us to go through five gallons of it in a week! It is adapted from a James Beard recipe, and I have added as little cream as possible to make it as chocolatey as I can.

1 CUP HEAVY WHIPPING CREAM

7 OUNCES BITTERSWEET CHOCOLATE, COARSELY CHOPPED

In a heavy saucepan, heat the cream over medium heat until small bubbles appear around the edges of the pan. Remove from the heat and add the chocolate. Let stand for 5 minutes and then stir until smooth.

Serve the sauce warm or cover and refrigerate for later use.

PLANNING AHEAD

The sauce may be made up to 2 weeks in advance, covered, and refrigerated. To reheat, warm the sauce in a double boiler (see page 18 for tips on using a double boiler) or in a microwave.

CARAMEL SAUCE

— MAKES ABOUT 2 CUPS —

I always like to keep some caramel sauce on hand in the refrigerator. This is James Beard's recipe, and it is wonderful spooned warm over ice cream or added to chantilly cream to make Caramel Cream (page 277). Wear oven mitts when you add the cream to the caramelized sugar. The combination of hot and cold ingredients causes the mixture to bubble up.

1½ CUPS GRANULATED SUGAR

½ CUP WATER

1 CUP HEAVY WHIPPING CREAM

In a heavy, nonreactive saucepan, stir together the sugar and water. Place over medium heat and cook, stirring occasionally, until the sugar dissolves and the mixture comes to a boil. Increase the heat to high and cook, without stirring, until the mixture becomes a golden amber color. (See page 20 for tips on making caramel.)

Remove from the heat and let the bubbles subside for a few seconds. Stir in 2 tablespoons of the cream. Be careful as you stir, as the caramel will bubble up when you add the cream. Continue adding the cream a little at a time until you have added about ½ cup. At this point, the caramel will have cooled enough and you can whisk in the remaining cream all at once.

Serve the sauce warm or cover and refrigerate for later use.

PLANNING AHEAD

The sauce may be made up to 2 weeks in advance, covered, and refrigerated. To reheat, warm the sauce in a double boiler (see page 18 for tips on using a double boiler) or in a microwave.

PLUM CARAMEL SAUCE

— MAKES 1½ CUPS —

Feel free to substitute peach, rhubarb, or apricot purée for the plum purée. This sauce is perfect for using up overripe fruit. Just make sure it is blemish free.

1 POUND RIPE PLUMS, HALVED AND PITTED
½ CUP GRANULATED SUGAR
¼ CUP WATER

In a food processor, purée the plums until smooth. Strain through a medium-mesh sieve placed over a bowl to eliminate any bits of skin. You should have about 1¼ cups.

Stir together the sugar and water in a heavy, nonreactive saucepan. Place over medium heat and cook, stirring occasionally, until the sugar dissolves and the mixture comes to a boil. Increase the heat to high and cook, without stirring, until the mixture becomes a golden amber color. (See page 20 for tips on making caramel.)

Remove from the heat and let the bubbles subside for a few seconds. Stir in 2 tablespoons of the plum purée. Be careful as you stir, as the caramel will bubble up when you add the plum purée. Then slowly stir in the rest of the purée.

Let cool to room temperature before serving.

PLANNING AHEAD
The sauce may be made 2 days in advance and kept refrigerated.

APPLE CARAMEL SAUCE

This sauce was created for Pumpkin Soufflé (page 111), but it can be served with Walnut Rum Steamed Pudding (page 52) and vanilla ice cream, or in a fall version of French Cream (page 45), replacing the berries and sauce with an apple or pear compote and this sauce.

1½ CUPS GRANULATED SUGAR

¾ CUP WATER

1 CUP APPLE JUICE

In a heavy, nonreactive saucepan, stir together the sugar and water. Place over medium heat and cook, stirring occasionally, until the sugar dissolves and the mixture comes to a boil. Increase the heat to high and cook, without stirring, until the mixture becomes a golden amber color. (See page 20 for tips on making caramel.)

Remove from the heat and let the bubbles subside for a few seconds. Stir in 2 tablespoons of the apple juice. Be careful as you stir, as the caramel will bubble up when you add the juice. Then slowly stir in the rest of the juice.

Let cool to room temperature before serving.

··· ⦿ ···

PLANNING AHEAD
The sauce may be made 3 days in advance, covered, and refrigerated.

ESPRESSO CARAMEL SAUCE

— MAKES ABOUT 2 CUPS —

Serve this sauce with any chocolate cake.

1¾ CUPS GRANULATED SUGAR

½ CUP WATER

6 TABLESPOONS BREWED ESPRESSO,
AT ROOM TEMPERATURE

¾ CUP HEAVY WHIPPING CREAM

In a heavy, nonreactive saucepan, stir together the sugar and water. Place over medium heat and cook, stirring occasionally, until the sugar dissolves and the mixture comes to a boil. Increase the heat to high and cook, without stirring, until the mixture becomes a golden amber color. (See page 20 for tips on making caramel.)

Remove from the heat and let the bubbles subside for a few seconds. Stir in 2 tablespoons of the espresso. Be careful as you stir, as the caramel will bubble up when you add the espresso. Slowly adding 2 more tablespoons espresso. Then add the remaining 2 tablespoons. Stir in the cream.

Serve the sauce warm. If it cools, reheat it in a double boiler. (See page 18 for tips on using and making a double boiler.)

PLANNING AHEAD

The sauce may be made 3 days in advance, covered, and refrigerated. Reheat before serving.

CHOCOLATE CARAMEL SAUCE

— MAKES ABOUT 2 CUPS —

Sometimes it is hard to decide whether I should use a caramel sauce or a chocolate sauce on a dessert. This recipe remedies the problem.

3 OUNCES BITTERSWEET CHOCOLATE,
FINELY CHOPPED

1½ CUPS CARAMEL SAUCE (PAGE 285), WARMED

Melt the chocolate. (See page 19 for tips on melting chocolate.) Whisk until smooth.

Whisk the chocolate into the caramel sauce. Serve the sauce warm. If it cools, reheat it in a

double boiler. (See page 18 for tips on using and making a double boiler.)

PLANNING AHEAD

The sauce may be made up to 2 weeks in advance, covered, and refrigerated. Reheat before serving.

BERRY SAUCE

You can use this basic method for making strawberry, raspberry, or blackberry sauce. The amount of sugar you use will depend on the sweetness of the berries. Frozen berries often need more sugar than fresh.

1 PINT FRESH STRAWBERRIES, RASPBERRIES, OR BLACKBERRIES (ABOUT 2 CUPS), OR 12 OUNCES FROZEN UNSWEETENED BERRIES, THAWED

2 TABLESPOONS GRANULATED SUGAR

½ TEASPOON FRESHLY SQUEEZED LEMON JUICE

PINCH OF KOSHER SALT

Hull the strawberries if using them. Pass the berries through a food mill or purée them in a food processor.

Strain the purée through a medium-mesh sieve placed over a bowl to eliminate any seeds. Stir in the sugar, lemon juice, and salt. Taste and adjust the sweetness with more sugar if needed.

Cover and refrigerate until serving.

PLANNING AHEAD

The berry sauce may be made 2 days in advance and kept refrigerated.

MANGO SAUCE

— MAKES ABOUT 1½ CUPS —

In many Asian countries, the mango is as popular as the apple is in America. A sauce made from the fruit brightens up many desserts, especially in winter when colorful berries and stone fruits are out of season.

2 LARGE RIPE MANGOES (ABOUT 1 POUND 14 OUNCES), PEELED AND PITTED

1½ TABLESPOONS SUGAR

SMALL PINCH OF KOSHER SALT

In a food processor, purée the mango pulp until smooth. Strain through a medium-mesh sieve placed over a bowl. Stir in the sugar and salt.

Taste and adjust the sweetness with more sugar if needed.

Cover and refrigerate until serving

PLANNING AHEAD

The mango sauce may be made a day in advance and kept refrigerated.

TART AND PIE DOUGH

— EACH RECIPE MAKES ONE 9½-INCH TART CRUST OR PIE CRUST AND 1 LATTICE TOP
OR TOP CRUST, OR SIX 4-INCH TARTLET CRUSTS WITH 1-INCH SIDES —

Here are two recipes for tart and pie pastry. One is made with water and the other is made with cream and egg yolk. I usually use water for pies and egg and cream for tarts, but they are interchangeable. Make them both and see which one you prefer. I don't use vegetable shortening in pie crusts. Some bakers prefer it over butter because it produces a particularly flaky pastry. But if you handle dough made with butter properly, you will get both the flakiness and the great flavor of butter. Also, keep in mind that the trick to making a good pastry crust is not to add too much water and not to overwork the dough. Both will make the dough tough.

DOUGH WITH WATER

2½ CUPS ALL-PURPOSE FLOUR

1½ TABLESPOONS GRANULATED SUGAR

¼ TEASPOON KOSHER SALT

10 OUNCES (20 TABLESPOONS) COLD UNSALTED
    BUTTER, CUT INTO ½-INCH PIECES

3½ TO 4½ TABLESPOONS ICE WATER

FLOUR FOR DUSTING

DOUGH WITH CREAM AND EGG YOLK

1 LARGE EGG

2 TO 3 TABLESPOONS HEAVY WHIPPING CREAM

2½ CUPS ALL-PURPOSE FLOUR

2 TABLESPOONS GRANULATED SUGAR

¼ TEASPOON KOSHER SALT

7 OUNCES (14 TABLESPOONS) COLD UNSALTED
    BUTTER, CUT INTO ½-INCH PIECES

FLOUR FOR DUSTING

To Make the Dough with Water

Combine the flour, sugar, and salt in the bowl of a stand mixer fitted with the paddle attachment and mix on low speed until combined. Scatter the butter pieces over the top and mix on low speed until the butter is the size of small peas.

Add 3½ tablespoons of the ice water and mix on low speed for about 10 seconds. Stop the mixer and gently squeeze a small amount of the dough in your hand. If the dough comes together and does not have any dry pieces, it has enough water. If it is dry, mix in another tablespoon of water and test again. Continue to mix on low speed until the dough almost comes together in a ball. (Alternatively, cut the butter into the dry ingredients with a pastry blender until the butter is the size of small peas, and then slowly add the ice water, stirring and tossing with a fork until the dough comes together.)

Form the dough into a 5-inch disk, wrap in plastic wrap, and refrigerate for 30 minutes before rolling it out.

To Make the Dough with Cream and Egg Yolk

In a small bowl, whisk together the egg and 2 tablespoons of the cream. Proceed as directed for the dough made with water, substituting the egg-and-cream mixture for the ice water. If the dough is dry, add another tablespoon of cream.

To Roll Out the Dough

For a 9½-inch pie crust and top, divide the dough in half and roll out each half into a circle 13 inches in diameter and ¼ inch thick. If making a lattice top, roll out the second half into a circle 13 inches in diameter and ⅛ inch thick and cut into ½-inch-wide strips.

For a 9½-inch tart crust and lattice top, divide the dough in half. For the crust, roll out one-half into a circle 12 inches in diameter and ¼ inch thick. For the lattice top, roll out the second half into a circle 12 inches in diameter and ⅛ inch thick and cut into ½-inch-wide strips.

For six 4-inch tartlet crusts, roll out the dough ⅛ inch thick and cut into 6 circles, each 5 inches in diameter.

To roll out the dough, place it on a lightly floured work surface. Dust the top lightly with flour. Roll the dough from the center toward the edges into a circle, rotating the dough a quarter turn after each roll. Occasionally loosen the dough from the work surface with a metal or plastic pastry scraper to prevent sticking and lightly flour the top and bottom of the dough as needed.

To Line a Pie Pan

Wrap the dough around the rolling pin, carefully center it over the pie pan, and then unwrap it from the pin. Using your fingers, gently press the dough into the bottom and sides of the pan. Fold the overhang under itself, forming a high edge on the pan rim. Flute the edge with your fingers or crimp it with the tines of a fork. Refrigerate the lined pan for at least 30 minutes before baking.

To Line a Tart Pan

Wrap the dough around the rolling pin, carefully center it over a tart pan with a removable bottom, and then unwrap it from the pin. Gently ease it into the bottom and sides of the pan. Fold the overhang inward and press gently, creating a double thickness along the inside edge of the pan. This helps to strengthen the sides of the tart crust. Trim the top of the dough even with the pan rim by cutting it away with a small knife, working from the inside edge outward. Refrigerate the lined pan for at least 30 minutes before baking.

To Line a Tartlet Pan

Center a dough circle over a tartlet pan and gently ease it into the bottom of the pan, pressing it into the corners and sides. Trim the top of the dough even with the pan rim. Refrigerate for at least 30 minutes before baking.

To Make a Lattice Top

For a simple lattice top, lay half of the strips of dough across the pie or tart, spacing them about 1¼ inches apart. Make sure the ends reach to the edge of the pie or tart crust. Lay the remaining strips at a right angle to the first strips, again spacing them

CONTINUED...

1¼ inches apart. Trim the excess and press the ends gently against the crust to adhere.

To Prebake a Pie or Tart Crust or Tartlet Crusts

Preheat the oven to 350°F. Line the unbaked pie crust, tart crust, or tartlet crusts with parchment paper and fill with pie weights, uncooked rice, or dried beans. If baking tartlet crusts, put them on a baking sheet for easy transport to the oven. Bake until the edges of the crust are golden brown, about 35 minutes for large tarts and pies and 25 minutes for tartlets. Remove the weights and the parchment. Continue baking until the bottom is golden brown, about 10 minutes for tartlet and tart crusts and 15 minutes for pie crusts.

If your tart, pie, or tartlet crust cracks on the bottom, make a thick paste out of a little flour and water and seal the crack. Place back in the oven for a few minutes to dry the "glue."

··· ❧ ···

PLANNING AHEAD

The dough may be made a day ahead and kept refrigerated. Let stand at room temperature for about 15 minutes before rolling it out, or it will be too hard to roll. Or, you can wrap the dough well, freeze it for up to 2 weeks, and thaw it in the refrigerator. If you are making a tart crust with no lattice top, or a pie crust with no lattice top or top crust, store the remaining half of the dough the same way. You may also line the pie or tart pan or tartlet pans with the dough and refrigerate overnight or freeze for up to 2 weeks before baking, then bake directly from the refrigerator or freezer. For crusts with the best flavor and texture, eat the tarts, pies, or tartlets the same day they are baked.

BRIOCHE

— MAKES 2 LOAVES —

Here is a delicious bread to have on hand, in and out of the freezer.
I use it in many desserts, such as Summer Pudding (page 145) and Pear
Charlotte (page 106). Extra pieces are marvelous for breakfast,
toasted, buttered, and sprinkled with cinnamon sugar or drizzled
with wild Tasmanian honey.

3½ TEASPOONS ACTIVE DRY YEAST

½ CUP WARM WATER

2 TABLESPOONS GRANULATED SUGAR

4 LARGE EGGS, AT ROOM TEMPERATURE

4 CUPS ALL-PURPOSE FLOUR

1½ TEASPOONS SALT

8 OUNCES (16 TABLESPOONS) UNSALTED BUTTER, AT
   ROOM TEMPERATURE, CUT INTO 1-INCH PIECES

BUTTER FOR THE PANS

In the bowl of a stand mixer, stir together the yeast
and warm water. Stir in the sugar and let stand for
about 5 minutes until foamy.

Fit the mixer with the paddle attachment,
add the eggs to the yeast mixture, and beat on
medium-low speed until combined. Add the flour
and salt and beat until incorporated. Switch to the
dough hook and add the butter 1 piece at a time
at 5 second intervals until all the butter has been
incorporated and the mixture comes together in a
dough. Increase the speed to medium and knead
until smooth and elastic, about 5 minutes. The
dough will be a little sticky.

Put the dough in a large bowl, cover the bowl
with a kitchen towel, and let the dough rise in a
warm place until doubled in bulk, about 2 hours.

Butter two 8½-by-4½-by-2¾-inch loaf pans.
Divide the dough in half and press each half into
a prepared loaf pan. Cover the pans with a kitchen
towel and let the dough rise in a warm place until
doubled in bulk, about 2 hours.

Preheat the oven to 350°F. Bake the loaves until
they are a deep golden brown, about 30 minutes.
Remove from the oven, turn out onto wire racks,
and let cool to room temperature.

PLANNING AHEAD

The dough may be made a day in advance and
allowed to rise in the refrigerator overnight. Because
the dough will be cold, the second rising in the pans
may take a little longer than 2 hours. The baked
loaves may be wrapped in plastic wrap and stored
at room temperature for 3 days. Or, they may be
wrapped in plastic wrap and then aluminum foil
and frozen for up to 1 month.

PUFF PASTRY

— MAKES 1¾ POUNDS —

Don't be afraid to make your own puff pastry. It just requires a little concentration. You may need to make it a few times before you master the technique, but be patient and you will soon be able to produce flaky, light puff pastry. The actual working time is not long, but it seems long because you must allow time for the dough to rest. I usually wait until after the third turn before I clean up the flour on the countertop. There is no use in cleaning it three times! For a particularly flavorful pastry, use butterfat-rich European-style butter.

2 CUPS ALL-PURPOSE FLOUR

½ TEASPOON KOSHER SALT

1 POUND COLD UNSALTED BUTTER, CUT INTO ¼-INCH CUBES

½ CUP ICE WATER

FLOUR FOR DUSTING

Combine the flour and salt on a work surface. Scatter the butter cubes over the flour and then toss together until all the cubes are coated with the flour. Shape the mixture into a mound and form a well in the center.

Pour the water into the well. With your fingertips, as though you were tossing a salad, work the water into the flour-butter mixture until a rough dough begins to form. It will look like torn and knotted rags. Gently press the dough together so that all the dry flour is absorbed.

Form the dough into a rectangle about 6 by 8 inches and 1¼ inches thick. Wrap the dough in plastic wrap and refrigerate for 1 hour.

On a lightly floured work surface, roll out the dough into a 7-by-16-inch rectangle about ½ inch thick. (See Tips for Rolling Out Puff Pastry, facing page.) With a short side of the rectangle facing you, fold the dough as you would a business letter: fold down the top two-thirds toward you and then fold the bottom third over the top. This is a single turn.

Give the dough a quarter turn so that the open seam is on your right and the closed seam is on your left. If necessary, lightly flour the work surface so the dough doesn't stick. Repeat the rolling and folding process; this is another single turn. Wrap and refrigerate the dough for 1 hour.

Give the dough 2 more single turns, rolling and folding each time and making sure to give it a quarter turn between the 2 turns so the open seam is on your right. Wrap and refrigerate for 1 hour.

Once more, give the dough 2 single turns, folding and rolling as before, and refrigerate for 1 hour before rolling out as directed in individual recipes.

Tips for Rolling Out Puff Pastry
Flour the work surface lightly before putting the pastry on it. If you notice the butter breaking through the flour, let the dough sit at room temperature for about 5 minutes before attempting to roll it. Sprinkle a little flour on top of the pastry and roll from the center outward in all 4 directions to the thickness specified. Keep the sides of the puff pastry straight and even as you roll. Occasionally loosen the dough from the work surface with a metal or plastic pastry scraper to prevent sticking and lightly flour the top and bottom of the dough as needed.

When the pastry is the desired size, brush off the excess flour and cut into pieces as needed. When cutting, press the knife down with a rocking motion to make a clean cut. Do not drag the knife through the pastry. Refrigerate or freeze pastry pieces until needed (see Planning Ahead).

To Create Mille-Feuille (Thousand Layers) for Napoleons
Using the tines of a fork, pierce holes all over the rolled-out dough either just after you have rolled it out or after it has been refrigerated. If you are freezing the rolled-out dough, pierce it before freezing. This is called docking and it prevents the dough from rising.

··· ⌇⌇ ···

PLANNING AHEAD
The pastry dough may be made 3 days ahead and kept refrigerated. The rolled-out dough may be refrigerated overnight, or frozen for up to 2 weeks and thawed in the refrigerator.

SPONGE CAKE

— MAKES ONE 11½-BY-17½-INCH CAKE —

This cake has a spongy consistency, which is perfect for soaking, and when it is soaked, it doesn't disintegrate like more delicate cakes. It will be easier to cut if you make it several hours ahead. A chocolate variation follows.

BUTTER FOR THE PAN
1¼ CUPS ALL-PURPOSE FLOUR
2½ TEASPOONS BAKING POWDER
PINCH OF KOSHER SALT
5 LARGE EGGS, SEPARATED
1¼ CUPS GRANULATED SUGAR
5 TABLESPOONS BOILING WATER
1 TEASPOON VANILLA EXTRACT

Preheat the oven to 350°F. Grease the bottom of an 11½-by-17½-inch baking sheet with 1-inch sides, then line the bottom with parchment paper.

Sift together the flour and baking powder onto a piece of parchment paper or into a bowl. Add the salt and set aside.

Whip the egg yolks and sugar in the bowl of a stand mixer on high speed until thick, about 2 minutes. Reduce the speed to medium-low, add the boiling water and vanilla, and mix until combined. Scrape the sides of the bowl as necessary. Increase to high speed and beat until thick, about 2 minutes. Reduce the speed to low, add the dry ingredients, and mix until incorporated.

Wash and dry the whip attachment. Put the egg whites in a clean mixer bowl, fit the mixer with the clean whip, and whip on medium speed until frothy. Increase to high speed and whip until soft peaks form. They should be smooth and not clumpy. Using a spatula, fold half of the whipped whites into the yolk mixture. Then fold in the remaining whites just until no white streaks remain. Spread the batter into the prepared pan.

Bake until the cake is golden brown and springs back when lightly touched, about 15 minutes. Let cool in the pan to room temperature.

To remove the cake from the pan, run a small knife around the inside edge of the pan. Invert the pan onto a work surface, lift off the pan, and carefully peel off the parchment paper.

VARIATION

Chocolate Sponge Cake: Reduce the flour to 1 cup and add ¼ cup sifted unsweetened cocoa powder to the dry ingredients.

PLANNING AHEAD

The cake may be made up to 2 days ahead. Wrap in plastic wrap and store at room temperature. Or, freeze the cake for up to 1 month and thaw at room temperature.

CRÊPES

Crêpes are quick and easy to make and are ideal to have on hand for a fast dessert: fold them into quarters and warm them in some fresh fruit juice, a knob of butter, and a little sugar (confectioners', superfine, or brown) and you have a simple, satisfying dessert.

2 LARGE EGGS

½ CUP WATER

½ CUP PLUS 2 TABLESPOONS MILK

½ TEASPOON VANILLA EXTRACT

1 CUP ALL-PURPOSE FLOUR

1 TABLESPOON GRANULATED SUGAR

PINCH OF KOSHER SALT

1 OUNCE (2 TABLESPOONS) UNSALTED BUTTER, MELTED

In a food processor or blender, combine the eggs, water, milk, and vanilla and process until smooth. Add the flour, sugar, and salt and again process until smooth. Finally, add the butter and process until mixed. Cover and refrigerate for at least 1 hour.

Heat a 6-inch nonstick or seasoned crêpe pan over medium heat. Pour in about 1½ tablespoons of the batter and quickly rotate the pan, spreading it in a thin layer over the entire bottom. Cook the crêpe until golden brown, about 30 seconds. Loosen the edge of the crêpe with the edge of a knife or your fingers and turn it over. Cook until the second side is lightly golden, about 10 seconds. Transfer the crêpe to a plate. Continue to make crêpes in this manner until you have used all of the batter, stacking the crêpes so that they overlap slightly.

PLANNING AHEAD

The batter may be made a day in advance and kept refrigerated. The crêpes may be made a day in advance, covered, and refrigerated. They may also be stacked, with pieces of waxed paper between them, well wrapped in plastic wrap, and frozen for up to 1 week.

CHOCOLATE CRÊPES

— MAKES 20 CRÊPES —

These crêpes have a great bittersweet chocolate flavor. They are delicious rolled around hazelnut cream (page 87) or served with your favorite ice cream and either Chocolate Sauce (page 284) or Caramel Sauce (page 285).

2 LARGE EGGS

¼ CUP GRANULATED SUGAR

1 CUP MILK

½ TEASPOON VANILLA EXTRACT

½ CUP ALL-PURPOSE FLOUR

1 TABLESPOON UNSWEETENED COCOA POWDER

PINCH OF SALT

1 TABLESPOON UNSALTED BUTTER, MELTED

In a food processor or blender, combine the eggs, sugar, milk, and vanilla and process until smooth. Add the flour, cocoa powder, and salt and process again until smooth. Finally, add the butter and process until mixed. Cover and refrigerate for at least 1 hour.

Heat a 6-inch nonstick or seasoned crêpe pan over medium heat. Pour in about 1 tablespoon of the batter and quickly rotate the pan, spreading it in a thin layer over the entire bottom. Cook the crêpe until set on the bottom, about 1 minute. Loosen the edge of the crêpe with the edge of a knife or your fingers and turn it over. Cook until the second side is set, about 15 seconds. Continue to make crêpes in this manner until you have used all of the batter, stacking the crêpes so that they overlap slightly.

PLANNING AHEAD

The batter may be made a day in advance and kept refrigerated. The crêpes may be made 1 day ahead, covered, and refrigerated. They can also be stacked, with pieces of waxed paper between them, well wrapped in plastic wrap, and frozen for up to 1 week.

VANILLA ICE CREAM

— MAKES ABOUT 1½ QUARTS —

This recipe makes a good vanilla ice cream and can also be used
as a base for other flavors. Ice creams are an essential and delicious part
of the dessert repertoire, whether they are served by themselves or
as an accompaniment. When serving them with other desserts, make
sure the ice cream is a necessary part of the overall composition,
or the result may be too rich.

6 LARGE EGG YOLKS

1 CUP GRANULATED SUGAR

PINCH OF KOSHER SALT

2 CUPS HEAVY WHIPPING CREAM

1½ CUPS MILK

1 VANILLA BEAN, SPLIT LENGTHWISE

Prepare an ice bath. (For tips on using an ice bath, see page 18.) In a stainless-steel bowl, whisk together the egg yolks, sugar, and salt until blended. Set aside.

In a heavy, nonreactive saucepan, combine the cream and milk. Using a knife blade, scrape the seeds from the vanilla bean halves into the milk and then add the pod halves. Place over medium heat until small bubbles appear around the edges of the pan.

Remove from the heat and, while whisking constantly, pour the cream mixture into the egg mixture in a slow, steady stream. Pour the mixture back into the pan, place over medium-low heat, and cook, stirring constantly with a heat-resistant spatula, until it coats the spatula and reaches 175°F on an instant-read thermometer, about 5 minutes.

Strain the custard through a medium-mesh sieve back into the bowl and place in the ice bath. Let cool to room temperature, whisking occasionally. Cover and refrigerate until well chilled, at least 4 hours.

Freeze the custard in an ice-cream maker according to the manufacturer's instructions. Transfer to a covered container and place in the freezer until scoopable, about 2 hours, depending on your freezer.

··· ⧼⧽ ···

PLANNING AHEAD

The custard base for the ice cream may be made a day in advance. The ice cream may be made up to a week in advance.

CARAMEL ICE CREAM

— MAKES ABOUT 2 PINTS —

Caramel ice cream can stand on its own—you don't need to serve anything with it to make it delicious. But when you do, it's even better.

8 LARGE EGG YOLKS

½ TEASPOON KOSHER SALT

2¼ CUPS HEAVY WHIPPING CREAM

2¼ CUPS MILK

1 CUP GRANULATED SUGAR

½ CUP WATER

Prepare an ice bath. (For tips on using an ice bath, see page 18.) In a stainless-steel bowl, whisk together the egg yolks and salt until blended. Set aside.

In a heavy, nonreactive saucepan, combine the cream and milk and heat until small bubbles appear around the edges of the pan. Remove from the heat.

In another heavy, nonreactive saucepan large enough to hold the cream mixture eventually, stir together the sugar and water. Place over medium heat and cook, stirring occasionally, until the sugar dissolves and the mixture comes to a boil. Increase the heat to high and cook, without stirring, until the mixture becomes a golden amber. (See page 20 for tips on making caramel.)

Remove from the heat and let the bubbles subside for a few seconds. Stir in 2 tablespoons of the cream mixture. The caramel will bubble up as you add the cream mixture, so stir carefully and

make sure the bubbles subside before slowly adding 2 more tablespoons.

Continue adding the cream mixture 2 tablespoons at a time until the mixture stops bubbling, then slowly stir in the remaining cream mixture. When all of the cream mixture has been added, whisk in the egg yolk mixture.

Pour the mixture back into the pan, place over medium-low heat, and cook, stirring constantly with a heat-resistant spatula, until it coats the spatula and reaches 175°F on an instant-read thermometer, about 5 minutes.

Strain the custard through a medium-mesh sieve back into the bowl and place in the ice bath. Let cool to room temperature, whisking occasionally. Cover and refrigerate until well chilled, at least 4 hours.

Freeze the custard in an ice-cream maker according to the manufacturer's instructions. Transfer to a covered container and place in the freezer until scoopable, about 2 hours.

PLANNING AHEAD

The custard base for the ice cream may be made a day in advance. The ice cream may be made 2 days in advance.

PUMPKIN PURÉE

— MAKES 2½ CUPS —

Making your own pumpkin purée is simple, and the results are superior to canned pumpkin. Use small Sugar pumpkins, which have the sweetest, most flavorful flesh.

2½ POUNDS SUGAR PUMPKINS

¼ CUP WATER

Preheat the oven to 325°F. Cut each pumpkin into sixths. Scrape out the seeds and any stringy pulp. Put the pumpkin pieces, cut-side up, and the water in a baking pan and cover the pan with aluminum foil. Bake until soft when pierced with a fork, about 1 hour and 10 minutes.

Remove from the oven and, when cool enough to handle, scoop out the flesh with a spoon and purée in a food mill or a food processor. If the purée is watery, place it in a large sauté pan and cook over medium heat, stirring frequently, until thick. The timing will depend on how watery the purée is.

Let cool, cover, and refrigerate until using.

··· ⌒⌒ ···

PLANNING AHEAD

The purée may be made a week in advance and kept refrigerated, or it may be frozen for up to 1 month.

ALMOND PRALINE

— MAKES ABOUT 1 POUND —

You can enjoy this praline many ways: by itself in 1-inch pieces,
chopped and served with Baked Apricots (page 123), or finely ground
as a garnish for your favorite chocolate cake.

BUTTER FOR THE BAKING SHEET

1½ CUPS GRANULATED SUGAR

½ CUP WATER

1 CUP (4 OUNCES) WHOLE NATURAL ALMONDS,
TOASTED (SEE PAGE 20)

Butter the bottom of a baking sheet or line it with a nonstick baking liner.

In a heavy, nonreactive saucepan, stir together the sugar and water. Place over medium heat and cook, stirring occasionally, until the sugar dissolves and the mixture comes to a boil. Increase the heat to high and cook, without stirring, until the mixture becomes a golden amber color. (See page 20 for tips on making caramel.)

Remove from the heat, let the bubbles subside for a few seconds, and then carefully stir in the almonds. Pour the mixture onto the prepared baking sheet and, using an offset spatula, spread into an even layer. Let stand at room temperature until hard, about 1 hour.

Gently tap the baking sheet against the countertop to loosen the praline. Break it into pieces with your hands. If you are using the praline as a garnish, coarsely grind it in a food processor, using quick pulses.

PLANNING AHEAD

The praline will keep for 1 week, depending on the humidity. Store in an airtight container at room temperature.

— ACKNOWLEDGMENTS —

TO THE ENTIRE STAFF OF STARS, who made it such a
magical place to work, especially Carolyn Weil and Jules Vranian,
who preceded me as the Stars pastry chefs, and Hollyce Snyder,
Julia Orenstein, and Tim Grable, who worked alongside me.

To everyone who attended the weekend recipe bake-athons
and participated in recipe testing: Susan Berger, Robin David,
Erin Loftus Sweetland, Janet Rikala Dalton, Angela Brassigna,
Cynthia Schmae, Cassia O'Black, Kathy and Larry Kahn, Suzannah
McFerran (also typist extraordinaire), Heather Lee, Ed Chen,
Lauren Vasallo, Emily Guzzardi, Rachael Stella, and Stephen Clark.
Your help was invaluable.

To Peter Palmer, for his contagious enthusiasm and easygoing
approach to dessert wines.

To Jennifer Creager and Terri Wu, for maintaining a professional,
creative, and fun day-to-day pastry operation at Farallon. I literally
could not do what I do without them.

And to my literary team: Jane Dystel, Bill LeBlond,
Amy Treadwell, photographer Sheri Giblin, food stylist
Dan Becker, and prop stylist Leigh Noe, who have enabled
me to put my sweets on paper.

A

Almonds
  Almond Biscotti, 232–33
  Almond Praline, 302
  Butter Almond Cake with
    Strawberries and Caramel
    Cream, 202
  Caramel Almond Tartlets with
    Warm Blueberries, 162–63
  Chinese Almond Cookies, 222
  Chocolate Almond Bark, 251
  Coconut Sesame Cookies, 227
  Cranberry Linzertorte, 160–61
  Spiced Nuts, 255
  toasting, 20
  Warm Bittersweet Chocolate Tartlets
    with Spiced Almonds, 164
Apples
  Apple Caramel Sauce, 287
  Apple Pandowdy, 104–5
  Apple Turnovers, 270–71
  French Apple Tartlets, 165
  Gingerbread with Warm Apples
    and Cider Sabayon, 206–7
Apricots
  Apricot Custard Tart, 154
  Baked Apricots with Vanilla Ice
    Cream and Almond Praline, 123

B

Baked Apricots with Vanilla Ice
  Cream and Almond Praline, 123
Bananas
  Banana Cream Pie, 178
  Banana Napoleons with Warm
    Caramel Walnut Sauce, 170–71

Banana Pecan Bread, 264
  Maple Banana Compote with Ginger
    Ice Cream, 94–95
Banyuls, 31
Beating, 19
Berries. *See also individual berries*
  Berry Sauce, 289
  French Cream with Berries, 45
  Goat Cheese Cake with Mixed
    Berries, 188
  Orange Spice Cake with Berries,
    196–97
  Savarin with Grand Marnier Sabayon
    and Mixed Berries, 134–35
  Summer Pudding, 145
Bing Cherry Tart, 155
Biscotti
  Almond Biscotti, 232–33
  Double-Chocolate Biscotti, 234–35
  Macadamia Nut Biscotti, 231
Bittersweet Chocolate Frosting, 208–9
Bittersweet Chocolate Soufflé with
  Espresso Caramel Sauce, 112–13
Black-and-White Brownies, 238
Blackberries
  Blackberry–Sour Cream Muffins,
    269
  Blackberry Streusel Tart, 157
  Cornmeal Pound Cake with Black-
    berries and Double Cream, 194
  French Cream with Berries, 45
  Summer Trifle, 46
Blintzes, Nectarine Blueberry, 102
Blueberries
  Blueberry Cornmeal Muffins, 268
  Blueberry Lemon Cheesecake with
    a Cornmeal Crust, 186–87

Blueberry-Peach Brown Betty, 110
  Blueberry Pie, 176
  Blueberry Sauce, 48
  Blueberry Steamed Pudding, 54–55
  Caramel Almond Tartlets with
    Warm Blueberries, 162–63
  Lemon Blueberry Trifle, 48–49
  Nectarine Blueberry Blintzes, 102
  Nectarine Blueberry Compote, 102
  Oat Crisps with Blueberries and
    Crème Fraîche, 120
Bombe, Plum Vanilla Creamsicle, with
  Plum Caramel Sauce, 122
Botrytis cinerea, 25
Boysenberry Cobbler, Peach, 108–9
Brachetto, 30–31
Bread
  Banana Pecan Bread, 264
  Blueberry-Peach Brown Betty, 110
  Brioche, 293
  Chocolate Caramel Bread Pudding,
    64
  Pear Charlotte, 106–7
  Summer Pudding, 145
Brioche, 293
Brown Betty, Blueberry-Peach, 110
Brown Butter Madeleines, 228–29
Brownies
  Black-and-White Brownies, 238
  Chocolate-Peppermint Brownies, 237
  Three-Chocolate Brownies, 236
Brown Sugar Pastry Cream, 280
Butter
  room-temperature, 18–19
  unsalted, 14
Butter Almond Cake with Strawberries
  and Caramel Cream, 202

C

Cakes

Blueberry Lemon Cheesecake with a Cornmeal Crust, 186–87

Butter Almond Cake with Strawberries and Caramel Cream, 202

Chocolate-Hazelnut Pound Cake with Espresso-Cinnamon Cream, 192–93

Chocolate Sponge Cake, 296

Cornmeal Pound Cake with Blackberries and Double Cream, 194

Drunken Chocolate Cake, 204–5

Espresso–Chocolate Chip Angel Food Cake, 184–85

French Silk, 200–201

Gâteau Royale, 88–89

Gingerbread with Warm Apples and Cider Sabayon, 206–7

Ginger Mascarpone Cheesecake with a Chocolate Crust, 190–91

Goat Cheese Cake with Mixed Berries, 188

Grandmothers' Chocolate Cake, 208–9

Lemon Curd Cake, 210–11

Orange Spice Cake with Berries, 196–97

Peach Streusel Coffee Cake, 265

Plum-Cardamom Upside-Down Cake, 198–99

Pumpkin Cheesecake, 189

Savarin with Grand Marnier Sabayon and Mixed Berries, 134–35

Sponge Cake, 296

Torta Regina, 195

Tuscan Cream Cake, 203

Warm Bittersweet Chocolate Pudding Cakes, 62–63

Candies

Chocolate Almond Bark, 251

Coffee Toffee, 254

Spiced Nuts, 255

White Chocolate–Mint Truffles, 252–53

Caramel

Apple Caramel Sauce, 287

Caramel Almond Tartlets with Warm Blueberries, 162–63

Caramel Cream, 277

Caramel Custards, 38–39

Caramel Ice Cream, 300

Caramel Sauce, 285

Caramel Walnut Sauce, 172

Chocolate Caramel Bread Pudding, 64

Chocolate Caramel Sauce, 288

Espresso Caramel Sauce, 288

Lemon Caramel Sorbet, 130

making, 20–21

Plum Caramel Sauce, 286

Champagne Sabayon, 281

Chantilly Cream, 276

Charlotte, Pear, 106–7

Cheesecakes

Blueberry Lemon Cheesecake with a Cornmeal Crust, 186–87

Ginger Mascarpone Cheesecake with a Chocolate Crust, 190–9

Goat Cheese Cake with Mixed Berries, 188

Pumpkin Cheesecake, 189

Chenin Blanc, 27–28

Cherry Tart, Bing, 155

Chestnut Crêpes with Orange Honey Ice Cream, 100–101

Chinese Almond Cookies, 222

Chocolate

Bittersweet Chocolate Frosting, 208–9

Bittersweet Chocolate Soufflé with Espresso Caramel Sauce, 112–13

Black-and-White Brownies, 238

Chocolate Almond Bark, 251

Chocolate "Brûlée" Ginger Custards, 42–43

Chocolate Caramel Bread Pudding, 64

Chocolate Caramel Sauce, 288

Chocolate Chip Cookies, 216

Chocolate Cream, 82–83, 86

Chocolate Crêpes, 298

Chocolate Custard Sauce, 283

Chocolate Espresso Frozen Cream Sandwiches, 82–83

Chocolate-Filled Filo Triangles, 73

Chocolate Glaze, 204–5

Chocolate Hazelnut Crêpes, 87

Chocolate-Hazelnut Pound Cake with Espresso-Cinnamon Cream, 192–93

Chocolate Meringue Cookies, 224

Chocolate–Peanut Butter Terrine with Sugared Peanuts, 76–77

Chocolate-Peppermint Brownies, 237

Chocolate Pudding, 74

Chocolate Sauce, 284

Chocolate Shortbread, 239–40

Chocolate Sponge Cake, 296

Chocolate Truffle Tart, 158
Chocolate Zabaglione Trifle, 75
Cocoa Wafers with Frozen Hazelnut
    Sabayon, 80–81
Coconut Haystacks, 226
Coconut Macaroons, 225
Coffee Toffee, 254
Double-Chocolate Biscotti, 234–35
Drunken Chocolate Cake, 204–5
Espresso–Chocolate Chip Angel
    Food Cake, 184–85
French Silk, 200–201
Gâteau Royale, 88–89
Ginger Mascarpone Cheesecake with
    a Chocolate Crust, 190–91
Grandmothers' Chocolate Cake,
    208–9
melting, 19
shaving, 21
Stareos, 239–40
tempering, 19
Three-Chocolate Brownies, 236
Tiramisu, 51
Torta Regina, 195
Triple-Striped Chocolate
    Semifreddo, 78–79
Tuscan Cream Cake, 203
types of, 14
Warm Bittersweet Chocolate
    Pudding Cakes, 62–63
Warm Bittersweet Chocolate Tartlets
    with Spiced Almonds, 164
White Chocolate–Mint Truffles,
    252–53
Cider Sabayon, 281
Cinnamon Custard Sauce, 283
Cinnamon Pastry Cream, 280

Cinnamon Rolls, 260–61
Cinnamon Shortbread, 221
Cinnamon Sugar Cookies, 217
Cobbler, Peach Boysenberry, 108–9
Cocoa Wafers with Frozen Hazelnut
    Sabayon, 80–81
Coconut
    Coconut Cream Pie with Mango and
        Blackberry Sauces, 179
    Coconut Haystacks, 226
    Coconut Macaroons, 225
    Coconut Sesame Cookies, 227
    Macaroon Nut Tart, 159
    toasting, 22
Coffee
    Chocolate Espresso Frozen Cream
        Sandwiches, 82–83
    Chocolate Zabaglione Trifle, 75
    Coffee Custard Sauce, 283
    Coffee Toffee, 254
    Espresso-Amaretto Sauce, 84
    Espresso Caramel Sauce, 288
    Espresso–Chocolate Chip Angel
        Food Cake, 184–85
    Espresso-Cinnamon Cream, 192–93
    Espresso Cream, 82–83
    Espresso Granita with Chocolate
        Cream, 86
    Espresso Pastry Cream, 280
    Espresso Shortbread, 221
    Tiramisu, 51
    White Chocolate–Espresso Parfait,
        84–85
Coffee Cake, Peach Streusel, 265
Compotes
    Maple Banana Compote with Ginger
        Ice Cream, 94–95

Nectarine Blueberry Compote, 102
Plum Compote, 124–25
Strawberry Compote with Rhubarb
    Ice Cream, 96–97
Cookies
    Almond Biscotti, 232–33
    Black-and-White Brownies, 238
    Brown Butter Madeleines, 228–29
    Chinese Almond Cookies, 222
    Chocolate Chip Cookies, 216
    Chocolate Meringue Cookies, 224
    Chocolate-Peppermint Brownies, 237
    Chocolate Shortbread, 239–40
    Cinnamon Shortbread, 221
    Cinnamon Sugar Cookies, 217
    Coconut Haystacks, 226
    Coconut Macaroons, 225
    Coconut Sesame Cookies, 227
    Date Bars, 250
    Double-Chocolate Biscotti, 234–35
    Espresso Shortbread, 221
    Ginger Cookies, 218–19
    Hazelnut Shortbread, 221
    Lemon Squares, 249
    Macadamia Nut Biscotti, 231
    Marmalade Window Cookies, 230
    Orange Shortbread, 221
    Pistachio Tuiles, 128–29
    Russian Tea Cakes, 223
    Shortbread Cookies, 220–21
    Stareos, 239–40
    Three-Chocolate Brownies, 236
    Vanilla Wafers with Zinfandel-
        Marinated Raspberries, 146–47
Cornmeal Pound Cake with Blackberries
    and Double Cream, 194

Cornmeal Tartlets with Orange Crème
    Fraîche and Strawberries, 168–69
Cornstarch, 15
Cranberry Linzertorte, 160–61
Cream, 14
Cream cheese
    Apple Turnovers, 270–71
    Black-and-White Brownies, 238
    Blueberry Lemon Cheesecake with
        a Cornmeal Crust, 186–87
    Pumpkin Cheesecake, 189
Creaming, 19
Creams. See also Pastry Cream
    Caramel Cream, 277
    Chantilly Cream, 276
    Chocolate Cream, 82–83, 86
    Crème Fraîche, 279
    Double Cream, 278
    Espresso-Cinnamon Cream,
        192–93
    Espresso Cream, 82–83
    Hazelnut Cream, 87
    Lemon Cream, 48
    Mascarpone Cream, 51
    Peach Cream, 46
    Walnut Cream, 132–33
Creamsicle Bombe, Plum Vanilla, with
    Plum Caramel Sauce, 122
Crème Caramels, Orange, with
    Raspberries, 40–41
Crème Fraîche, 279
    Orange Crème Fraîche, 168–69
Crêpes, 297
    Chestnut Crêpes with Orange Honey
        Ice Cream, 100–101
    Chocolate Crêpes, 298
    Chocolate Hazelnut Crêpes, 87

Crêpes Suzette, 99
    Nectarine Blueberry Blintzes, 102
Custards
    Caramel Custards, 38–39
    Chocolate "Brûlée" Ginger Custards,
        42–43
    French Cream with Berries, 45
    Lemon Custards, 44
    Orange Crème Caramels with
        Raspberries, 40–41
Cutting, 22

D
Date Bars, 250
Dessert wines, 23–33
Double boilers, 18
Double-Chocolate Biscotti, 234–35
Double Cream, 278
Drunken Chocolate Cake, 204–5

E
Equipment, 15–17
Espresso. See Coffee

F
Figs
    Honey-Marsala Baked Figs with
        Ginger Sabayon, 126–27
    Lemon Mascarpone Tart with Figs
        and Raspberries, 156
Filo Triangles, Chocolate-Filled, 73
Flour
    as thickener, 15
    types of, 14
Folding, 19–20
French Apple Tartlets, 165
French Cream with Berries, 45

French Silk, 200–201
Frosting, Bittersweet Chocolate,
    208–9
Frozen Kir Royale, 136

G
Gâteau Royale, 88–89
Ginger
    Gingerbread with Warm Apples and
        Cider Sabayon, 206–7
    Ginger Cookies, 218–19
    Ginger Ice Cream, 94
    Ginger Mascarpone Cheesecake
        with a Chocolate Crust, 190–91
    Ginger Pastry Cream, 280
Goat Cheese Cake with Mixed Berries,
    188
Grand Marnier
    Grand Marnier Sabayon, 281
    Orange Grand Marnier Soufflé
        with Chocolate Custard Sauce,
        114–15
    Strawberry Grand Marnier Trifle, 50
Grandmothers' Chocolate Cake, 208–9
Granita, Espresso, with Chocolate
    Cream, 86
Grapes, varieties of, 25–33
Gratin, Strawberry, 103

H
Hazelnuts
    Chocolate Hazelnut Crêpes, 87
    Chocolate-Hazelnut Pound Cake
        with Espresso-Cinnamon Cream,
        192–93
    Double-Chocolate Biscotti, 234–35
    Hazelnut Cream, 87

Hazelnut Sabayon, 80–81
Hazelnut Shortbread, 221
Hazelnut Shortcakes with Plum
    Compote, 124–25
toasting and skinning, 20
Torta Regina, 195
Hollyce's Oatmeal Scones, 266
Honey-Marsala Baked Figs with Ginger
    Sabayon, 126–27

I

Ice, Tangerine, with Pistachio Tuiles,
    128–29
Ice baths, 18
Ice cream
    Caramel Ice Cream, 300
    Ginger Ice Cream, 94
    Orange Honey Ice Cream, 100–101
    Plum Vanilla Creamsicle Bombe
        with Plum Caramel Sauce, 122
    Raspberry Spritzer, 121
    Rhubarb Ice Cream, 96
    Vanilla Ice Cream, 299
    White Chocolate–Espresso Parfait,
        84–85
    White Chocolate Ice Cream, 84

K

Key Lime Pie, 173
Kir Royale, Frozen, 136

L

Lemons
    Blueberry Lemon Cheesecake with a
        Cornmeal Crust, 186–87
    Lemon Blueberry Trifle, 48–49
    Lemon Caramel Sorbet, 130

Lemon Cream, 48
Lemon Curd Cake, 210–11
Lemon Custards, 44
Lemon Mascarpone Tart with Figs
    and Raspberries, 156
Lemon-Raspberry Pudding
    Soufflé, 98
Lemon Squares, 249
Lime Pie, Key, 173
Linzertorte, Cranberry, 160–61

M

Macadamia nuts
    Macadamia Nut Biscotti, 231
    Macaroon Nut Tart, 159
    toasting, 20
Macaroon Nut Tart, 159
Macaroons, Coconut, 225
Madeira, 29–30
Madeleines, Brown Butter, 228–29
Mango Sauce, 289
Maple Banana Compote with Ginger
    Ice Cream, 94–95
Maple Pecan Pie, 175
Marmalade Window Cookies, 230
Mascarpone cheese, 14
    Blueberry Lemon Cheesecake with a
        Cornmeal Crust, 186–87
    Espresso-Cinnamon Cream, 192–93
    French Cream with Berries, 45
    Ginger Mascarpone Cheesecake with
        a Chocolate Crust, 190–91
    Hazelnut Cream, 87
    Lemon Mascarpone Tart with Figs
        and Raspberries, 156
    Mascarpone Cream, 51
    Nectarine Blueberry Blintzes, 102

Pumpkin Cheesecake, 189
    Stareos, 239–40
    Summer Trifle, 46
    Tiramisu, 51
Measuring, 22
Mille-feuille, 295
Mixing, 19–20
Muffins
    Blackberry–Sour Cream Muffins, 269
    Blueberry Cornmeal Muffins, 268
    Pear Ginger Muffins, 267
Muscat, 25–26

N

Napoleons
    Banana Napoleons with Warm
        Caramel Walnut Sauce, 170–71
    Pear Napoleons with Ginger Pastry
        Cream, 172
Nectarines
    Nectarine Blueberry Blintzes, 102
    Nectarine Blueberry Compote, 102
Noble rot, 25
Nuts. *See also individual nuts*
    Spiced Nuts, 255
    toasting, 20

O

Oats
    Hollyce's Oatmeal Scones, 266
    Oat Crisps with Blueberries and
        Crème Fraîche, 120
Oranges
    Orange Crème Caramels with
        Raspberries, 40–41
    Orange Crème Fraîche, 168–69
    Orange Custard Sauce, 283

Orange Honey Ice Cream, 100–101
Orange Shortbread, 221
Orange Spice Cake with Berries,
    196–97
Ovens, 22

P

Pandowdy, Apple, 104–5
Pans
    greasing, 20
    types of, 15–16
Parchment paper, 21
Parfait, White Chocolate–Espresso,
    84–85
Passion Fruit–Meringue Tartlets, 166–67
Pastry Cream, 280
    Brown Sugar Pastry Cream, 280
    Cinnamon Pastry Cream, 280
    Espresso Pastry Cream, 280
    Ginger Pastry Cream, 280
Patrick's Peach Pie, 177
Peaches
    Blueberry-Peach Brown Betty, 110
    Patrick's Peach Pie, 177
    Peach Boysenberry Cobbler, 108–9
    Peach Cream, 46
    Peach Streusel Coffee Cake, 265
    Riesling-Poached Peaches, 131
    Summer Trifle, 46
Peanuts
    Chocolate–Peanut Butter Terrine
        with Sugared Peanuts, 76–77
    toasting, 20
Pears
    Pear Charlotte, 106–7
    Pear Ginger Muffins, 267
    Pear Napoleons with Ginger Pastry
        Cream, 172

Pear Riesling Trifle, 47
Poached Pears with Walnut Cream,
    132–33
Pecans
    Apple Pandowdy, 104–5
    Banana Pecan Bread, 264
    Cinnamon Rolls, 260–61
    Date Bars, 250
    French Silk, 200–201
    Macaroon Nut Tart, 159
    Maple Pecan Pie, 175
    Russian Tea Cakes, 223
    Spiced Nuts, 255
    toasting, 20
Persimmon Pudding, 57
Pies
    Banana Cream Pie, 178
    Blueberry Pie, 176
    Coconut Cream Pie with Mango and
        Blackberry Sauces, 179
    Key Lime Pie, 173
    Maple Pecan Pie, 175
    Patrick's Peach Pie, 177
    Pumpkin Pie, 174
    Tart and Pie Dough, 290–92
Pistachio Tuiles, 128–29
Plating, 17
Plums
    Plum Caramel Sauce, 286
    Plum-Cardamom Upside-Down
        Cake, 198–99
    Plum Compote, 124–25
    Plum Syrup, 198
    Plum Vanilla Creamsicle Bombe
        with Plum Caramel Sauce, 122
    Poached Pears with Walnut Cream,
        132–33

Poppyseed Shortcakes with Strawberries,
    148–49
Port, 31–33
Praline, Almond, 302
Puddings
    Blueberry Steamed Pudding, 54–55
    Chocolate Caramel Bread Pudding,
        64
    Chocolate Pudding, 74
    Persimmon Pudding, 57
    Pumpkin Steamed Pudding, 56
    Summer Pudding, 145
    Walnut Rum Steamed Pudding,
        52–53
Puff Pastry, 294–95
    Banana Napoleons with Warm
        Caramel Walnut Sauce, 170–71
    French Apple Tartlets, 165
    Pear Napoleons with Ginger Pastry
        Cream, 172
Pumpkin
    Pumpkin Cheesecake, 189
    Pumpkin Pie, 174
    Pumpkin Purée, 301
    Pumpkin Soufflé with Apple
        Caramel Sauce, 111
    Pumpkin Steamed Pudding, 56

R

Raspberries
    French Cream with Berries, 45
    Lemon Mascarpone Tart with Figs
        and Raspberries, 156
    Lemon-Raspberry Pudding Soufflé,
        98
    Orange Crème Caramels with
        Raspberries, 40–41

Raspberry-Cassis Sorbet, 136
Raspberry Spritzer, 121
Summer Trifle, 46
Vanilla Wafers with Zinfandel-
    Marinated Raspberries, 146–47
Recipes, reading, 18
Rhubarb Ice Cream, 96
Riesling, 26–27
    Pear Riesling Trifle, 47
    Riesling-Poached Peaches, 131
    Riesling Sabayon, 281
Rolls
    Cinnamon Rolls, 260–61
    Walnut Roll, 262–63
Rum
    Rum Custard Sauce, 283
    Walnut Rum Steamed Pudding,
        52–53
Russian Tea Cakes, 223

S

Sabayon
    Champagne Sabayon, 281
    Cider Sabayon, 281
    Grand Marnier Sabayon, 281
    Hazelnut Sabayon, 80–81
    Riesling Sabayon, 281
Salt, 15
Sandwiches, Chocolate Espresso Frozen
    Cream, 82–83
Sauces. *See also* Creams; Sabayon
    Apple Caramel Sauce, 287
    Berry Sauce, 289
    Blueberry Sauce, 48
    Caramel Sauce, 285
    Caramel Walnut Sauce, 172
    Chocolate Caramel Sauce, 288

Chocolate Custard Sauce, 283
Chocolate Sauce, 284
Cinnamon Custard Sauce, 283
Coffee Custard Sauce, 283
Espresso-Amaretto Sauce, 84
Espresso Caramel Sauce, 288
Mango Sauce, 289
Orange Custard Sauce, 283
Plum Caramel Sauce, 286
Rum Custard Sauce, 283
Vanilla Custard Sauce, 282–83
Zabaglione, 281
Sauternes, 26
Savarin with Grand Marnier Sabayon
    and Mixed Berries, 134–35
Scones, Hollyce's Oatmeal, 266
Semifreddo, Triple-Striped Chocolate,
    78–79
Sherry, 29
Shortbread
    Chocolate Shortbread, 239–40
    Cinnamon Shortbread, 221
    Espresso Shortbread, 221
    Hazelnut Shortbread, 221
    Orange Shortbread, 221
    Shortbread Cookies, 220–21
Shortcakes
    Hazelnut Shortcakes with Plum
        Compote, 124–25
    Poppyseed Shortcakes with
        Strawberries, 148–49
Sifting, 20

Sorbets
    Lemon Caramel Sorbet, 130
    Raspberry-Cassis Sorbet, 136
Soufflés
    Bittersweet Chocolate Soufflé with
        Espresso Caramel Sauce, 112–13
    Lemon-Raspberry Pudding Soufflé,
        98
    Orange Grand Marnier Soufflé
        with Chocolate Custard Sauce,
        114–15
    Pumpkin Soufflé with Apple Caramel
        Sauce, 111
Spiced Nuts, 255
Sponge Cake, 296
Spritzer, Raspberry, 121
Stand mixers, 20
Stareos, 239–40
Strawberries
    Butter Almond Cake with Straw-
        berries and Caramel Cream, 202
    Cornmeal Tartlets with Orange
        Crème Fraîche and Strawberries,
        168–69
    Poppyseed Shortcakes with
        Strawberries, 148–49
    Strawberry Compote with Rhubarb
        Ice Cream, 96–97
    Strawberry Grand Marnier Trifle, 50
    Strawberry Gratin, 103
Sugar, 15
Sugared Peanuts, 76–77
Summer Pudding, 145
Summer Trifle, 46